Costs in Employment Tribunals

Costs in Employment Tribunals

Daniel Barnett
Barrister, Temple Garden Chambers

Kate Palka
Solicitor, Palka Downton Solicitors

Benjamin Hay
Barrister, Temple Garden Chambers

Published by
Jordan Publishing Limited
21 St Thomas Street
Bristol BS1 6JS

British Library Cataloguing-in-Publication Data

A catalogue record for this book is available from the British Library.

ISBN 978 1 84661 208 4

Typeset by Letterpart Ltd, Reigate, Surrey

Printed and bound in Great Britain by Antony Rowe Limited, Chippenham, Wiltshire

ACKNOWLEDGMENTS

Daniel Barnett would like to thank Miranda Barnett, Eugenie Verney, Neil Russell, Michael Creamore, Dean Morris, Tim Kevan and everyone at Temple Garden Chambers.

Kate Palka acknowledges and thanks Sean for all his patience and encouragement and Nigel Astbury for his assistance with the practice to allow her time off to write. Thanks also to Nigel Brain of EFDL Ltd for his input and the lunches.

Benjamin Hay wishes to thank James Arney for his advice and assistance, everyone at Temple Garden Chambers for their support and, of course, Davina for her constant encouragement

In addition, the authors would like to thank the solicitors and barristers who sent us copies of the written reasons for tribunal decisions which are summarised in this book (and without whose help we would not have been able to establish and distil the way in which tribunals implement the costs rules up and down the country). Many of you are identified in the text, but some of you – including a small handful of tribunal judges who sent us transcripts – have asked to remain anonymous. If you did not request anonymity, you are (in no particular order): Neil Russell of BD Laddie; Tony Bertin of Employment Relations Solicitors; Shaman Kapoor of 1 Temple Gardens; Paul Housego of Beers Solicitors and fee-paid Employment Judge; Marc Jones of Turbervilles; Christopher Nott, Employment Judge; James Arnold of 5 Essex Court; Andrea Baller of the Treasury Solicitors; Rosa Brennan of Clarkson Wright & Jakes LLP; Elizabeth Lang at Bird & Bird; John Sturzaker of Russell Jones & Walker; Claire Brattey of SJ Berwin; Alison Peat of MacRoberts; Belinda Lester of CKFT Solicitors; Victoria Wright of Thackray Williams LLP; Kimberley Shaw of Irvine and Partners; Lee Rogers of Weightmans LLP; Vicky Parker of Legal Services, Isle of Wight Council; Louise Taft of JR Jones Solicitors; Jane Liddington, fee-paid Employment Judge at Croydon; Phil Bramhall of Bramhalls; Gwenno Hughes of Hugh James; Stefan Hagan of Clarkson Wright & Jakes; Andrew Midgley of Old Square Chambers; Mel Sangster of Dundas and Wilson; Christopher Newman of Littleton Chambers; Gina Wilson of MacRoberts; Paul Manson of WH Smith; Gina Wilson of MacRoberts; Karen Harvie of TC Young; Alex Colson of Taylor Walton LLP; Lynden Lever of Stone

King; Simon Martin of Battens Solicitors; Gina Wilson of MacRoberts LLP; Catherine Daw of Brachers; Nadim Dathi of Sternberg Reed; Gareth Rosser-Davies of BrookeStreet des Roches; Rob Whitaker of Stanley Tee; Jayne Harrison of Chattertons; Diarmuid Deeney of Halliwells LLP; Rebecca Fox of MAB Law; Clive Thomas of Watkins & Gunn Solicitors; Guy Guinan of Halliwells LLP; Natalie Roach of Brethertons; Lindsay Anderson of Morton Fraser LLP; Kathryn Lloyd of Bates Wells & Braithwaite; Simon Whitehead of Brabners Chaffe Street; Guy Guinan of Halliwells LLP; Jessel Gair of Biggart Baillie LLP; Catherine Daw of Brachers Law; Guy Hollebon of Bevans; Alec Colson of Taylor Walton LLP; Elizabeth Williams of Turcan Connell; Edward Brown of Bar Pro Bono Unit; Claire Tiffney of Directorate of Legal Services, Central Services Agency; Kiran Daurka of Russell Jones and Walker; Claire McCann of Cloisters; Harry Coll of EDG Legal; Andrew Knorpel of ASB Law; Andrea Bateman of BPE Solicitors; Rashmi Chopra of Comptroller and City Solicitor's Office; Simon Price of Chadwick Lawrence; James Humphrey of Trethowans; Jamie Anderson of Counsel; Gina Wilson of MacRoberts; Malcolm Lawrence of Copley Clark & Bennett; Saira Ali of Hill Dickinson LLP; Lindsey Cartwright of Maclay Murray & Spens; Mel Sangster of Dundas and Wilson; Claire Tiffney of Directorate of Legal Services, Central Services Agency; John MacKenzie, Solicitor Advocate; Kym Beeston of The Learning Trust; Andrew Brown of Anderson Strathern LLP; Lee Xavier of Bevans Solicitors; Philip Cameron of CMS Cameron McKenna LLP; Tanushree Sehmbi of Clarks Legal; Aoife MacManus of Donnelly & Kinder; Gerry Daly of Francis Hanna & Co Solicitors.

ABOUT THE AUTHORS

Daniel Barnett is a leading employment barrister practising from Temple Garden Chambers. He has a high-profile practice, acting principally for firms of solicitors against whom employment claims are made, FTSE-250 companies and NHS Trusts. He is a frequent interviewee in broadcast media commenting on legal issues. This is his eighth book.

Kate Palka was called to the Roll in 1990 and specialised in commercial litigation until 1996 when she became a Senior Lecturer in Business, Commercial and Employment law on the LPC and LLB at Bournemouth University. Since 2001, Kate has worked in private practice as a sole practitioner specialising in employment law and advises both employers and employees on contentious and non contentious issues. She has recently completed an LLM in Employment Law at Leicester University.

Benjamin Hay was called to the Bar in 2004 and is a scholar of Robinson College, Cambridge, the Inns of Court School of Law and the Middle Temple. Benjamin has a busy common law practice with particular expertise in employment law and costs litigation.

CONTENTS

TABLE OF CASES

References are to paragraph numbers.

TABLE OF STATUTES

References are to paragraph numbers.

TABLE OF STATUTORY INSTRUMENTS

References are to paragraph numbers.

CHAPTER 1

INTRODUCTION

When industrial tribunals were set up in 1964 the intention was to create, 'an easily accessible, speedy, informal and inexpensive procedure for the settlement of disputes ...' (Donovan Report, 1968). Whether or not this has been achieved is the subject of another debate, but the intention was certainly to create a forum for the quick resolution of workplace disputes in which as a general rule each party would bear its own costs. Rule 14 of the Employment Tribunal (Constitution and Rules of Procedure) 1967 made this clear: 'a tribunal shall not normally make an award in respect of costs or expenses'.

This is altogether different from the system in the civil courts costs where, subject to the court's discretion, the general rule is that the unsuccessful party will be ordered to pay the costs of the successful party (CPR, r 44.3(2)). Even though in general Employment Tribunals do not award costs, there are circumstances in which they may or must do so, but if they do, the rules differ from those which apply in the courts: in Employment Tribunals an award of costs is related to the conduct of the parties rather than to whether they win or lose.

1.1 RATIONALE OF COSTS RULES

1.1.1 Exception and not the rule

Costs orders are very much the exception and not the rule. In *Gee v Shell Ltd*,[1] Sedley LJ stated (para 35):

> 'It is nevertheless a very important feature of the employment jurisdiction that it is designed to be accessible to people without the need of lawyers, and that – in sharp distinction from ordinary litigation in the United Kingdom – losing does not ordinarily mean paying the other sides costs ... The governing structure remains that of a cost free user-friendly jurisdiction in which the power to award costs is not so much an exception as a means to protecting its essential character.'

The statistics at **1.2** below show that the proportion of the Employment Tribunal contested cases in which costs orders are made remain low. In

---

[1]   [2003] IRLR 82.

the majority of cases, the unsuccessful party will not be ordered to pay the successful party's costs – see *McPherson v BNP Paribas*,[2] paras 2 and 25, per Mummery LJ. However, the question is not whether the case is exceptional, but whether a party brings himself within the tribunal costs rules.

HHJ McMullen, in *Dean & Dean Solicitors v Mrs Dionissiou*,[3] said:

> '... the regime set up by the 2002 Act and the 2004 Regulations is there as a jurisdiction bar to make sure that parties take the opportunity to try and resolve issues between them. Although the CPR regime is not the same as that in the Employment Tribunal, the objective is. You should not bring claims unless they have been foreshadowed one way or another to the other side and you should not bring claims to assert matters outside the dispute, out of revenge or for some reason collateral to the dispute. In the employment field, costs are often threatened by Respondents but applications are rare, findings of unreasonable conduct are unusual and awards highly exceptional.'

1.1.2   Compensation and not punishment

The aim of an order for costs is compensation of the party which has incurred expense in winning the case and not punishment of the losing party. In *Lodwick v London Borough of Southwark*,[4] Pill LJ stated (para 23):

> 'Costs are rarely awarded in proceedings before an employment tribunal. Costs remain exceptional ... and the aim is compensation of the party which has incurred expense in winning the case, not punishment of the losing party ...'

1.1.3   Discretion that is not to be fettered by case law

In *Salinas* (below), Burton J noted that there would be something special or exceptional required before a costs order would be made, and even if the necessary requirements were established, there would still remain discretion.

OLIVAS SALINAS v BEAR STEARNS INTERNATIONAL HOLDINGS INC (1) MR J CAMBLAIN (2)

UKEAT/0596/04/DM

The Employment Tribunal at Stratford found that the bringing and conducting of proceedings by the Claimant had been misconceived➡

---

2   [2004] IRLR 558.
3   [2008] UKEAT 0140_08_1407.
4   [2004] IRLR 554.

and that she had acted unreasonably in conducting the proceedings and so ordered her to pay the costs of both Respondents, to be assessed by way of detailed assessment in the county court. Her claim for sex discrimination had previously been unanimously dismissed. The costs amounted to £120,000; the case had involved 324 pages of witness statements and a hearing lasting five days.

The Employment Tribunal had that the claim clearly had no reasonable prospects of success, having decided that many of the incidents about which the Claimant complained either did not happen at all or not in the way in which she alleged. Furthermore, they found no discriminatory element to the incidents that had occurred, for instance the dismissal itself. They found that she had not been honest about a particular incident concerning a date and her recording it in her diary and they also did not accept the Claimant's version of events in a number of other matters. The tribunal believed that she had behaved unreasonably in calling a number of witnesses whose evidence was, 'at best, irrelevant, and at worst not helpful to her case at all'. Finally, they were very concerned about a late allegation of a post dismissal incident concerning inappropriate touching, which was not made until a very late stage of the proceedings.

The Respondent had sent a letter to the Claimant at an early stage warning her that they considered her behaviour to be 'scandalous and vexatious' and that there were potential cost consequences of pursuing the claim in the way she did.

The EAT dismissed the Claimant's appeal. The fact that costs orders are exceptional and unusual is because there is a high hurdle to be surmounted before a costs order can be considered i e satisfaction of the requirements of (what was) r 14, but in this case they held that there was no error of law in the Employment Tribunal's reasoning that the proceedings were misconceived and unreasonably conducted.

It is clear also that the discretion given to tribunals and courts is not to be fettered – *Benyon and ors v Scadden.*[5]

BENYON & ORS v SCADDEN & ORS

[1999] IRLR 700

Mrs Beynon and 12 other Claimants presented complaints to an Employment Tribunal alleging that there had been a transfer of the business in which they were employed and that the employers had➡

---

5   [1999] IRLR 700.

failed to comply with the consultation requirements in reg 10 of the TUPE Regulations 1981. From the outset, the Claimants' union, Unison, supported their claims. The Employment Tribunal dismissed the claims on the ground that there had been no transfer of an undertaking within the meaning of the Regulations. There had been a sale of shares of the employing company but it was well-established that a sale and purchase of shares was not of itself a relevant transfer for the purposes of TUPE. The tribunal rejected the argument advanced by the Unison representative that the share sale was only part of the picture and that it was necessary to look at the reality of the situation and the effective control.

In this case the Judge found that the union was either aware or, by making proper inquiries, could have been aware that the claims had no reasonable prospect of success, they had continued to pursue them not only for their own sake but with the collateral object of attempting to force the employers to recognise the union. He concluded that this was both vexatious and unreasonable and an abuse of the tribunal process.

The EAT upheld the order for costs and so did the Court of Appeal. There was no reason to disturb the exercise of the Judge's unfettered discretion. Lindsey J stated:

> '... discretion like other judicial discretions (is) the exercise according to common sense and according to justice and if there is a miscarriage in the exercise of it, it will be reviewed but still it is a discretion ... So in our case whilst we shall examine the cases to which we have been referred we must be at pains to remember, firstly, that those cases cannot fetter the jurisdiction as to costs conferred upon the Employment Tribunal by the Rules and secondly, we must avoid the common error of construing the cases rather than the statute. The proper test for the Employment Tribunal was not whether its order accorded with this authority or that but, ultimately, whether it was just to have exercised as it did the power conferred upon by the Rule.'

The discretion of an Employment Tribunal under the costs rules is not limited to those costs that are caused by or are attributable to the unreasonable conduct found (see *McPherson v BNP Paribas*,[6] paras 40–41).

1.1.4   No legal aid

There has never been Legal Help available for parties in employment disputes in the UK. In 2000 proposals were put forward in Scotland[7] to

---

[6]   [2004] IRLR 558.

[7]   Jim Wallace's proposals on 12 December 2000 to the Justice and Home Affairs Committee of the Scottish Parliament.

allow publicly funded legal representation before Employment Tribunals for difficult and complex cases, following several cases before Employment Tribunals in Scotland which argued that the failure to make legal assistance available for Employment Tribunal proceedings amounts to a violation of the right to a fair hearing under Art 6(1) of the ECHR. These proposals were never put into place.

Legal Help is available for appeals from Employment Tribunals to the Employment Appeal Tribunal, to the Court of Appeal and to the House of Lords. It may also be available in some circumstances in respect of a contract claim pursued through the courts rather than at an Employment Tribunal.

1.1.5 Proportionality

The case of *AnnMaria Brash-Hall v Getty Images Limited*[8] highlighted what the Court of Appeal (per Wall, LJ) considered to be a 'substantial disproportionality between the award of damages and the costs incurred in achieving it'.

MRS ANNMARIA BRASH-HALL v GETTY IMAGES LIMITED

[2006] EWCA Civ 531

The Claimant succeeded in her claims of unfair dismissal, direct sex discrimination and wrongful dismissal. The Employment Tribunal awarded her a total of £27,787.16 and she appealed against the decision on remedies. When the EAT did not uphold her appeal she went to the Court of Appeal, which allowed her appeal but only to a limited extent. Her compensation was not, therefore, increased to the sum she had hoped for.

The case required two hearings of two days each with third days in chambers, although with hindsight the Court of Appeal believed that it was clear that the Respondent should not have contested liability, and the Appellant had substantially overstated her case at the remedies hearing. Neither the Employment Tribunal nor the EAT made costs orders and the Court of Appeal noted that both decisions not to award costs were plainly correct. The consequences for the Appellant were that by the time she had applied to the Court of Appeal, she had incurred more than £52,000 in pursuing the claim. Mummery LJ observed that if she had succeeded in the Court of Appeal and obtained an order for her costs of the appeal, she may have had some money left depending on the extent to which she was successful. However, if she was unsuccessful the normal rule was that she would have to pay the Respondent's costs. ➡

---

8   [2006] EWCA Civ 531.

> Furthermore, if she was successful, it was likely that the court would remit the matter for reconsideration by a different tribunal.
>
> Wall LJ had no answer 'to the manifestly disproportionality between the amount of the award and the costs incurred in achieving it'. However, he said that 'such considerations ... leave an uncomfortable feeling behind, and render the prospect of a remission to the tribunal deeply unattractive ...'

1.2　STATISTICS

Statistics have been published annually between 1999 and 2007 by the Employment Tribunals Service showing the costs awarded in Employment Tribunal cases in all jurisdictions.

1999 – 2000	
Costs	**No of cases**
£0 – £25	4
£26 – £50	9
£51 – £75	11
£76 – £100	26
£101 – £150	24
£151 – £200	12
£201 – £300	28
£301 – £400	7
£401 – £500	60
£501 – £1000	1
£1000 +	4
All	**186**

2000 – 2001	
Costs	**No of cases**
£0 – £25	6
£26 – £50	13
£51 – £75	6
£76 – £100	29
£101 – £150	32
£151 – £200	26
£201 – £300	41
£301 – £400	10

2000 – 2001

Costs	No of cases
£401 – £500	78
£500 – £1000	4
£1000 +	2
All	**247**
Maximum award	**£1,500**
Median award	**£250**
Average award	**£295**

2001 – 2002

Costs	No of cases	
	Claimant	**Respondent**
£0 – £25	5	2
£26 – £50	5	33
£51 – £75	3	17
£76 – £100	15	33
£101 – £150	13	22
£151 – £200	10	18
£201 – £300	13	73
£301 – £400	13	25
£401 – £500	21	89
£500 – £1000	23	80
£1000 +	48	75
All	**169**	**467**
Maximum award	**£15,000**	
Median award	**£500**	
Average award	**£983**	

2002 – 2003

Costs	No of cases	
	Claimant	**Respondent**
£0 – £200	59	133
£201 – 400	37	87
£401 – 600	43	121
£601 – 800	26	44
£801 – £1000	28	70
£1001 – £2000	44	94

2002 – 2003

Costs	No of cases	
	Claimant	**Respondent**
£2001 – £4000	40	73
£4001 – £6000	12	31
£6001 – £8000	7	18
£8001 – £10000	11	20
£10000 +	0	0
All	**307**	**691**
Maximum award	**£10,000**	
Median award	**£703**	
Average award	**£1,524**	

2003 – 2004

Costs	No of cases	
	Claimant	**Respondent**
£0 – £200	49	84
£201 – 400	53	81
£401 – 600	38	78
£601 – 800	19	39
£801 – £1000	23	61
£1001 – £2000	65	106
£2001 – £4000	40	97
£4001 – £6000	29	53
£6001 – £8000	6	16
£8001 – £10000	10	29
£10000 +	0	0
All	**332**	**644**
Maximum award	**£10,000**	
Median award	**£1,000**	
Average award	**£1,859**	

2004 – 2005

Costs	No of cases	
	Claimant	**Respondent**
£0 – £200	30	84
£201 – 400	33	75
£401 – 600	42	117

2004 – 2005		
Costs	**No of cases**	
	Claimant	**Respondent**
£601 – 800	20	52
£801 – £1000	28	87
£1001 – £2000	60	140
£2001 – £4000	33	110
£4001 – £6000	13	51
£6001 – £8000	10	12
£8001 – £10000	12	26
£10000 +	0	1
All	**281**	**755**
Maximum award	**£15,000**	
Median award	**£1,000**	
Average award	**£1,828**	

2005 – 2006		
Costs	**No of cases**	
	Claimant	**Respondent**
£0 – £200	16	35
£201 – 400	14	47
£401 – 600	15	58
£601 – 800	5	36
£801 – £1000	14	38
£1001 – £2000	35	81
£2001 – £4000	20	60
£4001 – £6000	19	32
£6001 – 8000	5	16
£8001 – 10000	4	27
£10000 +	1	2
All	**148**	**432**
Maximum award	**£20,000**	
Median award	**£1,136**	
Average award	**£2,256**	

2006 – 2007

Costs	No of cases	
	Claimant	**Respondent**
£0 – £200	16	35
£201 – 400	26	34
£401 – 600	21	49
£601 – 800	6	24
£801 – £1000	23	44
£1001 – £2000	33	54
£2001 – £4000	22	54
£4001 – £6000	5	23
£6001 – 8000	7	9
£8001 – 10000	7	15
£10000 +	0	2
All	**166**	**343**
Maximum award	**£65,000**	
Median award	**£1,000**	
Average award	**£2,078.88**	

2007 – 2008

No statistics were published for this year, during which responsibility for the Employment Tribunal Services passed from the DTI to the Ministry of Justice.

2008 – 2009

Costs	No of cases	
	Claimant	**Respondent**
£0 – £200	9	27
£201 – 400	20	21
£401 – 600	16	24
£601 – 800	6	20
£801 – £1000	8	29
£1001 – £2000	21	46
£2001 – £4000	8	45
£4001 – £6000	5	19
£6001 – 8000	2	14
£8001 – 10000	4	18
£10000 +	3	2
All	**102**	**265**

2008 – 2009		
Costs	No of cases	
	Claimant	**Respondent**
Maximum award	**£25,000**	
Median award	**£1,100**	
Average award	**£2,470**	

The information relates only to costs awarded and does not include awards of compensation where a claim has been successful. In addition, the information does not include preparation time orders.

A brief analysis of the statistics reveals the following:

- there are consistently more awards against Respondents than Claimants;

- while the average award has increased overall since 1999, and the increase in 2003 over the previous few years was considerable, the increase has not been significant since 2003 and indeed has fallen in some years from the previous year;

- the number of awards in the higher brackets (£8001 – £10,000) has been below 40 each year and has decreased in more recent years. However, the reports do not include costs orders of over £10,000 which have been assessed in the county courts and so it is likely that there are more high costs awards than are revealed by the statistics;

- while the number of awards over £10,000 remains very low (no more than 5 in any one year) the tribunals have been increasingly more willing to award significant amounts – up to £65,000 in 2006/2007.

1.3   CHANGES IN APPROACH

The original regulations governing industrial tribunals (SI 1965/1101 and SI 1985/16) were both replaced with effect from 16 December 1993 by the Employment Tribunals (Constitution and Rules of Procedure) Regulations 1993, SI 1993/2687 (SI 1993/2688 for Scotland) and by the Employment Tribunals (Constitution and Rules of Procedure) Regulations 2001, SI 2001/1171 (SI 2001/1170 for Scotland) with effect from 16 July 2001. These in turn, were replaced in 2004.

The earlier Rules provided that a costs order should not normally be made, with the exception of where a party has acted frivolously or vexatiously.

In 1993, the scope was expanded to include conduct whereby the tribunal considers a party to be acting abusively, disruptively or otherwise unreasonably, as well as frivolously or vexatiously.

Regulation 12 Employment Tribunals (Constitution and Rules of Procedure) Regulations 1993

Where, in the opinion of the tribunal, a party has in bringing or conducting the proceedings acted frivolously, vexatiously, abusively, disruptively or otherwise unreasonably, the tribunal may make an order containing an award against that party in respect of the costs incurred by another party.

In addition, a limit of £500 was imposed on the amount of costs which could be awarded.

The 1993 Rules gave specific power to the tribunal to make a costs order against a party who had successfully applied for a postponement or adjournment of a hearing (restricted to the costs incurred or allowances paid as a result of the postponement or adjournment).

Regulation 12(7) provided that where a deposit had been ordered as a condition of a party being permitted to continue to participate in proceedings and that party had been unsuccessful, a tribunal 'shall' consider whether to award costs against them on the ground that that party unreasonably persisted with the claim. The tribunal had to consider the reasons for the order of the deposit and could not award costs unless the reasons which caused it to find against the party were 'substantially the same' as the reasons recorded for considering that the party had no reasonable prospect of success. The deposit paid was to be paid in part or full settlement of the award.

2001

The 2001 Employment Tribunal Rules took the same form as the 1993 Rules but with some significant differences.

The limit was increased to £10,000. In addition, the 2001 Rules (reg 14) omitted the reference to acting 'frivolously' and the high threshold set by Parliament in reg 12 of the 1993 Regulations was lowered with a reformulation of the costs rule by the introduction in r 14 of the concept of a tribunal's discretion to make an award where the bringing or conducting of the proceedings by a party had been 'misconceived'.

14.—(1)   Where, in the opinion of the tribunal a party has in bringing the proceedings, or a party or party's representative has in conducting the proceedings, acted vexatiously, abusively, disruptively, or otherwise unreasonably, **or the bringing or conducting of the proceedings by a party has been misconceived**, the tribunal shall consider making, and if it so decides may make [an order for costs].

In *Gee v Shell (UK) Ltd* the Court of Appeal were dealing with the application of the 1993 Regulations but they (per Scott-Baker LJ, at para 22) recognised that the lowering of this threshold post 1993 emphasised the extreme unlikelihood of the tribunal making a costs order against Mrs Gee if she had proceeded with her claim and failed. The change is generally considered to mean that tribunals would be more easily persuaded to order costs under the 2001 rules than they were under the 1993 Rules. This view was given support by the EAT in *Parkins v Sodexho Ltd*[9] which pointed out that under the 2001 Rules, a tribunal can award costs 'on the ground that there is no reasonable prospect of success' whereas previously under the 1993 Rules it could only do so if it 'came to the conclusion that an application was bound to fail'.

The provisions relating to costs orders where postponements and adjournments of hearings were caused by a party and cases in which deposits had been paid were retained.

2004

The Employment Tribunal (Constitution and Rules of Procedure) Regulations 2004, SI 2004/1861 considerably widened the scope of tribunals to make orders for costs. The rules were expanded to reflect the provision in the Employment Act 2002 for costs powers over and above awards to parties who were legally represented. These introduced 'preparation time' orders to parties who were not legally qualified and 'wasted costs orders' which could be awarded against the parties' representatives themselves.

The Rules themselves provided far more detail as to when applications could be made, the circumstances in which a tribunal **must** make an award and when they can exercise their discretion and consideration is given to the circumstances in which a tribunal can have regard to the paying party's means.

1.4   POSSIBLE ALTERNATIVE STRUCTURES

There have been criticisms of Employment Tribunals for a number of years. The DoE 1994 Paper, 'Resolving Employment Rights Disputes – Options for Reform' stated:

> 'Concern has grown that the industrial tribunals have departed from their original objectives – to provide a readily accessible and cost effective means of redress with a minimum of formality and delay.'

---

[9]   [2002] IRLR 109.

Since 1994, the changes in the costs regimes have resulted in a lowering of the threshold and it is arguable that the increased risk of costs orders being made against parties will push those objectives away further.

In its response to the Gibbons Report (BERR (2008) *Resolving disputes in the workplace consultation – Government Response)* the Government confirmed that there would be no change to the costs regime in the tribunal in relation to any failure of either party to comply with the new ACAS Code of Practice. The recommendations of the Gibbons Report had included:

- ensuring that there are incentives to comply with the new guidelines, by maintaining and expanding employment tribunals' discretion to take into account reasonableness of behaviour and procedure when assessing (awards and) costs orders (recommendation 3, p 55);

- considering whether employment tribunals have powers to deal with weak and vexatious claims and whether tribunals use them consistently (recommendation 17, p 57);

- offering incentives to use early resolution techniques by giving employment tribunals' discretion to take into account parties' efforts to settle the dispute when making (awards and) costs orders (recommendation 9, p 56).

CHAPTER 2

OVERVIEW OF COSTS RULES

2.1 BASIC OUTLINE OF THE 2004 RULES

Rule 38 sets out the basic principles and these apply to costs orders made under rr 39, 40 and 47.

2.1.1 Who can make costs orders?

- Costs orders can be made by a tribunal panel or by an Employment Judge sitting alone (r 38(1)).

2.1.2 What costs can be ordered?

- 'Costs' means fees, charges, disbursements or expenses incurred by or on behalf of a party in relation to the proceedings (r 38(3)).

- Costs orders can be made against the paying party in respect of costs incurred by another party to the proceedings, or to the Secretary of State where payments or allowances have been made to:
  (a) assessors appointed to assist in tribunal matters;
  (b) anyone who has prepared a report under the Equal Pay 1970 relating to whether any work is of equal value (s 2A(1)(b) of the Equal Pay Act 1970);
  (c) any other person in connection with their attendance at employment tribunals. This would include expenses paid to witnesses.

2.1.3 Against whom can a costs order be made?

- Only against a party to the proceedings (r 38(1)(a)), and not to a third party.

- If a costs order is made under r 39, 40 or 47 it is the paying party and not their representative that is liable for payment. Payments by representatives are made under the provisions for wasted costs order in r 48.

- A costs order may be made against or in favour of a Respondent even if they have not had a response accepted, in so far as it relates to their conduct of any part which they have taken in the proceedings (r 38(4)).

- Costs orders can only be made where the receiving party is legally represented either at the hearing at which a costs order is made or, where there is no hearing, when the proceedings are otherwise determined (r 38(2)). As to what being 'legally represented' means, see chapter 3 below. If the party is not legally represented, a time preparation order may be made.

- There are restrictions on making a costs order and a preparation time order in the same proceedings.

Both parties can apply for costs order to be made against the other, as in *Ms S Raza v Dimension Data Network Services Ltd.*[1]

MS S RAZA v DIMENSION DATA NETWORK SERVICES LTD READING EMPLOYMENT TRIBUNAL

Case No 2700580/2006
Supplied by James Arnold, Barrister, 5 Essex Court

The Claimant succeeded in her claims for unfair dismissal and discrimination. Both parties then sought their costs. The Claimant said that the Respondent had behaved in an unreasonable manner throughout the litigation. The Respondent claimed that the Claimant's conduct had been unreasonable.

The Tribunal examined each of the allegations and concluded that the situation was, 'in football terms a no score draw'. Both sides had been unreasonable on occasion; both sides had taken action which had resulted in hearings which may have been made marginally shorter if they had been less devious or inflexible. The Tribunal concluded that it could technically make an order for costs in relation to either or both of the parties. In a situation like this, the Tribunal did not feel it appropriate to make any order for costs.

2.1.4 When and how can an application be made (r 38(7))

- Orally at the end of a hearing or in writing to the employment tribunal office.

- At any time during proceedings.

---

[1] Case No 2700580/2006.

- Within 28 days from the issuing of the judgment determining the claim, which is the date of the hearing if judgment was delivered orally or the date of the written judgment sent after the hearing. If a later application is made, it shall not be accepted or considered unless the tribunal or chairman considers that it is in the interests of justice to do so.

- In circumstances when it has not been possible for the party against whom the order is to be made to provide oral reasons as to why it should not be made (e g at the end of a hearing), an order cannot be made unless the tribunal has written to the party against whom the order may be made giving them the opportunity to provide those reasons.

- Where a costs order has been made, a request for written reasons can be made although it must be made within 14 days of the costs order.

Any application should be supported by a costs schedule and although it is not necessary to produce a detailed schedule drawn up by a professional costs draftsman, it should be sufficiently detailed to assist the Employment Tribunal.

The onus is on the party making the application to make a compelling case, as in *Ioannou v Ministry of Justice*[2] (below) and *Woolf v Kingston Upon Hill City Council (1) & The Governors of Pickering High School Sports College (2)*[3] (below).

MRS S A IOANNOU v MINISTRY OF JUSTICE
LONDON CENTRAL EMPLOYMENT TRIBUNAL

Case No 2201017/2007
Supplied by Andrea Baller of the Treasury Solicitors

The claim for unfair dismissal was dismissed. A costs application was made by the Respondent on the grounds that the Claimant had failed to comply with the tribunal's directions concerning disclosure, further and better particulars and witness statements, that claims that had been withdrawn, were vexatious, that the Claimant's case had 'changed' and that her schedule of loss was a 'mystery novel'.

The tribunal decided not to award costs. They made it clear that a party seeking costs must make a compelling case and that the obligation is all the more weighty where the party on the receiving end does not have the benefit of legal representation, noting that they would 'decline the implicit invitation to trawl through the file in ➡

---

[2]   Case No 2201017/2007.
[3]   Appeal No UKEAT/0631/06/DA.

search of instances of unreasonable behaviour on the Claimant's part or to hypothesise about the merits or demerits of the withdrawn claims'.

MR B WOLFF v KINGSTON UPON HULL CITY COUNCIL (1) THE GOVERNORS OF PICKERING HIGH SCHOOL SPORTS COLLEGE (2)

Appeal No UKEAT/0631/06/DA

The Employment Tribunal had made an award of costs where the Claimant persisted unreasonably in pursuing his claim for re-engagement. He had been guided to take advice in a CMD but appeared to have ignored that guidance, and persisted with his claim long after it had become 'blindingly obvious that no such remedy was remotely practicable'. The Respondent had made a settlement offer of £1,000, which was almost twice what the Claimant received as a compensatory award.

Before the EAT Mr Wolff argued that this was an unlawful exercise by the tribunal of its discretion. He said that as a Claimant who had succeeded in establishing that he had been unfairly constructively dismissed, and who had only ever sought reengagement as a remedy, he was entitled to pursue that remedy to a remedies hearing.

The EAT (per HHJ Wilkie) held that in order for Mr Wolff to establish that the exercise by the Employment Tribunal of their discretion was unlawful, he had to surmount a high hurdle. It was not enough to persuade the EAT that it might have done something different. What he had to do was to establish that the Employment Tribunal was unreasonable in exercising its discretion in the way that it did. They were unable to accede to his argument that the tribunal, in awarding costs against him, acted unreasonably and therefore his appeal failed.

2.2 WHEN AN EMPLOYMENT TRIBUNAL *MUST* MAKE COSTS ORDER (RULE 39)

When a costs or expenses order must be made

39.—(1) Subject to rule 38(2), a tribunal must make a costs order against a respondent where in proceedings for unfair dismissal a Hearing has been postponed or adjourned and –

    (a)   the claimant has expressed a wish to be reinstated or re-engaged which has been communicated to the respondent not less than 7 days before the Hearing; and

(b)   the postponement or adjournment of that Hearing has been caused by the respondent's failure, without a special reason, to adduce reasonable evidence as to the availability of the job from which the claimant was dismissed, or of comparable or suitable employment.

(2) A costs order made under paragraph (1) shall relate to any costs incurred as a result of the postponement or adjournment of the Hearing.

In an unfair dismissal claim, where a Claimant has informed their employer of their wish to be re-engaged or reinstated (in the ET1 or in subsequent correspondence) not less than seven days before a hearing, the Respondent employer is required to adduce reasonable evidence as to the availability of the Claimant's former job (or of comparable or suitable employment). Where there is a failure to adduce that evidence without a 'special' reason, and this results in a postponement or adjournment of the hearing, the tribunal must make a costs order and has no discretion not to do so.

Regulation 39(2) limits the amount of the order to the costs incurred as a result of the postponement or adjournment of the hearing, for example, costs of attendance at the postponed hearing or correspondence relating to the delay.

The costs award in these circumstances will be necessarily made against the employer; indeed, r 39(1) specifically refers to a 'respondent'. In order to be entitled to costs under r 39, a claimant must be legally represented at the point of determination, whether this is at a hearing or not (r 38(2)). Where a claimant is not legally represented, there is no jurisdiction to make an order under r 39 and instead r 38(2) provides that the tribunal 'may' make a preparation time order. There is therefore discretion in circumstances where an unrepresented claimant applies for costs under r 39.

2.3   WHEN AN EMPLOYMENT TRIBUNAL *MAY* MAKE COSTS ORDER

General power to make costs and expenses orders

38.—(4)   A costs order may be made against or in favour of a respondent who has not had a response accepted in the proceedings in relation to the conduct of any part which he has taken in the proceedings.

When a costs or expenses order may be made

40.—(1) A tribunal or chairman may make a costs order when on the application of a party it has postponed the day or time fixed for or adjourned a Hearing or pre-hearing review. The costs order may be against or, as the case may require, in favour of that party as respects any costs incurred or any allowances paid as a result of the postponement or adjournment.

(2) A tribunal or chairman shall consider making a costs order against a paying party where, in the opinion of the tribunal or chairman (as the case may be), any of the circumstances in paragraph (3) apply. Having so considered, the tribunal or chairman may make a costs order against the paying party if it or he considers it appropriate to do so.

(3) The circumstances referred to in paragraph (2) are where the paying party has in bringing the proceedings, or he or his representative has in conducting the proceedings, acted vexatiously, abusively, disruptively or otherwise unreasonably, or the bringing or conducting of the proceedings by the paying party has been misconceived.

(4) A tribunal or chairman may make a costs order against a party who has not complied with an order or practice direction.

The tribunal 'may' make a costs award when the hearing or PHR has been postponed on the application of a party (r 40(1)).

With a slightly different emphasis, set out in r 40(2), a tribunal 'shall consider' making a costs award in the following circumstances:

- when a party or their representative has acted vexatiously, abusively, disruptively or otherwise unreasonably (r 40(3));

- when the bringing or conducting of the proceedings by the paying party has been misconceived (r 40(3));

- where a party has failed to comply with a tribunal order or a practice direction (r 40(4)).

2.3.1   Two-stage process

Case law has developed a two-stage test that should be applied by Employment Tribunals when considering a costs award – see *Monaghan v Close Thornton,*[4] para 22, per Lindsay J.

The two stage process is:

a)   Was the costs threshold triggered, for example, was the conduct of the party against whom costs is sought unreasonable, and if so,

b)   Ought the tribunal to exercise their discretion in favour of the receiving party, having regard to all the circumstances?

An example of a case in which the costs threshold was not triggered is *Miller v Bromley Primary Care Trust.*[5] If the tribunal is satisfied that there was some aspect in the claim (or in each of the heads of claim) that

---

[4]   EAT/0003/01 (unreported) 22 February 2002.
[5]   Case No 1101248/07, 1101716/07, 1101976/07.

contained an arguable point which has to be tested on the evidence, then it is unlikely the costs application will get past the first stage.

MS S MILLER v BROMLEY PRIMARY CARE TRUST
ASHFORD EMPLOYMENT TRIBUNAL

Case No 1101248/07, 1101716/07, 1101976/07

The Claimant claimed that she had suffered a detriment and dismissal on the ground of having made a protected disclosure, that she had suffered disability discrimination and that she had been unfairly dismissed. The Employment Tribunal found that she had not suffered a detriment nor had she been dismissed due to the protected disclosure and that she did not suffer from a disability as defined by the DDA 1995. Finally they found against her on the issue of dismissal. The Respondent made an application for costs and written representations were made.

The tribunal concluded that a number of the points made by the Claimant in support of her claim were arguable and had to be determined on the balance of probabilities, having weighed up all the evidence before the tribunal. They were therefore unable to conclude that she had been vexatious, abusive or unreasonable in bringing the proceedings. This was not, therefore, a case in which it was appropriate to make a costs order.

As pointed out by Mummery J in *Khan v Kirklees Borough Council*[6] (see below) at para 8, it is not possible to list exhaustively what all the circumstances at the second stage might be. However, considerations of conduct, proportionality and the merits of the case and also whether a person is represented or unrepresented are potentially relevant circumstances.

The Regulations make it clear that this is discretionary (*'shall consider making'*). Because an order for costs is an exceptional action, where an Employment Tribunal makes an award of costs, the reason for and the basis for the costs order should be set out clearly – Pill LJ in *Lodwick v London Borough of Southwark,*[7] para 26. In some cases, a subsequent appeal has been successful on the basis that the tribunal had failed to set out its reasons adequately, or to explain how it reached the conclusion it did. Reasons are to be given in the normal way, that is, at the conclusion of a hearing and/or in writing after the hearing.

---

[6]   [2007] EWCA Civ 1342.
[7]   [2004] IRLR 554.

2.3.2 Exercise of discretion

LEWALD – JEZIERSKA v SOLICITORS IN LAW LTD

UKEAT/0165/06/ZT

The Employment Tribunal awarded the Respondents the costs of the entire claim on the basis that the Claimant had throughout acted unreasonably in the presentation of her claims and was misconceived in placing them before the tribunal. Her behaviour included a 90-page Further and Better Particulars, quantification of her claim at £9.5 million (rising to £13.05 million during the hearing) and bizarre and erratic behaviour.

The question of costs was dealt with under the 2001 Rules and the tribunal dealt with this in a single paragraph, stating:

> 'It is the Tribunal's finding that the Claimant has throughout acted unreasonably in the presentation of her claims and was misconceived in placing them before the Tribunal. Accordingly, the Tribunal orders under r 14(1), 3(c) and Sch 1 that the Claimant pays the costs of the three Respondents as assessed by taxation by the county court'.

The costs were assessed in excess of £40,000.

The EAT disagreed that the claims could be described as misconceived, in circumstances where three of the four heads of claim were conceded at the beginning of the hearing. Furthermore, the Employment Tribunal's reasoning showed that it did not follow the two stage approach as required by the regulations: the tribunal should first decide whether in conducting the proceedings a party has acted vexatiously, abusively, disruptively or otherwise unreasonably, or the bringing of the proceedings by a party has been misconceived and then decide whether it should exercise its discretion and make an order. Here the Employment Tribunal had done no more than decide that the Claimant's conduct was unreasonable and immediately proceeded to order her to pay the whole of the costs.

The case was remitted to the same tribunal to reconsider whether an award should be made (as well as the substantive issues). HHJ Reid made it clear that:

> '... we should add that we have every sympathy with the employment tribunal in having had to deal with a Claimant who was plainly extremely difficult and thoroughly unreasonable, as was apparent even before the EAT, where she was largely protected from her own excesses by experienced counsel acting pro bono, to whom we are ➡

more than usually grateful. She should not assume that this success means that she will ... necessarily be immune to an order for costs.'

MARLER (ET) LTD v ROBERTSON

[1974] ICR 72 NIRC

The employers appealed the refusal of an Employment Tribunal to award them the costs of the hearing of a complaint of unfair dismissal. The tribunal proceeded on the basis that tribunals should not normally award costs and that they could only do so where a party had acted frivolously or vexatiously. Consequently, as it was incumbent on the employer to show the reasons for dismissing an employee, a complainant employee was entitled to have those reasons tested before a tribunal and although there could be cases where a complaint would be frivolous and vexatious, they were of the opinion that the complaint in this instant was not such a case.

The EAT dismissed the appeal, holding that costs were a matter of discretion for the tribunal and an appeal against the exercise of that discretion could only succeed if it were shown that the tribunal had misdirected itself in law. In the present case the court could see nothing in the tribunal's reasoning to lead them to the opinion that the tribunal did not exercise their discretion correctly.

MR B SAKA v FITZROY ROBINSON LTD

EAT/0241/00

Mr Saka appealed against an order made by the Employment Tribunal that he should pay the employer's costs of his race discrimination claim, which amounted to about £16,000. He argued that the tribunal had erred in law in its interpretation of the way in which the evidence was given at the hearing so as to conclude that his conduct in pursuing his claim was capable of being frivolous, vexatious or otherwise unreasonable (but not abusive), when there had been no strike out proceedings on the basis of a lack of merits and no costs warning. The tribunal found four reasons for so deciding. Firstly, he had given no evidence of any comparators who had been treated more favourably than him but were of different ethnic origin. Secondly, he had givenno cogent evidence as to why he considered that he had been dismissed because of his ethnic origin as opposed to his lack of competence on which the employers relied. Thirdly, the tribunal had no hesitation in concluding that he had been dismissed because of his conduct; and fourthly, the tribunal ➡

took into account that Mr Saka had presented a similar application to the tribunal in relation to previous employers, which had failed.

The EAT made it clear that tribunals should always have in mind the very real difficulties which face a Claimant in a discrimination claim:

> 'Very rarely is there overt evidence of discrimination; and thus it may be and often is very difficult for the claimant to know whether or not he has real prospects of success until the explanation of the employers' conduct which is the subject of complaint is heard, seen and tested ... Secondly, and it follows from that, a costs order against a claimant in a discrimination claim is always likely in the absence of misconduct to be made only in a very rare and even an exceptional case.'

However, it is for a tribunal to decide whether, in its opinion, a party has behaved in bringing or conducting proceedings before it frivolously, vexatiously or otherwise unreasonably and to decide whether to make a costs order. In so doing it is exercising a discretionary jurisdiction.

The EAT did not accept that a tribunal cannot make a costs order against an applicant in a discrimination claim or any other claim simply because there has been previous application to strike out or no application under r 7(4) or no costs warning. These are factors which a tribunal may or may not wish to take into account in the exercise of its broad discretion.

In addition, the EAT did not accept that the tribunal was not entitled to take into account the previous claim against the previous employers which had failed. It was a factor which the tribunal was entitled to take into account and the weight which they gave to it was a matter for the tribunal and not the EAT.

MISS C H SWEETMAN v MITIE SECURITY (LONDON) LIMITED (1) & DANIELLE WHITE (2)
LONDON SOUTH EMPLOYMENT TRIBUNAL

Case No 2301897/2007
Supplied by Rosa Brennan of Clarkson Wright & Jakes LLP

The claim for disability discrimination succeeded and the Claimant made an application for her costs of the proceedings. The tribunal considered oral and written submissions at a hearing. An issue was the fact that the tribunal did not have to identify any causative link between the unreasonable conduct found and the costs ordered. The tribunal applied the two stage test and found, firstly, that in ➡

defending the proceedings, the Respondent had acted unreasonably. The Respondents' actions that resulted in this decision included:

- the Respondents' evidence about the causes of the dismissal was 'unsatisfactory and incoherent;

- the First Respondent had the benefit of legal advice, a qualified HR officer and considerable resources; and

- the Respondents were 'mendacious or wholly incompetent'.

The tribunal therefore exercised its discretion to make an award of costs and then considered various countervailing features, which included the following:

- although the Claimant had also brought claims for sex and disability discrimination, these were withdrawn and there were no additional facts necessary to be considered by the tribunal as a result;

- the heart of the matter was the Respondents' evidence about the circumstances of the dismissal, which was either inadequate, misleading or irrelevant.

The tribunal considered without prejudice correspondence which had been disclosed and took into account the fact that the Respondents had made no reply to the Claimant's various offers to settle her claim until after the judgment in the substantive hearing.

However, they also considered that the defence had some substance in it. They concluded that, having regard to the nature, gravity and effect of the Respondents' unreasonable conduct, it was appropriate to award 75% of the reasonable costs of the Claimant. They considered what the reasonable costs might be and having investigated the schedule of costs, decided that the Counsel's fee of £1,650 and Claimant's costs of the solicitors of £10,000 were reasonable and that an award of 75% (£8,737.40) would be made.

2.3.3 Conditions

Can the Employment Tribunal attach conditions to the payment of costs? It was clear from *Cooper and anor v Weatherwise (Roofing and Walling) Ltd*[8] that an Employment Tribunal's power to regulate its own procedure did not extend to the imposition of a condition regarding payment of costs.

---

[8]   [1993] ICR 81.

COOPER AND ANOR v WEATHERWISE (ROOFING AND WALLING) LTD

[1993] ICR 81

Three weeks before his claim for unfair dismissal was due to be heard, the Claimant instructed new solicitors. The day before the hearing his solicitors contacted the employers' solicitors and suggested an adjournment. A request was also faxed to the Employment Tribunal but was refused by the Judge. On the day of the hearing the Claimant was neither present nor represented. The tribunal adjourned the hearing and made an order requiring him to pay by a specified date the employers' costs, fixed in the sum of £4,000. The order also provided that if that sum was not paid, the employee would be deprived of the right to restore his application.

The employee appealed and the EAT held that r 12(2)(b) contained no provision for conditions to be attached either with regard to payment of costs or otherwise.

The EAT also held that it was wrong in principle for an award of costs to be made on a punitive as opposed to a compensatory basis, and as such £4,000 was an excessive figure to cover the costs or expenses resulting from the adjournment and therefore must have contained a punitive element. Accordingly, the appeal was allowed and the matter remitted to a different tribunal for reconsideration.

2.4 INTERACTION OF RULES 38–40 WITH STRIKING OUT PROCEEDINGS UNDER RULE 18(7)

Regulation 2 of the 2004 Rules specifically provides that 'misconceived' includes having no reasonable prospect of success. The phraseology 'no reasonable prospect of success' is identical to that of r 18(7)(b), which deals with the powers of the Employment Tribunal to strike out proceedings where, in the opinion of the tribunal, those proceedings have no reasonable prospect of success. It is laid down in the authorities that an Employment Tribunal should be slow to exercise the power under r 18(7)(b) where there are factual issues to be resolved. It is therefore likely to be rare that proceedings would be struck out under r 18, especially if at that stage the evidence of the various parties had not been disclosed (*North Glamorgan NHS Trust v Ezsies*).[9]

On the issue of costs, a claimant will sometimes argue that the proceedings could not have been misconceived or there would have been

---

[9]   [2007] IRLR 603, CA.

an application to strike out under r 18(7). The issue of whether a similar approach should be adopted in relation to r 40 as that adopted in relation to r 18(7)(b) was considered in *Mr R Coathup v Norman Jackson Contractors*.[10]

MR R COATHUP v NORMAN JACKSON CONTRACTORS MANCHESTER EMPLOYMENT TRIBUNAL

Case No 2406893/2006

At the conclusion of the two day hearing, the Claimant withdrew his claim for constructive dismissal, commencedafter his resignation arising out of alleged disciplinary proceedings. He withdrew after the evidence had been heard and just before the Employment Tribunal were about to find against him. The Respondent argued that the claim had been misconceived either (a) from the outset or (b) on exchange of witness statements some two weeks earlier.

The issue for the tribunal was – it is not just a question of whether the Claimant believed (as he clearly did in these circumstances) that his employer had committed a fundamental breach of contract but whether there were reasonable grounds for that belief (Sedley LJ in *Scott v Commissioners for Inland Revenue*).[11] A Claimant may reasonably hold a completely unreasonable view of the chances of success. The question to ask was, did the Claimant, either when commencing proceedings or at the later stage of exchange of witness statements, have 'real or reasonable chances of success'? It was clear that by the time the witness evidence was exchanged, there were no reasonable grounds for the Claimant's belief that the Respondent intended to hold a disciplinary meeting. He had also known this by the time he commenced proceedings because it had been made clear to him at a grievance meeting that the Respondent had no such intention.

In relation to reconciling r 18(7)(b) with r 40, the Claimant submitted that the proceedings could not have been misconceived because there would have been either an application to strike out or a submission of no case to answer at the conclusion of the evidence. He criticised the tribunal for not warning him that his case was hopeless at the conclusion of his evidence.

The tribunal believed that faced with an application by a Respondent to strike out the claim, it may reasonably have come to the conclusion that there were at that stage factual issues that needed to be resolved at a full hearing. The tribunal felt that it is➡

---

[10]   Case No 2406893/2006.
[11]   [2004] IRLR 713.

rare that a claim for constructive dismissal is ever dismissed before the Respondent's evidence is heard on the basis of a submission that there is no case to answer and stated that tribunals are advised that it is rare to entertain such a submission, let alone grant it. If one must apply the same construction to r 40 as to r 18, then arguably costs would never be awarded if the claim would not have been struck out under r 18(7)(b).

The costs of the whole proceedings since commencement were awarded against the Claimant, such sum to be determined by assessment in the county court.

Rule 40(3) clearly envisages a different situation to r 18(7)(b) because the tribunal under r 40 is normally being required to determine, looking backwards, whether there was any point at which the Claimant (or for that matter the Respondent) had no reasonable prospects of success, either in bringing or defending the proceedings or in continuing them. The power of the tribunal to intervene under r 18 will usually be exercised before any of that evidence has been tested.

CHAPTER 3

COSTS V PREPARATION TIME ORDERS

3.1 COST ORDERS

3.1.1 Who is eligible?

Until 2004 costs were only awarded in respect of the costs of a legal representative acting for a party in proceedings and the costs of a litigant in person could not be recovered. A person represented by a non-lawyer is a litigant in person (*Dunnachie v Kingston Upon Hull CC (No 3)*.[1] Thus in *Khan and King v Home Office*,[2] despite success for the Claimants, who were represented by a non legally qualified representative, the Employment Tribunal wrongly ordered costs where an eight day hearing had to be aborted due to the conduct of the Respondent's HR Director.

KHAN/KING v HOME OFFICE

UKEAT/0026/06/LA & UKEAT/0250/06/LA

The HR Director was the principal HR witness for the Respondent. His wife was a lay member and on the penultimate day of the eight day hearing, he asked to speak to the Employment Judge. When he was told that he could not speak to the tribunal he said, 'can you give the (Judge) a message that my wife [name given but omitted here], who he sat with on panels in the tribunal, sends her regards'. As a result, the tribunal had to recuse itself and a year passed before the case could be reconstituted at a different tribunal location, with the Claimants having to resubmit their evidence again. The costs claimed were £14,000 and the tribunal awarded £9,000 on the basis that the Respondent, through its HR Director, had conducted the proceedings unreasonably. ➡

---

[1] [2004] ICR 227.
[2] UKEAT/0026/06/LA & UKEAT/0250/06/LA.

The Respondents appeal against the costs order was upheld because the Claimants were represented by a non-legally qualified representative, although it is clear that this was done reluctantly by the EAT. HHJ McMullen said:

> 'What happens when one of Britain's least impressive managements, by its sole consistent attribute of procrastination, drives two long-service Asian women to become uncooperative and dismissive? The answer is systemic race and sex discrimination against them and dismissals unfair according to every tenet in the canon, rightly found by an Employment Tribunal and wisely not appealed. Sophisticated employment procedures applicable to the two cases, collectively consulted on and agreed over the years, have been left in wreckage by the mismanagement over 15 years of no less than 101 HR professionals and managers, some disingenuous and blind to discrimination. It reached its nadir when its HR director, steering this organisation of 8,000 people, single-handedly by his misjudgement caused the hearing to be aborted after eight days at enormous cost to the women and to the public purse, with the result that they had to give their evidence all over again, one year later, before a different Employment Tribunal and at a different hearing centre.'

3.1.2   How much can be ordered?

Under r 41, there are three ways in which the amount of a costs order can be determined:

- the tribunal can specify the amount (r 41(1)). In this case, the amount cannot exceed £10,000 and this can be ordered without any kind of detailed assessment;

- the parties may agree an amount, in which case the amount is that agreed between them (r 41(2)). The amount can exceed £10,000;

- where the tribunal believes that an award exceeding £10,000 is appropriate, r 41(3) applies. It may order that the costs be assessed in the normal way under the Civil Procedure Rules 1998 (or in Scotland, taxed in the Sheriff Court according to the fee table).

The amount of a costs or expenses order

41.—(1) The amount of a costs order against the paying party shall be determined in any of the following ways –

    (a)   the tribunal may specify the sum which the paying party must pay to the receiving party, provided that sum does not exceed £10,000;

    (b)   the parties may agree on a sum to be paid by the paying party to the receiving party and if they do so the costs order shall be for the sum so agreed;

    (c)   the tribunal may order the paying party to pay the receiving party the whole or a specified part of the costs of the receiving party with the amount to be paid being determined by way of detailed assessment in a County Court in accordance with the Civil Procedure Rules 1998 or, in Scotland, as taxed according to such part of the table of fees prescribed for proceedings in the sheriff court as shall be directed by the order.

(2) The tribunal or chairman may have regard to the paying party's ability to pay when considering whether it or he shall make a costs order or how much that order should be.

(3) For the avoidance of doubt, the amount of a costs order made under paragraphs (1)(b) or (c) may exceed £10,000.

The relevant CPR Part relating to costs is Part 48.

In relation to the £10,000 limit, in *Kovacs v Queen Mary and Westfield College CA*[3] (see below), Chadwick LJ stated that this limit should not result in an award, 'which is less than proper compensation for the costs incurred by the receiving party by reason of the culpable conduct which has led to the decision [to award costs]'.

It is possible for the Employment Tribunal to make orders for a series of unassessed awards, each up to £10,000, in one case.

MR ANTHONY JAMES v BLOCKBUSTER ENTERTAINMENT LTD

UKEAT/0601/05/DM

Mr James appealed in respect of two costs orders made at the London Central Tribunal. The substantive order was a sum of £10,000 ordered to be paid towards the Respondent's costs of defending the proceedings, following the striking-out of the two claims Mr James had brought, together with a further sum of £1,000 incurred in respect of a subsequent costs hearing. One ground of Mr James' appeal was that the costs order was effectively one order, namely that of £11,000 and therefore that sum was in excess of the Tribunal's powers to award up to £10,000.

In the EAT HHJ Ansell was satisfied that:

> 'on a proper interpretation of r 14, … it is open to a Tribunal to make a whole series of a costs awards throughout proceedings if it is felt necessary.'

Therefore a series of unassessed awards, each up to £10,000, may be made in one case. ➡

---

3   [2002] EWCA Civ 352, [2002] IRLR 414.

This was subsequently applied by the Employment Tribunal and on 20 January 2009 Blockbuster was awarded three orders of costs of £5,000, £10,000 and £10,000 for different periods of time in the same proceedings.

3.1.3   Quantifying the costs order

*   A fixed sum is preferable.

LOTHIAN HEALTH BOARD v JOHNSTONE

[1981] IRLR 321, EAT

The Respondent, a ward sister, was dismissed for what was stated to be professional misconduct. An employment tribunal upheld her complaint of unfair dismissal on the ground that the employer had not shown the reason for dismissal. Her solicitors applied for their costs to be awarded on the ground that the employers had acted frivolously, in that by the end of the second day of the four-day hearing it was apparent that the employers would not prove their case. The Employment Tribunal made an order of 'one half of their costs'.

On appeal by the employers the EAT held that frivolous conduct was different from cases where proceedings were unnecessary, improper or vexatious, and had to comprise something exceptional. The test was whether the party in question knew or ought to have known, if he had gone about the matter sensibly, that his case was hopeless. In this case it could not be said that the employers had acted precipitately in dismissing the Respondent and were not entitled to defend the proceedings. The appeal was allowed.

The EAT also stated that it was preferable for an order for costs to refer to a fixed sum rather than 'one half' of the costs.

*   The tribunal should ensure that the reasons for assessing costs at a certain figure are set out and that figures should not be 'plucked out of thin air'

RICHMOND v DEVON DOCTORS ON CALL

UKEAT/0314/06/DA

The Employment Tribunal dismissed the claim for unfair dismissal and ordered the Claimant to pay £4,000 by way of costs to the Respondent. The panel accepted that the case had been brought➡

unreasonably, but they also took into account the late withdrawal of the Claimant's disability claim and her failure to comply with directions. In assessing the amount of costs to be ordered, they took into account her means but gave no indication in their reasoning of the extent to which, if any, they had had regard to the fact that the Claimant was unemployed.

However, on the appeal, HHJ Serota noted that:

> '... an Employment Tribunal is not obliged to have regard to the party's means but at least, it seems to us, it needs to give consideration to the questions of whether it should, and explain why it has or has not taken those means into account. It seems to us that the reasoning given by the Employment Tribunal is so brief that it looks as if they have simply plucked the figure of £4,000 out of the air without giving any adequate explanation as to why they have chosen this figure.'

The case was remitted to the same tribunal for a decision whether, in the circumstances of the case, it was appropriate to make an order for costs in the sum of £4,000 or any other sum.

MR J ESSIEN v JJ JOYCE & SON LTD

UKEAT/0137/06/DA

The Claimant was ordered to pay costs assessed in the sum of £4,000. The Employment Tribunal was critical of the way the claims for constructive dismissal, discrimination on the grounds of race (subsequently amended to racial harassment), unlawful deductions from salary and holiday pay had been conducted. Mr Essien appealed, claiming that the Employment Tribunal had failed to explain how the sum of £4,000 had been calculated and that it had failed to differentiate between his conduct and that of his solicitor, or to explain why an order had been made against him.

In its decision the Employment Tribunal made a number of findings in relation to delay, which was largely the responsibility of the Claimant's solicitors and the EAT therefore believed that the tribunal was entitled to find that a hearing should never have taken place and also that some three hours had been lost during the final hearing as a result of the Claimant's solicitor's conduct. They were therefore entitled to make an order for costs. However, the EAT felt that the tribunal had failed to give an adequate explanation as to how it had reached the sum of £4,000. They said:

> '... to say that it adopted a rough and ready approach in our opinion is no substitution for making proper enquiries as to the level of costs and ascertaining the extent of costs which had been wasted.' ➡

The EAT also said that the tribunal should have explained to what extent it regarded the Claimant as responsible for the costs as opposed to his solicitor, and to have worked out what proportion of the costs being claimed reflected the costs attributable to unreasonable behaviour and what proportion reflected the overall costs. In these circumstances, the EAT allowed the appeal and remitted the matter to the tribunal for reconsideration.

HUGH BRYANT AND REGINALD BENCH t/a BRYANT HAMILTON & CO v MS D WEIR

Appeal No UKEAT/0253/04/DM

The Employment Tribunal had concluded that the criteria for the making of a costs order (misconceived proceedings and unreasonable conduct) existed and that a costs order would be made in favour of the Respondent. The Respondent's costs amounted to £28,000 but the Tribunal awarded £750 saying only, 'the Tribunal has looked at the quantum in the round, and in this case the appropriate sum is £750.'

The EAT referred the case back to the Employment Tribunal in order to answer the question as to what were its reasons for arriving at the sum of £750, so that it could be seen whether it had any reasons at all, and if so whether those reasons can be regarded as valid in law. The EAT also expressly gave the employment tribunal the power to review its own motion, '... if it looks at this £750 order, gulps and realises that it cannot think of any reasons to justify it, or cannot remember what its reasons were'.

- Sometimes, it is disproportionate to attempt the task of systematically assessing the amount of costs

LEE v LONDON ATHLETIC RAIDERS SOCCER ACADEMY STRATFORD EMPLOYMENT TRIBUNAL

Case no 3201887/2003
Supplied by Neil Russell of BD Laddie

Costs of £350 were allowed to cover costs incurred by the Respondent as a result of the Claimant's failure to comply with an order for disclosure, resulting in chaser letters and the job of counsel being more difficult (although not affecting the refresher fee). The Employment Tribunal believed that that failure should be visited in costs. It decided that there was no clear basis upon which to assess➡

the costs and it was disproportionate to attempt the task in a systematic manner, so they assessed the costs generally, at £350.

MS E E HOWIE v H M PRISON SERVICE
LEEDS EMPLOYMENT TRIBUNAL

Case No 1802213/07
Supplied by John Sturzaker of Russell Jones & Walker

The Claimant's claim that she was subjected to detriments on the ground that she made a protected disclosure succeeded, the judgment being overwhelmingly in her favour. She was awarded damages and aggravated damages. The Employment Tribunal noted that in relation to the Respondent's conduct 'the word "travesty" is not inappropriate'. There were five principal issues (although there were others) and in relation to three of them the Tribunal found that the thread running through the Respondent's defence – that it had acted entirely properly – had no reasonable prospect of success. In relation to the fourth issue, there was no evidential basis to support the Respondent's position and it must therefore have failed. There was only one issue which was remotely arguable. The Tribunal did not believe that it should seek to carry out a detailed assessment of the percentage involvement of that one issue and they looked at the matter in the round. They concluded that the Claimant should be awarded 80% of her costs on the basis that four out of the five arguments run by the Respondent had no reasonable prospect of success.

- It is the conduct in the course of proceedings which alone must be considered

---

HEALTH DEVELOPMENT AGENCY v PARISH

[2004] IRLR 550

The originating application was presented on 15 January 2003, and the Notice of Appearance on 5 February. The costs application made by Mr Parish was for costs incurred after 2 December 2002, when the employers refused to comply with his request for written reasons. The Employment Tribunal awarded costs in respect of the period after 2 December 2002, on the basis that the employers had acted unreasonably, forcing the applicant to instigate proceedings in the tribunal and incur additional costs. ➡

The EAT made it clear (per HHJ Richardson at para 21) that an Employment Tribunal had no jurisdiction to award costs in respect of the conduct of a party prior to proceedings or unrelated to proceedings, and it was:

> '... necessary for there to be a causal relationship between the conduct of a party in bringing or conducting proceedings and the costs which are awarded under Rule 14 ... An employment tribunal, having found fault in the conducting of proceedings, needs to examine carefully what loss is attributable to that conduct. It does not need to conduct a minute examination or make individual findings about every hour of a solicitor's time. It may make a broad assessment; but it cannot, once having found vexatious or unreasonable behaviour in the conduct of proceedings, backdate its award to include costs which are not attributable to that conduct.'

- A tribunal should not go beyond the terms of the receiving party's application.

MR S DEMAN v VICTORIA UNIVERSITY OF MANCHESTER (1), PROFESSOR ANDREW STARK (2), PROFESSOR STUART TURLEY (3)

UKEAT/0211/06/RN

The Employment Tribunal considered that the Claimant had been guilty of conduct which amounted to vexatious, abusive and disruptive conduct; at times it was scandalous and at all times it was unreasonable. They concluded that they could consider making an order for costs against him.

The Respondent had limited its claim for costs to £10,000 and the Employment Tribunal ordered costs at a 20% reduction, noting that the Respondent's costs would have been at a minimum £1,500 per day, four of which were 'wilfully' wasted by the Claimant.

One of the Claimant's submissions on appeal was that a tribunal does not have power to make an award which goes outside the terms of a written application by the prospective receiving party. The EAT held that the tribunal could perfectly well have taken the view that the Respondents had incurred costs by way of unreasonable conduct far in excess of £10,000 and made an award of £10,000 overall. It was not open to the Respondents so to contend, neither was it open to Mr Deman to contend that limiting the reduction to £2,000 and the net total to £8,000 was outside the tribunal's discretion.

➡

The EAT considered para T1069 of *Harvey on Industrial Relations and Employment Law*:

> 'A tribunal has a mandatory duty to consider making an order for costs where it is of the opinion that any of the grounds for making of costs or preparation time order has been made out. The effect of this is that if a tribunal considers that there has been unreasonable conduct by a party or his representative or that the bringing or conducting of the proceedings has been misconceived it must actively address the question of a possible award whether or not an application for costs has been made. In doing so it must, of course, give the parties an opportunity to make representations as to why such an order should or should not be made. The fact that a tribunal has a duty to consider making an order does not, however, deprive it of its ultimate discretion of whether or not to award costs in the particular circumstances of the case.'

The EAT agreed with this and with the approach taken by the tribunal and dismissed the Claimant's appeal.

- Tribunals may allocate sums to individual aspects of claims.

MISS SUSAN JANE NICOL v MILLS GLOBAL SERVICES OF UK LTD (1), THE MILS CORPORATION (2) GLASGOW EMPLOYMENT TRIBUNAL

Case No S/125023/06
Supplied by Claire Brattey of SJ Berwin LLP

Both parties made applications for expenses against the other. Although the Claimant was unsuccessful, the Tribunal did not share the Respondent's view that the matter was so clear that embarking on litigation was an unreasonable course of conduct or that it had been unreasonable to commence or continue the proceedings for breach of contract. The Claimant's request for expenses against both Respondents was made on the basis that she would not have incurred expenses if it had been made clear to her that she was only entitled to a pro rata amount of shares. The Tribunal rejected this argument – as soon as the ET3 had been filed she would have known this and the Tribunal did not believe that the Respondents had acted unreasonably in contesting the claim. Both claims for expenses were therefore rejected.

There was an arguable case in her public interest disclosure claim but her claims for sex discrimination and dismissal for asserting a statutory right were wholly misconceived. The Claimant had received a clear warning from the Judge in relation to her claim for dismissal for asserting a statutory right but she had not heeded this➡

and the Tribunal felt that, 'a claimant is entitled to ignore such warnings but do (sic) so at their own risk'. She had not had a deposit ordered in respect of her sex discrimination claim but had offered very little evidence to support the claim at the hearing and the tribunal accepted the Respondent's assertion that the sex discrimination claim had been 'hooked on' as an afterthought to the claim.

The Respondent requested costs from the date of the pre hearing review but the Tribunal did not believe that this was appropriate because the hearing had been concerned mainly with the public interest disclosure claim and they had decided that no award would be made in respect of that part of the claim. The claims of dismissal for asserting a statutory right and sex discrimination were secondary and did not cause the length of the hearing or the preparation to be substantially longer. The award was therefore for £800 (less £300 already paid by way of deposit).

- Tribunals may order sums to be paid in instalments.

MR PAUL STEWART v WH MALCOLM LTD
GLASGOW EMPLOYMENT TRIBUNAL

Case No S/133867/07 & S/100161/08
Supplied by Alison Peat of MacRoberts

The unanimous judgment of the Tribunal was that the dismissal of the Claimant was fair and his claim was therefore dismissed. An award of expenses was made in the sum of £100, payable at the rate of £15 per month.

The power to order payment by instalments is not immediately apparent in the Rules. However, it is a sterile point since if the receiving party seeks to enforce the costs, the county court can order payment by instalments anyway (under s 71 of the County Courts Act 1984).

3.1.4   Relevance of paying party's means

Both the 1993 and the 2001 Rules contained no reference to the exercise of discretion or otherwise by the tribunal, or to a requirement to make enquiries as to the paying party's means. In the *Benyon* case the EAT said:

> '... even if it had been shown (as it was not) that the appellant employees in our case were unable to pay the costs they were ordered to pay, that of itself would not have vitiated the exercise of the Chairman's discretion. Each case ... depends upon its own circumstances and lies within the discretion of the

Tribunal. It is perhaps notable, as far as parties' means, that the present Rule 12 neither requires nor provides any machinery for an enquiry into a party's means ...'

Where the 1993 and 2001 Rules applied, ability to pay could of course be taken into account by the county court under s 71 of the County Courts Act 1984, which gives the court a wide power to take into account the ability of the paying party to pay.

Satisfaction of judgments and orders for payment of money

71.—(1) Where a judgment is given or an order is made by a county court under which a sum of money of any amount is payable, whether by way of satisfaction of the claim or counterclaim in the proceedings or by way of costs or otherwise, the court may, as it thinks fit, order the 'money to be paid either –

   (a)   in one sum, whether forthwith or within such period as the court may fix; or

   (b)   by such instalments payable at such times as the court may fix.

(2) If at any time it appears to the satisfaction of the court that any party to any proceedings is unable from any cause to pay any sum recovered against him (whether by way of satisfaction of the claim or counterclaim in the proceedings or by way of costs or otherwise) or any instalment of such a sum, the court may, in its discretion, suspend or stay any judgment or order given or made in the proceedings for such time and on such terms as the court thinks fit, and so from time to time until it appears that the cause of inability has ceased.

In *Kovacs v Queen Mary and Westfield College*,[4] the decision was made under the 2001 Rules, which meant that the tribunal did not need to have regard to the means of a party. The Court of Appeal upheld the tribunal's approach, which was that there was no intention that issues in respect of means should be binding or overwhelming when the tribunal was considering a costs application. There was approval of the tribunal's statement that:

'... it does not appear, on the face of the relevant Regulations, that it was intended that poor litigants may misbehave with impunity and without fearing that any significant costs order will be made against them, whereas wealthy ones must behave themselves because otherwise an order will be made. '

---

[4]   [2002] ICR 919, CA.

KOVACS v QUEEN MARY & WESTFIELD COLLEGE AND ANOR

[2002] EWCA Civ 352, [2002] IRLR 414

Dr Kovacs presented an application claiming unfair dismissal and unlawful race and sex discrimination against Queen Mary & Westfield College, and unlawful sex and race discrimination against The Royal Hospitals NHS Trust. The tribunal dismissed her claims against the Second Respondent, finding that there was not and never had been a genuine claim of race and sex discrimination against them and that the proceedings were entirely unmeritorious and a flagrant abuse of the purposes of litigation. The tribunal was satisfied, therefore, that the litigation had been conducted in a way which was frivolous, vexatious and unreasonable. Accordingly, the tribunal went on to consider whether to make an order for costs against Dr Kovacs.

Whilst recognising that her finances were restricted, the tribunal concluded that, in the exceptional circumstances of the case, it was appropriate to order that Dr Kovacs should pay the whole of the Second Respondent's costs.

On appeal to the EAT, Dr Kovacs argued that the Employment Tribunal had erred in failing to take her means into account in making the order for unlimited costs. The EAT dismissed the appeal. She appealed again and the Court of Appeal dismissed that appeal and refused leave to appeal to the House of Lords. It held that ability to pay is not a factor which an Employment Tribunal should take into account when deciding whether or not to make an order for costs under the power conferred by r 12 of the 1993 Rules. No order for costs can ever be made by an Employment Tribunal except against a person who, in terms of r 12(1), has behaved 'frivolously, vexatiously, abusively, disruptively or otherwise unreasonably'. Once that threshold of unreasonable behaviour has been crossed, there is no reason why the misbehaving party should not be required to compensate his opponent for costs which he plainly should not have had to incur. Where it was intended that an Employment Tribunal should take ability to pay into account (when deciding whether to order payment of a deposit as a condition of being permitted to continue to take part in proceedings), an express provision was made. In ordinary litigation, where Parliament has intended that the amount of costs ordered against an individual should be limited to the amount which it is reasonable for him to pay, it has done so in express terms.

The *Kovacs* decision that tribunals should not take means into account reversed a line of authority dating back to *Wiggin Alloys v Jenkins.*[5] However the 2004 Rules reinstated the *Wiggin* position. Rule 41(2) provides that the tribunal or Judge *may* have regard to the paying party's ability to pay when considering whether it or he shall make a costs order or how much that order should be.

So a tribunal is not obliged to take means into account, however if it does do so, it must state how it did so. In many cases it may well be desirable to take means into account before making an order; ability to pay may affect the exercise of an overall discretion. But if, for example, the paying party has not attended a costs hearing or has given unsatisfactory evidence about means, the tribunal may not be able to take ability to pay into account.

However, it was made clear in *Jilly v Birmingham and Solihull Mental NHS Trust & ors* (see below), per HHJ Richardson, that if the tribunal decides not to take means into account, it should express that conclusion and say why. If it decides to take means into account, it will then need to set out its findings about ability to pay, decide whether to make a costs order at all in the light of the paying party's means, and if it does so, what the order should be. Furthermore, it should give succinct reasons for its conclusions.

JILLY v BIRMINGHAM AND SOLIHULL MENTAL NHS TRUST & ORS

Appeal Nos UKEAT/0584/06/DA and UKEAT/0155/07/DA

Miss Jilley brought separate claims for race discrimination, harassment and victimisation, which were combined and listed for a lengthy hearing. At the beginning of the hearing the Trust applied to strike out the claims. The application was refused but the Employment Tribunal found that Miss Jilley had behaved unreasonably and that it was just, fair and proportionate that she should pay the costs of the strike out application. At the conclusion of the main hearing of the first two sets of proceedings, the tribunal dismissed Miss Jilley's claims in their entirety. The tribunal then granted the Trust's application for costs, ordering that the costs (which had been claimed in a schedule at, in round terms, £3,000 for the striking out application and £62,000 for the rest of the proceedings) should be referred to the county court for a detailed assessment. Ms Jilley appealed against the judgment as to costs.

One of the submissions on appeal was that the tribunal had not dealt properly or adequately with the question of Ms Jilley's means. ➡

---

[5]   [1981] IRLR 275.

The tribunal had evidence that her capital was limited to some £40,000 at most, and to a modest monthly net income, yet they awarded the whole of the Trust's costs, which (though subject to detailed assessment) were likely to exceed by far the capital she had available. No reasons were given for making such an order. She submitted that it is generally undesirable for a tribunal to make large awards for costs when it is clear on the information before it that an award cannot be enforced. There was no cap of any kind on the order and it was unclear whether the tribunal appreciated that it had a power to cap the award even if it was sending the award for detailed assessment.

The EAT did not think there was any error of law in the tribunal's reasoning in respect of costs and considered that the reasons properly and adequately explained the decisions, but they agreed that the tribunal has not dealt adequately with the question of Ms Jilley's means. It was recognised that r 41(2) gives a discretion whether to take into account the paying party's ability to pay but if a tribunal decides not to do so, it should say why. If it decides to take into account ability to pay, it should set out its findings in a succinct statement about ability to pay, say what impact this has had on its decision whether to award costs or on the amount of costs, and explain why. In this case the tribunal had not provided any such explanation.

The EAT also held that if a tribunal orders detailed assessment it is entitled, in the exercise of its discretion, to make an order for costs which takes account of ability to pay. It can, for example, order that only a specified part of the costs should be payable (r 41(1)(c)). Moreover rr 41(1) and (2) taken together are wide enough to allow a tribunal to take account of ability to pay by placing a cap on an award of costs even where it orders a detailed assessment. If a tribunal is satisfied that a paying party has been frank as to its means, it may be positively desirable to do so. It may, for example, render it unnecessary to go through the expense of a detailed assessment or it may assist parties to reach terms of payment.

BENJAMIN v INTERLACING RIBBON LTD

UKEAT/0363/05/LA & UKEAT/0420/05/LA

The Employment Tribunal dismissed the claim for constructive dismissal and made an order for costs of £5,000 against the Claimant, on the ground that the proceedings were misconceived. The EAT remitted the case back because they believed that there ➡

had been an error of law by the tribunal in the way in which it dealt with her sick pay, which meant that the decision as to costs was also remitted.

The EAT held that the tribunal had not adequately given reasons for exercising its discretion to award costs and also that the tribunal certainly ought to have had regard to the means of the paying party. HHJ Richardson said:

> 'It is now plain (in contra-distinction to the position before the 2004 Rules) that a Tribunal may take into account the means of a paying party. The Tribunal is not obliged to do so; there will be cases where the Tribunal will not need to do so, for example, where a party is an employer with very large financial resources. In our judgment where, as here, a Tribunal was asked to take into account the paying party's ability to pay under r 41(2), it ought to have stated in its reasons whether it did so and how it did so' and for that reason also, the Tribunal's decision on costs could not stand.'

There is therefore no requirement that a tribunal should look at a Claimant's personal means before making an order, but where that information is before the tribunal, they must take that information into account. For that reason, there will normally be good reason for a paying party's representative to give full details about their client's means to pay, if their means are such that this would prevent an otherwise certain costs order against them.

BAGGS v FUDGE
BRIGHTON EMPLOYMENT TRIBUNAL

Case No 1400114/05
Supplied by Daniel Barnett, Barrister, Temple Garden Chambers

Mr Baggs was a member of the BNP. He applied for a job as a practice manager with a medical practice and was rejected. He claimed direct discrimination under the Employment Equality (Religion or Belief) Regulations 2003, SI 2003/1660. His claim was dismissed on the basis that the claim did not come within the ambit of reg 2(1) of the 2003 Regulations.

The Respondent applied for costs of £2,800 plus VAT. They had put Mr Baggs on notice of their intention to do so. The Claimant accepted that the claim had been pursued to test the scope of the Regulations, although he denied that the BNP was supporting him. The Judge held that the claim had been doomed from the start, saying:

➡

'This is a political party. No sleight of hand or skilful oratory can transform it into a religious organisation or one that subscribes to particular religious or similar philosophical beliefs. It had no reasonable prospect of success and it is appropriate to consider awarding costs.'

He had regard to the Claimant's ability to pay in deciding whether costs should be awarded, under r 41(2). He took into account the fact that Mr Baggs' outgoings virtually matched his income and decided that awarding the full amount claimed would be unduly burdensome so he awarded £1,400 plus VAT to be paid.

There are a number of examples of Employment Tribunals awarding costs of nil due to the Claimant's straightened circumstances, even in circumstances where their claim has been dismissed.

MR T PIRIE v WA BAXTERS & SONS LTD
ABERDEEN EMPLOYMENT TRIBUNAL

Case No 101162/2004
Supplied by Claire Brattey of S J Berwin

The Claimant had failed to turn up to a hearing because his advisor did not tell him about it; the failure was the advisor's fault but the Rules at the time did not permit an award to be made against a party's advisor. The tribunal also took into consideration the Claimant's lack of means and felt that there was little point in making an order where the ability to pay was nil.

MR A MIRTAHMASEBI v TERSUS CONSULTANCY LTD
STRATFORD EMPLOYMENT TRIBUNAL

Case No 3202044/2007
Supplied by Belinda Lester of CKFT Solicitors

The Claimant's claims for unfair dismissal and a bonus payment were dismissed. The Respondent's solicitors had sent a costs warning to the Claimant's solicitors and they applied for £2,000 costs to cover Counsel's brief fee and the preparation of the bundle. The Tribunal held that the Claimant had been misconceived in pursuing the proceedings; it was clear on the Claimant's own evidence that the claims had no reasonable prospect of success. However, the Claimant also gave evidence of his means and in view of his significant debts the Tribunal declined to make any award against him.

MR M TAYLFORTH v IACS LTD
ASHFORD EMPLOYMENT TRIBUNAL

Case No 1101534/2008/CW
Supplied by Victoria Wright of Thackray Williams LLP

The Claimant did not attend the hearing. The Judge found that the claim had been misconceived and that the proceedings had been conducted unreasonably and he indicated that a costs award of £3,000 would be made. The Claimant had not been given notice of the costs application and so was given the opportunity to give reasons in writing why the order should not be made. Although the Judge did not accept the reason for the Claimant's non attendance, he did have regard to the Claimant's ability to pay. The Claimant was unemployed and being supported by his family and a costs award would, his representative said, lead to bankruptcy or a voluntary arrangement. The Judge held that the hardship likely to be suffered by the Claimant by making the order outweighed the hardship to the Respondent in not making such an order, and so no order was made.

MRS H M GINN v ADVANTAGE HEALTHCARE GROUP LTD (1), NOTTINGHAMSHIRE COUNTY COUNCIL (2)
NOTTINGHAM EMPLOYMENT TRIBUNAL

Case No 2600795/2006
Supplied by Kimberley Shaw of Irvine and Partners

The Employment Tribunal were satisfied that, in the light of their findings in the case for race discrimination and victimisation, the claim was misconceived and the continued pursuit of it was unreasonable. They considered that in the ordinary course, it would be entirely appropriate that the Claimant should pay a proportion of the costs. They noted that both Respondents had been put to 'inordinate' expense in defending the claims. However the Tribunal had regard to the Claimant's means and accepted that she realistically had no prospect of paying any sensible proportion of those costs. They accepted her evidence that she had substantial debts and no means to support herself, and decided that in the circumstances it was not appropriate to make an order for costs.

A tribunal can and will make judgments about the amounts of outgoings presented to them by the paying party.

MR T S THORPE v ROYAL MAIL GROUP PLC (1), MR J SPENCER (2)
ABERGELE EMPLOYMENT TRIBUNAL

Case No 2900195/2007
Supplied by Lee Rogers of Weightmans LLP

The Claimant's claims against the First Respondent were dismissed on the basis that the termination of his employment had been by mutual consent. The Employment Tribunal considered that because he had made his position clear to independent third parties (doctors) and to the First Respondent that he wished to avail himself of ill heath retirement, his claim for unfair dismissal was misconceived.

Although the Respondent's costs amounted to £6,131.70 it did not seek to recover its full costs but sought only counsel's fees of £750, which they agreed to accept in instalments. When the Tribunal considered the Claimant's means they noted that his outgoings exceeded his income by £363.17. They examined his monthly outgoings carefully and came to the conclusion that he could dramatically reduce these, for example, by spending less than £45 on dog food, £140 on diesel and £104 on gas and electricity. On that basis the Tribunal was of the view that the Claimant could afford to pay £750 in the instalments suggested by the First Respondent.

3.1.5   The costs of an in-house lawyer can be recovered

WIGGIN ALLOYS v JENKINS

[1981] IRLR 275

An employee was dismissed on grounds of suspected theft and he was subsequently prosecuted and imprisoned. His dismissal was found to be fair but the employers' application for costs was refused, the Employment Tribunal taking the view that the Respondent, being in prison, would be unlikely to be in a position to pay costs, and further that as the employers were represented by an in-house lawyer the costs incurred were not recoverable.

The employers appealed. The EAT held the inability of the employee to meet an order for costs was a proper matter to be taken into consideration under the Industrial Tribunal (Labour Relations) Regulations 1974, Schedule, r 10(1)(a). However, the tribunal had erred in considering that they would not be able to award the costs →

of an in-house lawyer. Such costs were as much recoverable as the costs incurred by employing an independent solicitor. The appeal would nevertheless be dismissed.

3.1.6 Trade union/CAB support

In *Omar v Worldwide News Inc*[6] the EAT held that only in exceptional cases should a tribunal consider the means of a party's trade union in making an award of costs but this was rejected by the EAT in *Benyon*. In that case, the EAT stated that this would place an unjustified fetter on the tribunal's discretion to award costs which the unrestricted terms in which it is conferred under the Rules does not permit. In that case, the means of the union were taken into account in making the order for costs against the Claimants and the EAT held that there is no authority for the proposition that the involvement of a supporting union can only be taken into account where the union has accepted that it would indemnify the individuals involved.

CARR v ALLEN BRADLEY ELECTRONICS LTD

[1980] ICR 603, IRLR 263, EAT

An employee was dismissed because of her persistent absence. She complained to an employment tribunal that her dismissal was unfair and at the hearing was represented by her union's unqualified regional organiser. The tribunal found that the employee's claim was without merit and they made an order for costs on the basis that her complaint was frivolous and vexatious. Furthermore, as she was assisted by her union, they ordered her to pay the employers' full costs, to be taxed by the county court registrar. The Claimant appealed against the order for costs.

The EAT held that although there was no evidence to support a finding that she had acted vexatiously, in the sense that she had brought her claim out of spite or some improper motive, the tribunal was justified in finding that she had acted frivolously, in that her claim was misconceived and they were therefore entitled to make an order for costs under the 1974 Rules. The High Court practice, however, of taking account of the fact that an employee was supported by her union when awarding costs was an inappropriate practice for tribunals to adopt. The tribunal was to consider the means of the Claimant and not the trade union when considering whether or not to order costs and the term of the order to be made. Accordingly the appeal would be allowed and the order for costs altered.

---

[6]   [1998] IRLR 291.

WALKER v HEATHROW REFUELLING SERVICES CO LTD

UKEAT/0366/04/TM

The Appellant was supported by his Trade Union, which had provided the costs of his representation. The EAT noted that in High Court proceedings (where of course costs are a much more live issue and arise much more regularly where claimants fail), in practice a Trade Union would pay any costs ordered to be paid by its member to the Respondent. They held that in considering 'ability to pay' account, should be taken of whether the party concerned has the backing of a trade union and the amount, if any, of any award in his favour.

There has therefore been conflicting case law on this issue but the position now seems to be that if a Claimant is supported by their union and an award of costs is made, the means of the union may be taken into account.

MRS M SULLIVAN v ISLE OF WIGHT COUNCIL
SOUTHAMPTON EMPLOYMENT TRIBUNAL

Case No 3101545/2008
Supplied by Vicky Parker of Legal Services, Isle of Wight Council

The Claimant's claim for unfair dismissal was dismissed. The Respondent made an application for costs at the conclusion of the hearing on the basis that the claim was misconceived. The Tribunal considered their findings of fact, in particular the facts that the Claimant had made a misleading entry in what she purported to be a contemporaneous record and had, in her disciplinary interview, admitted on three occasions that this amounted to lying or had the appearance of dishonesty. Nothing in the evidence had changed that initial view. On that basis the Tribunal felt that the Claimant would have had an uphill struggle to succeed and that the case was a very weak one so it did not have any reasonable prospect of success.

The Tribunal made an order for costs of £2,000 plus VAT (amounting to counsel's fees alone) but made it clear that they anticipated that the sum would be paid by the Claimant's union and that if this was not case, that would be a ground for the Claimant to apply for a review of their order, as the question of her means would then have to be examined.

3.1.7 Attributing costs

Does a costs order have to be precisely attributable to the amount of wasted costs, for example, if the Respondent acts unreasonably and extends the trial length by two days, should the Claimant be entitled to two days' costs or to all his costs? In *Health Development Agency v Parish*[7] the EAT held that an Employment Tribunal had no power to award costs against a party until after the date the party had brought or conducted proceedings. The matter was remitted to the tribunal to assess what costs were due to the employer's unreasonable conduct from the time of the notice of appearance, in other words, what costs were attributable to the unreasonable conduct. However, this approach was reversed in *McPherson v BNP Paribas,* when Mummery LJ said *Parish* was not authority for limiting costs to those caused by or attributable to *specific instances* of unreasonable conduct.

McPHERSON v BNP PARIBAS (LONDON BRANCH)

[2004] EWCA Civ 569

A costs order was made on withdrawal of a claim due to the Claimant's bad health only several weeks before the hearing, so there was no decision on the substantive merits. Nonetheless, the employment tribunal made an order for £90,747.82 costs against the Claimant.

The EAT rejected the Claimant's argument that as a matter of construction of r 14 of the 2001 Rules, the requirement that the costs in issue were 'attributable' to specific instances of unreasonable conduct by him meant that costs were limited and that the tribunal had therefore wrongly ordered payment of all the costs. HHJ McMullen stated that:

> '... rule 14(1) does not impose any such causal requirement in the exercise of the discretion. The principle of relevance means that the tribunal must have regard to the nature, gravity and effect of the unreasonable conduct as factors relevant to the exercise of the discretion, but that is not the same as requiring (the Respondent) to prove that specific unreasonable conduct by (the Claimant) caused particular costs to be incurred ... there is a significant contrast between the language of rule 14(1), which deals with costs generally, and the language of rule 14(4), which deals with an order in respect of the costs incurred 'as a result of the postponement or adjournment.'

So r 14(1) did not limit the tribunal's discretion to those costs that are caused by or attributable to the unreasonable conduct. ➡

---

7 [2004] IRLR 550.

However, the EAT held that because there was no evidence of unreasonable conduct of the proceedings before the Claimant's health issue was first raised with the tribunal, no reasonable tribunal, properly directing itself under r 14, would have ordered the Claimant to pay the costs of the whole of these proceedings without some evidence of the unreasonable conduct during the first eleven months that the proceedings had been in existence. The Court of Appeal allowed the appeal to the extent of varying the costs order so that Mr McPherson was liable to pay the costs of the proceedings incurred after the date of the application to the tribunal to adjourn on medical grounds.

KHAN v KIRKLESS METROPOLITAN BOROUGH COUNCIL

[2007] EWCA Civ 1342

The claim was struck out after a long hearing (50 days spread over three years) in which the Claimant's conduct gave adequate grounds for the tribunal to conclude that he had behaved unreasonably, and taking into account all the discretionary matters he ought to bear a large percentage of the costs.

The tribunal went into a lengthy examination of the history of the case and in particular the Appellant's unreasonable conduct throughout. They formed the view that the exceptional length of time taken to hear the case was almost entirely attributable to the conduct of the Appellant and the unreasonable manner in which he had conducted himself throughout the hearing. They accepted that a period of up to ten days would have been a reasonable period for him to have presented his case without incurring any unnecessary costs, and for that reason they only awarded a sum equal to 80% of the costs.

The Court of Appeal recognised that in the vast majority of cases it must be the normal rule that costs will not be ordered against a party because he fails but stated that in this case, there was 'no ordinary failure'. They said that the tribunal was not required to form a view as to the responsibility for each and every application and they took a sensible course in trying to assess what would have been a realistic time to deal with those issues that had any chance of success. They were satisfied that the tribunal took a careful view of the issue of costs and balanced the lengthy history of unreasonable behaviour throughout the litigation. The tribunal hearing the case was in the unique position of being able to form a view of the Appellant's conduct throughout, as well as being able to assess in broad terms how much of the original hearing had been justified in terms of realistic issues and how much was simply part of the ➡

> Appellant's time-wasting conduct. It was not necessary for the tribunal to identify with particularity a causal link between the unreasonable conduct found and the amount of costs ordered.

An employment tribunal will expect a Schedule of costs to be prepared. When doing this, it is important to consider showing the allocation of costs to particular stages of this case, if this is appropriate.

MRS D DADWHAL v REACH CONTACT LTD
LONDON SOUTH EMPLOYMENT TRIBUNAL

Case No 2327625/08
Supplied by Louise Taft of JR Jones Solicitors

The Claimant's claims failed because she was adjudged not to be an employee, although she was entitled to holiday pay. The Respondent made an application for costs on the ground that the Claimant had been late in withdrawing her application for non payment of wages, which they maintained she could have done immediately after disclosure of documents. They claimed £3,000 additional costs.

The Tribunal examined the Respondent's Schedule of Costs and found that a large proportion of the costs being claimed involved the preparation of witness statements which would in any event have had to be prepared for the hearing. They did not find that any substantive part of the Schedule was attributable to the wages claim and so declined to award costs to the Respondent.

3.1.8 Indemnity costs

The general rule is that costs are to be awarded on a standard basis but tribunals have the power to award indemnity costs. Costs which are unreasonably incurred or unreasonable in amount cannot be recovered on either basis. On a standard basis any doubts as to whether costs were reasonably incurred or are reasonable or proportionate in amount are resolved in favour of the paying party. On an indemnity basis those doubts are to be resolved in favour of the receiving party. Even if costs are awarded on an indemnity basis, this will not amount to a full recovery of costs unless all the costs have been reasonably incurred and are reasonable in amount; there has to be some added factor to justify departure from the general rule (Langley J, in *Amco (UK) Expiration Co v British Offshore Ltd*).[8]

Such a factor is most likely to be found in some conduct of the paying party which the court considers merits sufficient criticism beyond that

---

[8]   [2002] BLT 135.

which might ordinarily apply in the case of a party which has fought and lost. For example, in *Kew College Ltd v Mrs J Parsley*[9] in the judgment of the employment tribunal, the conduct of the Head, Deputy Head and the Governors justified an award of costs on an indemnity basis and costs were awarded for the whole of the proceedings up to determination of liability, excluding any deduction for an amount received from insurers.

3.2   PREPARATION TIME ORDERS

Until 2004, it was not possible to award costs in favour of a litigant in person, and it was made clear in *Khan and King v Home Office* that a person represented by a non lawyer for the purpose of the 2001 Rules is a litigant in person. The lacuna in the 2001 Rules for litigants in person was made good by the 2004 Rules, in rr 42–45, which provided for preparation time orders.

The power and circumstances in which an award may be made are essentially the same as the power to award legal costs.

General power to make preparation time orders

42.—(1) Subject to paragraph (2) and in the circumstances described in rules 43, 44 and 47 a tribunal or chairman may make an order ("a preparation time order") that a party ("the paying party") make a payment in respect of the preparation time of another party ("the receiving party").

(2) A preparation time order may be made under rules 43, 44 or 47 only where the receiving party has not been legally represented at a Hearing or, in proceedings which are determined without a Hearing, if the receiving party has not been legally represented when the proceedings are determined. (See: rules 38 to 41 on when a costs order may be made; rule 38(5) for the definition of legally represented; and rule 46 on the restriction on making a costs order and a preparation time order in the same proceedings).

(3) For the purposes of these rules preparation time shall mean time spent by –

  (a)   the receiving party or his employees carrying out preparatory work directly relating to the proceedings; and

  (b   the receiving party's legal or other advisers relating to the conduct of the proceedings;

up to but not including time spent at any Hearing.

(4) A preparation time order may be made against a respondent who has not had a response accepted in the proceedings in relation to the conduct of any part which he has taken in the proceedings.

(5) A party may apply to the tribunal for a preparation time order to be made at any time during the proceedings. An application may be made at the end of a hearing or in writing to the Secretary. An application for

---

[9]   UKEAT/0565/06/DA.

preparation time which is received by the Employment Tribunal Office later than 28 days from the issuing of the judgment determining the claim shall not be accepted or considered by a tribunal or chairman unless they consider that it is in the interests of justice to do so.

(6) In paragraph (5) the date of issuing of the judgment determining the claim shall be either –

(a)   the date of the Hearing if the judgment was issued orally; or,

(b)   if the judgment was reserved, the date on which the written judgment was sent to the parties.

(7) No preparation time order shall be made unless the Secretary has sent notice to the party against whom the order may be made giving him the opportunity to give reasons why the order should not be made. This paragraph shall not be taken to require the Secretary to send notice to that party if the party has been given an opportunity to give reasons orally to the chairman or tribunal as to why the order should not be made.

(8) Where a tribunal or chairman makes a preparation time order it or he shall provide written reasons for doing so if a request for written reasons is made within 14 days of the date of the preparation time order. The Secretary shall send a copy of the written reasons to all parties to the proceedings.

3.2.1   Who is eligible?

A preparation time order may be made in favour of a party who has not been legally represented at a hearing or, where proceedings have not been determined by a hearing, if they have not been legally represented at the date of determination.

Legal representation is defined in r 38(5).

Rule 38(5)

(5) In these rules legally represented means having the assistance of a person (including where that person is the receiving party's employee) who –

(a)   has a general qualification within the meaning of section 71 of the Courts and Legal Services Act 1990;

(b)   is an advocate or solicitor in Scotland; or

(c)   is a member of the Bar of Northern Ireland or a solicitor of the Supreme Court of Northern Ireland.

3.2.2   What is preparation time?

Rule 42(3) defines preparation time as time spent by the non legally represented receiving party carrying out preparatory work directly relating to the proceedings (but not time spent at the hearing), as well as time spent by their legal or other advisers relating to the conduct of the proceedings.

3.2.3   When can a preparation time order be made?

A tribunal may (or must) make a preparation time order in exactly the same cases as those in which it may (or must) make a costs order under rr 38 and 40.

When a preparation time order must be made

43.—(1) Subject to rule 42(2), a tribunal must make a preparation time order against a respondent where in proceedings for unfair dismissal a Hearing has been postponed or adjourned and –

    (a)   the claimant has expressed a wish to be reinstated or re-engaged which has been communicated to the respondent not less than 7 days before the Hearing; and

    (b)   the postponement or adjournment of that Hearing has been caused by the respondent's failure, without a special reason, to adduce reasonable evidence as to the availability of the job from which the claimant was dismissed, or of comparable or suitable employment.

(2) A preparation time order made under paragraph (1) shall relate to any preparation time spent as a result of the postponement or adjournment of the Hearing.

When a preparation time order may be made

44.—(1) A tribunal or chairman may make a preparation time order when on the application of a party it has postponed the day or time fixed for or adjourned a Hearing or a pre-hearing review. The preparation time order may be against or, as the case may require, in favour of that party as respects any preparation time spent as a result of the postponement or adjournment.

(2) A tribunal or chairman shall consider making a preparation time order against a party (the paying party) where, in the opinion of the tribunal or the chairman (as the case may be), any of the circumstances in paragraph (3) apply. Having so considered the tribunal or chairman may make a preparation time order against that party if it considers it appropriate to do so.

(3) The circumstances described in paragraph (2) are where the paying party has in bringing the proceedings, or he or his representative has in conducting the proceedings, acted vexatiously, abusively, disruptively or otherwise unreasonably, or the bringing or conducting of the proceedings by the paying party has been misconceived.

(4) A tribunal or chairman may make a preparation time order against a party who has not complied with an order or practice direction.

3.2.4   How much can be ordered?

Preparation time is assessed in terms of the number of hours spent in preparation. The tribunal will take into account information provided by the receiving party as well as the tribunal or Judge's own assessment of what it or he considers to be a 'reasonable and proportionate amount of time to spend on such preparatory work', with reference to the complexity of the proceedings, the number of witnesses and documentation required.

Time assessed cannot include any amount of time spent at a hearing (r 42(3)).

The number of hours assessed is then multiplied by the set rate (£28 as of 6 April 2010) and the total cannot exceed £10,000.

The ability of the paying party may be taken into account (r 45(3)).

Calculation of a preparation time order

45.—(1) In order to calculate the amount of preparation time the tribunal or chairman shall make an assessment of the number of hours spent on preparation time on the basis of –

(a) information on time spent provided by the receiving party; and

(b) the tribunal or chairman's own assessment of what it or he considers to be a reasonable and proportionate amount of time to spend on such preparatory work and with reference to, for example, matters such as the complexity of the proceedings, the number of witnesses and documentation required.

(2) Once the tribunal or chairman has assessed the number of hours spent on preparation time in accordance with paragraph (1), it or he shall calculate the amount of the award to be paid to the receiving party by applying an hourly rate of £25.00 to that figure (or such other figure calculated in accordance with paragraph (4)). No preparation time order made under these rules may exceed the sum of £10,000.

(3) The tribunal or chairman may have regard to the paying party's ability to pay when considering whether it or he shall make a preparation time order or how much that order should be.

(4) For the year commencing on 6th April 2006, the hourly rate of £25 shall be increased by the sum of £1.00 and for each subsequent year commencing on 6 April, the hourly rate for the previous year shall also be increased by the sum of £1.00.

3.2.5 Can a costs order and a preparation order both be made?

Costs orders and preparation time orders are mutually exclusive – a tribunal cannot order both in favour of the same party in the same proceedings. However, if there are two or more parties, separate costs and preparation time orders may be made as appropriate, as well as costs under r 38(1)(b).

Restriction on making costs or expenses orders and preparation time orders

46.—(1) A tribunal or chairman may not make a preparation time order and a costs order in favour of the same party in the same proceedings. However where a preparation time order is made in favour of a party in proceedings, the tribunal or chairman may make a costs order in favour of another party or in favour of the Secretary of State under rule 38(1)(b) in the same proceedings.

(2) If a tribunal or a chairman wishes to make either a costs order or a preparation time order in proceedings, before the claim has been determined, it or he may make an order that either costs or preparation time be awarded to the receiving party. In such circumstances a tribunal or chairman may decide whether the award should be for costs or preparation time after the proceedings have been determined.

CHAPTER 4

DEPOSITS

4.1 THE LEGAL TEST

Under r 18, an Employment Judge may carry out a preliminary consideration of the proceedings in a pre-hearing review. The main purpose is to enable the Judge to determine any interim matters relating to the proceedings including striking out hopeless cases or making an order that a deposit be paid in accordance with r 20 as a condition of being allowed to proceed (r 18(2)(c)).

The power (under r 18(7)(b)) is to strike out or amend all or part of a claim on various grounds, for example that it is scandalous or vexatious or has not been actively pursued or has 'no reasonable prospect of success'.

Rule 20(1) provides that where a Judge considers that a party's contentions have little reasonable prospect of success, that party can be ordered to pay a deposit as a condition of being allowed to continue to take part in the proceedings. A contrast can be made between r 7(4) of the 2001 Rules with r 20(1). Rule 7(4) required that there was 'no' reasonable prospect of success, whereas the 2004 Rules require 'little' reasonable prospect of success.

Requirement to pay a deposit in order to continue with the proceedings

20.—(1) At a pre-hearing review if a chairman considers that the contentions put forward by any party in relation to a matter required to be determined by a tribunal have little reasonable prospect of success, the chairman may make an order against that party requiring the party to pay a deposit of an amount not exceeding £500 as a condition of being permitted to continue to take part in the proceedings relating to that matter.

(2) No order shall be made under this rule unless the chairman has taken reasonable steps to ascertain the ability of the party against whom it is proposed to make the order to comply with such an order, and has taken account of any information so ascertained in determining the amount of the deposit.

(3) An order made under this rule, and the chairman's grounds for making such an order, shall be recorded in a document signed by the chairman. A

copy of that document shall be sent to each of the parties and shall be accompanied by a note explaining that if the party against whom the order is made persists in making those contentions relating to the matter to which the order relates, he may have an award of costs or preparation time made against him and could lose his deposit.

(4) If a party against whom an order has been made does not pay the amount specified in the order to the Secretary either –

(a)   within the period of 21 days of the day on which the document recording the making of the order is sent to him; or

(b)   within such further period, not exceeding 14 days, as the chairman may allow in the light of representations made by that party within the period of 21 days;

a chairman shall strike out the claim or response of that party or, as the case may be, the part of it to which the order relates.

(5) The deposit paid by a party under an order made under this rule shall be refunded to him in full except where rule 47 applies.

MS J E JANSEN VAN RENSBURG v THE ROYAL BOROUGH OF KINGSTON-UPON-THAMES & ORS

UKEAT/0095/07/MAA

The Employment Tribunal made a £100 deposit order under r 20 against the Appellant on the grounds that her claims had little prospect of success. In her reasons, the Employment Judge noted that:

> 'The Respondent submitted that the claims are weak and unclear. The Claimant demonstrated her difficulty in articulating them at the hearing. The equal pay claims were hopeless and her allegations of sex and race discrimination were not made during the course of her employment. The Claimant is seeking re-engagement which undermines her claim of constructive dismissal. The Claimant herself put forward the first Respondent for a diversity award on the ground that it was a leader in this field.'

The Claimant failed to pay the deposit as required. Initially, she had not done so because she was appealing to the EAT and she was apparently under the impression that the deposit need not be paid in those circumstances. She had sent a cheque but asked for it not to be banked until her appeal to the EAT had been determined. Because of this misunderstanding, the Judge of her own motion extended the time for lodging the payment for a further 21 days. However, the Claimant still failed to pay the deposit by that later date. That led to a further order being made in which the tribunal ordered that the claims be struck out because of the failure to remit the deposit. ➡

One issue raised in the appeal was whether the Judge was entitled to have regard to the likelihood of the facts being established when making a deposit order. The EAT held that the Judge could do so. Elias J said:

> '... the test of little prospect of success in rule 20(1) is plainly not as rigorous as the test that the claim has no reasonable prospect of success found in rule 18(7). It follows that a tribunal has a greater leeway when considering whether or not to order a deposit. Needless to say, it must have a proper basis for doubting the likelihood of the party being able to establish the facts essential to the claim or response.'

4.2   THE HEARING

Applications for a PHR can be can be made in writing or the tribunal may institute a hearing of its own motion. The PHR is at the discretion of the tribunal and it is usually conducted by an Employment Judge sitting alone.

The tribunal can refuse the application for a PHR without giving reasons and there is no right to appeal such a refusal. Rule 7(1) provides for consideration of:

(a)   the contents of the originating application and notice of appearance;

(b)   any representations in writing; and

(c)   any oral argument advanced by or on behalf of a party.

So no oral evidence is allowed.

4.3   THE AMOUNT

Until 2001 the amount of a deposit was £150 but it was increased to a maximum of £500 by the 2001 Rules and that amount was retained in 2004.

Rule 20(2) requires a Judge to take reasonable steps to ascertain the ability of a person to pay the deposit, and to take account of any information so ascertained. It is questionable whether an order that even the maximum deposit of £500 be paid would be sufficient to make many parties think twice about proceeding on financial grounds; the real disincentive to proceeding is the message that the claim has little reasonable prospect of success.

Rule 20(4) requires payment to be made within 21 days of the date of the 'document recording the making of the order' being sent to the paying party. It is the date of sending and not the date of service that is relevant – *Chelminksi* v *Gdynia American Shipping Lines*.[1]

If the paying party believes that there will be a difficulty in making the payment within that period, they can apply within 21 days for more time in which to make the payment (r 20(4)(2)) but that further period cannot exceed 14 days. The party's representations and reasons for making the request should be explained in the application. The funds have to be 'paid' but do not have to have cleared within the 21-day time limit. It is long-established, on high authority, that a cheque or bill, if duly honoured, is payment as from the time of its being given (*Belshaw* v *Bush*,[2] *Currie* v *Misa*[3]).

It is within the tribunal's power to extend the time for paying a deposit provided for in r 20(4), even after the time under the rule has expired – *Immigration Advisory Service* v *Oommen*,[4] confirmed in *Kuttapan* v *London Borough of Croydon*.[5]

4.4   GETTING A DECISION REVIEWED

An order for a deposit under r 20(1) is not a 'judgment' and so is not reviewable,

---

MAURICE v BETTERWARE UK LTD

EAT/1030/99

At a PHR hearing an Employment Judge refused to make an order requiring the Claimant to pay a deposit as a condition of proceeding with her complaint of unfair dismissal. Six months later the tribunal granted the Respondent's request to hold a second pre-hearing review. A different Judge subsequently held that the tribunal had jurisdiction to hear the second review and looked at the matter afresh. They found that the Claimant's contract was a contract for services, so that her complaint of unfair dismissal had no reasonable prospect of success, and they required her to pay a deposit as a condition of continuing with her claim. The Claimant then appealed against the order for a deposit.   ➡

---

[1]   [2004] EWCA Civ 871, [2004] IRLR 1523.
[2]   11 CB 191.
[3]   LR 10 Ex 153.
[4]   [1997] ICR 683.
[5]   EAT/1103/00.

The EAT held that although a decision under r 7 (as it then was) was not a 'decision' with reg 2(2) of the Employment Tribunals (Constitution and Procedure) Regulations 1993 and, accordingly, could not be reviewed under r 11, there was power under r 16(1), which enabled tribunals to 'give directions on any matter arising in connection with the proceedings', to reconsider an interlocutory decision of the kind in r 7.

The issue was considered in the light of the 2004 Rules in *Sodexho Ltd v Gibbons*[6] when it was confirmed that if a party wishes to have an order for a deposit revoked or varied, they would need to make an application under the general case management powers set out in r 10 (General power to manage proceedings).

SODHEXO LTD v GIBBONS

[2005] ICR 1647, EAT

The Claimant was ordered to pay a deposit but the deposit order was not received by her solicitors due to an administrative error (the Claimant gave the wrong post code for his solicitors). He therefore failed to pay the deposit and his claim was struck out as a result. He applied for a review of the strike out and succeeded in obtaining a revocation of the strike out as well as a variation of the deposit order to restart the time for payment from the date of the review order.

The Respondent's appeal was dismissed by the EAT, which held that a strike out order was a 'judgment' within r 28(1)(a) and therefore reviewable under r 34(1)(b). They agreed that the interests of justice required the strike out order to be reviewed and that the Judge had correctly adopted an approach consistent with the overriding objective.

The EAT also confirmed that a deposit order under r 20(1) was an 'order' within r 28(1)(b) and not a 'judgment' within r 28(1)(a), and as such not susceptible to review by virtue of r 34(1), but it could nevertheless be revoked or varied by a Judge under r 10(1)(2)(n).

If a deposit is ordered, it must be paid within 21 days of the date of the order. If the party fails to make the payment the Judge 'shall' strike out the claim or response, as appropriate (or the part to which the order for a deposit relates, if there are a number of claims). A strike out under r 20(4) is a 'judgment' within the meaning of r 28(1)(a) and as such is reviewable under r 34(1)(b).

---

6   EAT 2005.

4.5 SIGNIFICANCE OF DEPOSIT TO ULTIMATE COSTS ORDERS

If a deposit is ordered and paid and then at the conclusion of the hearing the tribunal's decision is against that party, the deposit will be forfeited and may be used to offset costs ordered against the party in respect of which the deposit was ordered.

Costs, expenses or preparation time orders when a deposit has been taken

47.—(1) When –

(a)   a party has been ordered under rule 20 to pay a deposit as a condition of being permitted to continue to participate in proceedings relating to a matter;

(b)   in respect of that matter, the tribunal or chairman has found against that party in its or his judgment; and

(c)   no award of costs or preparation time has been made against that party arising out of the proceedings on the matter;

the tribunal or chairman shall consider whether to make a costs or preparation time order against that party on the ground that he conducted the proceedings relating to the matter unreasonably in persisting in having the matter determined; but the tribunal or chairman shall not make a costs or preparation time order on that ground unless it has considered the document recording the order under rule 20 and is of the opinion that the grounds which caused the tribunal or chairman to find against the party in its judgment were substantially the same as the grounds recorded in that document for considering that the contentions of the party had little reasonable prospect of success.

(2) When a costs or preparation time order is made against a party who has had an order under rule 20 made against him (whether the award arises out of the proceedings relating to the matter in respect of which the order was made or out of proceedings relating to any other matter considered with that matter), his deposit shall be paid in part or full settlement of the costs or preparation time order –

(a)   when an order is made in favour of one party, to that party; and

(b)   when orders are made in favour of more than one party, to all of them or any one or more of them as the tribunal or chairman thinks fit, and if to all or more than one, in such proportions as the tribunal or chairman considers appropriate;

and if the amount of the deposit exceeds the amount of the costs or preparation time order, the balance shall be refunded to the party who paid it.

In considering a costs order, r 47 requires the tribunal or Judge to consider whether to make an order on the ground that the party conducted the proceedings unreasonably in persisting to have the matter determined despite the order for the deposit to be paid. In carrying out their consideration, the tribunal or Employment Judge must look at the original reasons given for making the deposit under r 20 and can only make a costs order if they believe that the grounds for their decision to find against the party at the main hearing are substantially the same as the grounds recorded in the order under r 20 for considering that the 'contentions of the party had little reasonable prospect of success'.

GARDINER v MOTORCAST

Appeal No EAT/0262/00

The claim was for unlawful deductions of wages. The Judge, sitting alone, ordered a pre-hearing review of the applications. The Judge ordered the Claimant to pay £50 by way of a deposit, having expressed the view that on the documentation there was little or no real prospect of success.

On the appeal, the EAT held that in those circumstances, mere persistence with the claim itself does not give rise to a conclusion of unreasonableness. Many factors come into play; the Claimant had, on the face of it, credible evidence to support the claim. There was a straightforward conflict of evidence and the result was not inevitable. Taking into account the witness evidence and other material available, the EAT did not believe that the Appellants were unreasonable in persisting in bringing the claim. The appeal was dismissed and the order for costs quashed.

Does the fact that a Respondent does not seek a deposit have any relevance when a tribunal considers an application for costs at the end of the hearing? In *Salinas v Bear Stearns*[7] there was a suggestion made by the Applicant that whether or not a deposit has been sought or ordered pursuant to r 7 of the Employment Tribunal Rules has some relevance. Burton J said:

> '... there may be some cases in which this might be so, particularly if there has been a pre-trial hearing at which such deposit has either not been sought or has been sought and not ordered, where the case remains the same at the end of the full hearing as it had been at a pre-trial hearing. But this was plainly not such a case. In a case like this, where evidence, not tested until the final hearing, and in the event disbelieved, was apparently available to support a case, it is only at and after the full hearing that the misconceived nature of the claim can be fully or at all appreciated.'

4.6 PRACTICAL CONSIDERATIONS

When should you apply for a deposit? This will be a matter for a party to consider early in the claim. The applying party will normally be the Respondent, although the application could be made by a Claimant in

---

7 UKEAT/0596/04/DM.

respect of a response. If it appears that the claim is factually hopeless or legally misconceived (for example, an equal pay claim brought in circumstances where there is no comparator of the opposite sex), a strike-out application should be considered with an application for a deposit made in the alternative. If there is a overwhelming raft of testimony (which could, in theory, be nullified by effective cross-examination, thus meaning strike-out is inappropriate but which may suffice to establish 'little' reasonable prospect of success), an application may be desirable. However, bear in mind the cost of bringing the application (which, since it will involve early drafting of witness statements, will be considerable) as well as the tactical disadvantage of giving the Claimant early sight of those statements.

There are other tactical considerations. If an application is made and refused, this may encourage a Claimant (particularly one who is unrepresented) to believe they have a strong case, possibly erroneously. If it succeeds, the deposit ordered may be so low as to be meaningless as a financial warning. However, whatever the size of the deposit ordered, a successful application will ultimately increase the chance of obtaining a costs order at the conclusion of the case. Not only would the deposit itself be forfeited (and paid to the successful party), but the tribunal's discretion is more likely to be applied in favour of a costs order from at least the date of the pre hearing review .

If the party against whom the order is made decides not to proceed, they can withdraw the claim(s) and do not have to wait for the case to be struck out. It may be more sensible in fact to withdraw rather than have a strike out order made, on the basis that in both cases the other party can apply for an order that the costs they have already incurred be paid but they may be more likely to succeed on a strike out.

If an application is made in a Response for a pre-hearing review to consider whether a deposit should be paid, this should be pursued as a tribunal may take this into account when considering its discretion to make a costs award – see *Mr A P Buhaj v Inchcape Retail Ltd.*[8]

MR AP BUHAJ v INCHCAPE RETAIL LTD
NOTTINGHAM EMPLOYMENT TRIBUNAL

Case No 2601644/08
Supplied by Beverley Sunderland of Crossland Employment solicitors

The claim for unfair dismissal failed and the Respondent made an application for costs amounting to about £7,500 including VAT, on the grounds that the proceedings had no reasonable prospect of success and that they had been unreasonably conducted. The ➡

---

8   Case No 2601644/08.

Tribunal agreed that the proceedings had no reasonable prospect of success because it was clear that the Claimant did not have twelve months' continuous service and would therefore have to bring himself within s 100 of the ERA 1996, which on his own account he could not. There was no evidence at all to support his contention that the reason for his dismissal was his complaint on a health and safety matter. He had had two costs warnings from the Respondent, the first when the Response was lodged and the second during disclosure. Nevertheless, he continued with the proceedings, which the Tribunal believed to be unreasonable conduct.

The Tribunal considered the Claimant's means, which were 'precarious', and also considered the fact that although the Respondent had originally made an application in the Response for a PHR to consider a Deposit Order, it did not pursue this. The Tribunal was not critical of the Respondent in that respect but said that 'it may be that it might have been appropriate to pursue that matter further'. Bearing in mind those two factors, the costs order was limited to £2,500.

4.7   THE RELEVANCE OF LEGAL ADVICE

DORNEY v CHIPPENHAM COLLEGE

(UNREPORTED) 28 MAY 1997, EAT

A deposit was ordered under r 7(4), where the tribunal considered that the case had no reasonable prospect of success. The employees, supported by their Union, nevertheless proceeded to a full hearing. Their cases were all dismissed and they were ordered to pay the Respondent's taxed costs. The deposit was forfeited. HHJ Peter Clark said:

> '... it is said that the full Tribunal fell into error when considering the costs application by basing its decision on the fact that the applicants had access to skilled legal advice ... (However) the Tribunal was at pains to make clear that it was not saying that the decision to go ahead following the PHR Order was automatically unreasonable; however, it took into account in finding that it was unreasonable so to do that the claimants had the advantage of being able to explore with their legal advisers the ramifications if they were to proceed with the matter.'

This approach was confirmed by Lindsay J in *Benyon* when he said:

'We underline the common sense of that observation; one does not necessarily judge a party who has had the benefit of advice as one would a lay person left only to his own perhaps inadequate devices.'

CHAPTER 5

COSTS WARNINGS AND SETTLEMENT OFFERS

5.1 COSTS WARNINGS

5.1.1 What are costs warnings?

Costs warnings are not referred to in the Rules but may be given at any stage of proceedings, including during a hearing, by either party or by the tribunal itself. Since 2004 it has become more normal for practitioners (particularly those acting for Respondents) to warn the other party that an application for costs will be made against them. This may be either in respect of the pursuing (or defending) a claim as a whole or in respect of particular applications, for example, where a Respondent refuses to accept that the Claimant has a disability and this is dealt with by way of a preliminary issue, resulting in costs to the Claimant of medical evidence and legal representation.

5.1.2 Warnings given by parties

Costs warnings are normally, but not exclusively, given by Respondents. It is not be good practice to issue them as a matter of course (see the *St Helens* case below) but one of the initial considerations for a Respondent should be whether the claim is one in which a costs warning is appropriate. Alternatively, during the process of the claim it may become relevant if either party is conducting their claim or defence unreasonably.

Pointers on how they should they be phrased:

- make it in open correspondence;

- keep it short, no longer than one page of A4 or you run the risk that the tribunal will take the view either that the issue is complicated rather than straightforward, or that you are unduly pressurising the other party;

- be polite but firm;

- set out clearly the reason why costs will be ordered e g that the claim is misconceived on the basis of lack of jurisdiction because of the lack of the qualifying period, or that no grievance was brought;

- avoid a costs warning if the case for costs is not clear-cut;

- ensure that the costs warning says exactly what you want the other party to do, eg:

  > '... we invite you to withdraw your claim within 14 days, failing which we will rely on this letter in support of an application for costs. If you do withdraw your claim within 14 days, we undertake not to make any application for our costs incurred to date.'

Tribunals can take exception to over zealous costs warnings or indeed any costs warnings – one region had, until recently, a practice of calling Respondents who issued costs warnings in standard costs before it to explain why they should not have the Response struck out for unreasonable conduct of proceedings.

BIRD v SYLVESTER

[2007] EWCA Civ 1052

The Respondent's solicitors sent a costs warning to the Claimant asserting that she had acted unreasonably, that the claim was misconceived, and that if it proved unsuccessful an application for costs would be made against her. Her claim (for race discrimination) was dismissed. The Employment Tribunal found Ms Bird an unimpressive witness who had exaggerated her evidence. The Respondent's solicitors issued an application for costs against her on the ground that the claim was unreasonable and misconceived. They wrote a 'without prejudice' letter in which they stated that Mr Sylvester was willing to accept 50% of the costs if Ms Bird would agree to resign from her employment without compensation, sign a compromise agreement, apologise to Mr Sylvester and two other employees of his and refrain from appealing against the Employment Tribunal's judgment.

Ms Bird rejected the proposal. The costs application was dismissed, as was a cross-application for costs brought by Ms Bird for the costs of that application. She then brought a second claim against both Mr Sylvester and his solicitors. She argued that Mr Sylvester's application for costs, together with the terms of the proposal for settlement and the subsequent pursuit of the application to the Employment Tribunal, amounted to victimisation within the meaning of s 2(1) of the Race Relations Act 1976. Mr Sylvester and his solicitors applied to strike out the claim. The Employment ➡

Tribunal struck out the claim in so far as it related to the costs application, on the basis that it was proper and appropriate to make an application for costs against Ms Bird, and that Mr Sylvester had been entitled to make proposals to compromise the claim for costs on the terms.

With regard to the claim against the solicitors, the Employment Tribunal held that it was contrary to public policy for a professional firm of solicitors to be at risk of becoming a respondent to proceedings simply by writing letters setting out the proposed course of action by their client, the employer, which the employee considered amounted to an act of discrimination or victimisation. Accordingly, they struck out the claim against the solicitors. The EAT dismissed Ms Bird's appeal, and the Court of Appeal upheld the EAT decision. Laws LJ stated:

> 'I have considered whether by force of the public interest in the integrity and effectiveness of the solicitor-client relationship, the court should go so far as to hold that a solicitor acting within the terms of his retainer can never be liable under s 33. But I doubt whether that is so. Extreme situations may be envisaged in which the solicitor himself actively promotes, perhaps for a malign motive, oppressive actions, and actively carries them along. I would, however, suggest that it is very difficult to see how a solicitor who confines himself to giving objective legal advice in good faith as to the proper protection of his client's interests, and acts strictly upon his client's instructions, could be at risk of an adverse finding under s 33 of the Race Relations Act. Something more than that, as it seems to me, is required if a person is to be shown to have knowingly aided an unlawful act within the meaning of that subsection.'

ADU v LONDON GENERAL TRANSPORT SERVICES
LONDON SOUTH EMPLOYMENT TRIBUNAL

Case No 2304213/2006
Supplied by Jane Liddington, fee-paid employment judge at London South Tribunal

The claims for disability discrimination and unfair dismissal were dismissed. At the end of the hearing, Counsel for the Respondents made an application for costs on the basis that at the end of the first day of the hearing it was quite clear that the Claimant's case would not succeed and that it was unreasonable or misconceived to go to the second day. There had been three interventions from the bench during the evidence on the first day as well as a clear warning from the judge at the end of the first day as to the weakness of the Claimant's claims. After the first day of the hearing Counsel for the Respondents offered to the Claimant's solicitor to 'drop hands' and➡

to not pursue them for costs should the Claimant withdraw his claim before the second day. A letter was subsequently faxed to the Claimant's solicitors putting them on notice that an application would be made to pay 'all of part of the costs to which our clients have been put.'

The Claimant's representative argued that it was not unreasonable to go to the second day as cross examination of the Respondent's witnesses was necessary to go to the question of failure to make reasonable adjustments. However the Tribunal believed that the cross examination of the Respondent's witnesses achieved 'virtually nothing in this respect' and that the Claimant's representative was not able to establish anything new as a result of the cross examination.

An award for costs was made in the sum of £250.

MR S PEMBERTON v PD TEESPORT LIMITED
NEWCASTLE UPON TYNE EMPLOYMENT TRIBUNAL

Case No 2513204/07
Supplied by Phil Bramhall of Bramhalls

The Claimant withdrew his claim for unfair dismissal a week before the hearing. The Respondent's solicitors had sent his solicitors a letter some six weeks earlier giving a costs warning. Upon exchange of witness statements it should have been clear to the Claimant that a witness upon whom he had intended to rely was in fact supporting the Respondent. It then took him four weeks to notify his withdrawal, by which time the Respondent had incurred costs of preparation and instructing counsel. Upon withdrawal the Respondent's solicitors sought costs. After considering the Claimant's case the Judge concluded that it had, on the balance of probabilities, no reasonable prospects from the start and so the threshold requirement for the making of a costs order was established. The Judge decided that as the claim had been misconceived from the start, all the costs were payable (although he reduced the Respondent's solicitor's charging rate from £200 to £100 per hour).

5.1.3 Impact on the exercise of discretion

A costs warning will usually be made in open correspondence and can therefore be considered by the tribunal on an application for costs. Whether to give a costs warning and, if so, when, should be a consideration early in the life of the claim. A clear warning means that the tribunal may be more likely to exercise discretion in favour of granting costs. Some thought should be given to the timing of a warning as it can sometimes amount to a longstop on the date for costs, for example if a costs warning is given on 1 March in a claim that was issued on 1 January, at a later hearing the tribunal may agree that the claim was misconceived, but take the view that the Claimant should have withdrawn his claim within 14 days of getting costs warning. This would result in a costs award from 15 March rather than 1 January.

5.1.4   Warnings given by tribunals

In *Gee v Shell*[1] (see below for a summary) Maurice Kay J in the EAT identified an all important dividing line between on the one hand 'robust, effective and fair case management' and on the other 'inappropriate pressure and unfairness'. Brown LJ (at para 40) recognised that the line is not a sharp one and stated that costs warnings 'cannot properly be characterised as having applied 'inappropriate pressure' or as being 'unfair' unless no reasonable tribunal would have given them. Given the obvious need for 'robust and effective case management' which might sometimes positively require a costs warning, there must be a wide margin of appreciation (a substantial area of discretionary judgment) open to the tribunal as to when and in what terms the warning should be given'.

The extent of the order and the terms and context in which the warning is given are also relevant. Brown LJ stated:

> '... it would be no less wrong to warn a litigant of the risk of a whole costs order being made when in reality only a limited or specified order could possibly become justified. Equally, it would be wrong to give the impression that a costs order was probable if in reality it was at most conceivable.'

GEE v SHELL UK LIMITED

[2003] IRLR 82

Mrs Gee brought a claim for unfair dismissal. Two issues arose for preliminary determination; whether the relationship between Shell and Mrs Gee was that of employer and employee and, if so, whether Mrs Gee had sufficient service for claiming unfair dismissal.

The Employment Tribunal expressed the view that there was considerable doubt as to whether Mrs Gee could satisfy the service qualification. They went on to say that she was at risk of a substantial costs award if she persisted in her claim and the tribunal then found that she lacked the necessary period of service. Concerned that her house may be at risk, Mrs Gee withdrew her ➡

---

[1]   [2003] IRLR 82.

claim. The EAT allowed her appeal on the ground that the Employment Tribunal had acted unfairly and oppressively in issuing the costs warning and had left Mrs Gee with no alternative but to withdraw.

On appeal the Court of Appeal were satisfied that there had been a miscarriage of justice because the Employment Tribunal had issued a costs warning in circumstances where it was unjustified (because the Claimant had a perfectly respectable argument) and where it had placed the unrepresented Claimant under improper pressure. At para 26 Scott Baker LJ stated:

> 'Against this background the 'costs warning' was unfair. It left Mrs Gee in no doubt (and in my judgment would have left any reasonable litigant in person standing in her shoes in no doubt) that if she continued and lost she was at a real risk of a substantial order for costs being made against her and that it might well be enforced against her house. Both she and her husband were unemployed. She simply could not afford to take the risk. There is no doubt that it was this that caused her to withdraw her claim and in my judgment the Employment Appeal Tribunal was correct in concluding that the pressure was unfair and accordingly that the employment tribunal acted unlawfully.'

Sedley LJ put the matter in this way at para 34:

> 'While plainly there cannot be one rule or legal principle for litigants in person and another for those who are represented (see *Divine-Bortey v London Borough of Brent*,[2] per Simon Brown LJ), it does not follow that an employment tribunal is entitled to treat every party as if it had the strength of advice and representation which, for example, Shell (UK) Ltd enjoyed in this case ... The tribunal's job, precisely because it cannot guarantee equality of arms, is to ensure equality of access to its processes for sometimes disparately powerful parties. This involves making a careful appraisal, case by case, of the parties and their respective capabilities. It must also, however, involve ultimate equality of treatment, so that whoever presses on with a doomed case after due warning faces the same risk on costs.'

ADESE v CORAL RACING

UKEAT/0760/04/CK

The Claimant's representative was not presenting the case competently. On the second day, the Judge made it clear that she was extremely concerned about the Claimant's case, in particular, in relation to the race discrimination case, as nothing of the ➡

---

[2]   [1998] ICR 886; [1998] IRLR 525.

discrimination case was put in cross-examination to the Respondent's witnesses. Further, neither the EIT1 nor the statement of the Claimant disclosed any detail of his race discrimination allegations. She said that she recognised that it was the tribunal's role to strike a balance between the parties given the inexperience of the Claimant's representative, but she could not help him any more. She made the Claimant aware that the Respondent could seek a costs order against him and suggested that the Representative speak to the Claimant about continuing with his case. After lunch the Claimant withdrew his claims for race discrimination, wrongful dismissal, breach of contract and failure to pay holiday pay. He subsequently appealed on the ground that he was treated unfairly by the Employment Tribunal when it gave him an 'unjust' costs warning, which placed such pressure upon him that he felt obliged to abandon those claims.

The EAT made it clear that they did not consider there was any question of the Employment Tribunal applying improper pressure. They also did not consider it could fairly be said that no reasonable Employment Tribunal could have given such a warning on the particular facts of this case, having regard in particular to the language in which the warning was couched, the fact that the Claimant was obviously at risk of an application for costs being made against him and fact that the risk of an order being made was very real.

MS S AUSTIN v ANGLIA NEWSPAPERS LTD (1), MRS KIM HARRIS (2)
BURY ST EDMUNDS TRIBUNAL

Case Nos 1501693/2007 & 1502152/2007
Supplied by Alison Peat of MacRoberts LLP

The claims for constructive dismissal based on the Respondent's alleged inappropriate rejection of the Claimant's flexible working request and sex discrimination were dismissed. The Tribunal accepted that by joining the Second Respondent to the claim, the Claimant had acted unreasonably if not vexatiously. The claim against the Second Respondent had no merit whatsoever and was misconceived. The First Respondent had been put to extra costs in its defence as a result and so an order was made for £250 as a nominal award and 'a marker' of the Tribunal's views.

The Claimant had also brought a claim for disability discrimination by association. The hearing took place before the ECJ's decision in ➡

Coleman v Attridge[3] and so the Tribunal stayed that part of its determination. However, it made clear to the Claimant that they had accepted without question the Respondent's evidence that its decision to refuse the flexible working request was made on its own merits and that discrimination of any kind was not nor could ever reasonably have been on the evidence a feature of the Respondent's refusal. On that basis they gave a clear costs warning that if the Claimant was to seek leave to carry that part of the claim forward following the ECJ judgment:

> '... she should expect an award representative of the additional costs of the Respondent on the basis that part of her claim cannot ... stand any reasonable prospect of success on the facts alone, irrespective of any subsequent legal entitlement to prosecute that claim.'

5.1.5 What if a party heeds a costs warning?

MADARASSY v NOMURA INTERNATIONAL PLC

[2007] EWCA Civ 33

Ms Madarassy lodged a very long notice of appeal (108 paragraphs, 31 pages) in which she made allegations of bias and improper conduct on the part of the Employment Tribunal. HHJ Peter Clark ordered her to lodge an affidavit giving details in support of her allegations of bias or improper conduct. He also gave a costs warning to the effect that the unsuccessful pursuit of the allegations might give rise to an award of costs. In her affidavit. Ms Madarassy expressly withdrew some of the allegations, but not all of them.

One issue was whether the EAT had erred in making a costs order against her after she had acted upon the costs warning by withdrawing parts of her appeal. She argued that such orders would denude costs warnings of any effect and would discourage parties from abandoning weak allegations at an early stage.

The Court of Appeal agreed that it would be contrary to the purpose of a costs warning to make the party warned liable for costs incurred after the party had heeded the warning and ceased the conduct warned against, but in this case they concluded that the EAT had concluded correctly that Ms Madarassy had behaved improperly and unreasonably in making the allegations in the first place and that Nomura's costs in relation to the written submissions were incurred in consequence of the allegations, so the order stood.

---

3   [2008] IRLR 722 .

5.1.6   Does a costs warning have to be given in order to obtain costs?

In some cases, in a defence to a costs application a party may raise the argument that costs should not be awarded because the other party failed to issue a costs warning.

TOWU v LEWISHAM HOSPITAL NHS TRUST

UKEAT/0314/05/DM

One of the points raised by the Claimant in his appeal against a costs order of £10,000 made by the Employment Tribunal was that he did not have any, or any adequate, warning as to the likely award of costs. He said that there was no pre-hearing review; no application for a costs warning or deposit and no warning to him that legal advice was required.

One of the reasons given by the EAT in rejecting this point was that Mr Towu was himself a professional man who had already brought one tribunal claim. HHJ Richardson stated:

'... the desirability of obtaining independent advice before pursuing claims of this kind which are inevitably expensive and time-consuming for all concerned, should have been apparent to him; all the more so when the allegations that he was making were allegations of some seriousness – allegations of discriminatory conduct by fellow professionals and people in senior positions within the Trust.'

What was not clear from this is what the position would have been had the Claimant not been a professional person with previous experience of litigation. However, the general principle was considered in *ISTC v ASW in liquidation*.[4] Burton J's response was unequivocal:

'We do not encourage, indeed we would not welcome, a situation in which threats of costs are fired across the bows as a matter of course between the parties. There are many cases in which this will be seen almost to amount to emotional or financial blackmail, and certainly in any sort of race or sex discrimination cases it could be said, and has been I think in some cases said, that a threat of costs could amount to victimisation. Therefore, we do not agree ... that there is some kind of condition before it can be said that a case has been brought or continued unreasonably for there to have been a threat of costs.'

In *Salinas v Bear Stearns*[5] the Respondent had sent the Claimant at an early stage a letter warning her that they considered her behaviour to be

---

[4]   UKEAT/0452/04/SM.
[5]   UKEAT/0596/04/DM.

'scandalous and vexatious' and that there would be potential cost consequences of pursuing the claim in the way she did. The Respondent made a discrete complaint that there was no adequate costs warning. The tribunal found that there had been, but in any event they were far from clear that a costs warning is a necessary, or indeed desirable, pre-condition. Burton J pointed out that there was no such warning in *Kovacs* and the existence of the tribunal's costs warning in *Gee* had caused real problems.

5.1.7   Costs warnings and victimisation

The view in *ISTC v ASW* (above) was that in the context of discrimination cases a threat of costs could amount to victimisation. In *Chief Constable of West Yorks Police & ors v Khan*[6] the question was whether the refusal to supply a reference could amount to victimisation but the House of Lords stated as a general rule that it is legitimate to take into account that that, 'once proceedings have been commenced, a new relationship is created between the parties. They are not only employer and employee but also adversaries in litigation. The existence of that adversarial relationship may reasonably cause the employer to behave in a way which treats the employee less favourably than someone who had not commenced such proceedings' (Lord Mackay).

As Lord Nicholls said in *Khan* (para 31) that:

> 'Employers, acting honestly and reasonably, ought to be able to take steps to preserve their position in pending discrimination proceedings without laying themselves open to a charge of victimisation ...'

The difficult job of applying the victimisation provisions stemming from the tensions inherent in the antagonistic litigation situation identified by Lord Hoffman in the *Khan* case were recognised in *Derbyshire & Ors v St Helens Metropolitan Borough Council*.[7]

DERBYSHIRE & ORS v ST HELENS METROPOLITAN BOROUGH COUNCIL

[2005] EWCA Civ 977, [2006] ICR 90

The claims for victimisation were founded on the sending of two letters by the Council two months before the hearing of the equal pay claims fixed. The Claimants claimed that they had been pressurised by intimations made by the Council that school meals would become more expensive and that bonuses would not be paid if they were to continue with their claims. There was no costs➡

---

6   [2001] UKHL 48; [2001] ICR 1065; [2001] 1 WLR 1947; [2001] IRLR 830.
7   [2005] EWCA Civ 977, [2006] ICR 90.

warning in the letters but it was the issue of the pressure the employees felt to withdraw their claims that resulted in a decision in their favour at the House of Lords.

Lord Hope stressed that the employer's conduct should be seen from the employees' standpoint pointing out that an employer 'must avoid doing anything that might make a reasonable employee feel that she is being unduly pressurised to concede her claim'.

Lord Bingham of Cornhill stated:

> '... the object of sending the letters was to put pressure on the [women] to drop their claims. The Council may very well have had compelling reasons for wanting the claims to be dropped. It cannot possibly be criticised for advancing a bona fide defence to the claims. It was fully entitled to seek to settle them. But the letters which it sent were found by the tribunal to treat the [women] less favourably than employees who had not brought and continued Equal Pay claims. The letters caused the [women] a detriment. The letters were sent because the [women] had persisted in their claims and the Council wished to put pressure on them to settle.'

5.2 SETTLEMENT OFFERS

In the civil courts it has long been established that where a reasonable offer marked, 'without prejudice save as to costs' has been made and rejected, that offer can be relied upon in an application for costs (the *Calderbank* rule from *Calderbank v Calderbank*[8]). The Rule is in Part 36 of the Civil Procedure Rules 1998 and the strict application of the principle does not automatically apply to proceedings before an Employment Tribunal.

However, in an employment dispute where a party makes an offer to settle a case, which is refused by the other side, costs can be awarded if the tribunal considers that the party refusing the offer has thereby acted unreasonably, as in *Kopel v Safeway Stores Plc*.[9]

KOPEL v SAFEWAY STORES PLC

[2003] IRLR 753, ALL ER (D) 05 (Sep)

The Claimant brought proceedings which claimed, inter alia, sex discrimination, constructive dismissal and breaches of Arts 3 and 4 of the European Convention on Human Rights. The Employment Tribunal rejected her claims. After the tribunal had given its➡

---

[8]   [1975] 3 All ER 333.
[9]   [2003] IRLR 753, All ER (D) 05 (Sep).

> decision, the employer's representative gave to the tribunal a letter written to the employee in which it had offered £5,700 in full and final settlement. The offer had been rejected. The tribunal then ordered the Claimant to pay £5,000 towards the employer's costs
>
> The employee appealed and the EAT dismissed the appeal. The tribunal was entitled to conclude that the rejection of the offer had been unreasonable. An offer of the *Calderbank* type was a factor that the tribunal could take into account under r 14. It did not follow that a failure by a party to beat a *Calderbank* offer should, by itself, lead to an order for costs being made against them. However, in the instant case the employee had rejected a generous offer and had made a manifestly misconceived claim under the convention. There was no material error of law or fact in the tribunal's reasoning.

Therefore, a failure by a party to beat a Calderbank offer would not, of itself, result in an award of costs against that party. The tribunal must first conclude that the conduct in rejecting the offer was unreasonable before the rejection becomes a relevant factor in the exercise of its discretion.

This had already been applied by the EAT in 1998, in *Coleman v Secureop (UK) Ltd.*[10]

> ## COLEMAN v SECUREOP (UK) LTD
>
> **EAT/483/98**
>
> The applicant had recovered £2,222.88 in proceedings before the Employment Tribunal. Before the proceedings had begun, the employer had made an offer of £6,000 marked without prejudice so far as the hearing was concerned but not as to costs. The tribunal thought that this was a very generous offer and found that that Mr Coleman had acted unreasonably in refusing it. The tribunal, therefore, made an order for £500 costs against him.
>
> On appeal the EAT held that the award of £500 costs is not something which is outside the discretion of the tribunal, and that anyone considering an offer of £6,000 might say he was acting unreasonably to refuse it.

The *Kopel* principle that refusal of a *Calderbank* offer was a factor for consideration in looking at costs was an issue in *Power v Panasonic.*[11] The Claimant argued that, contrary to *Kopel,* the tribunal had looked at the

---

[10] EAT/483/98.
[11] UKEAT/0439/04/RN.

Calderbank offer in isolation and had acted as if the *Calderbank* principle applied directly to the tribunal's jurisdiction. The EAT, upholding the tribunal's award, stated that the Claimant's approach to negotiations had been intransigent and that her Schedule of Loss was unrealistically optimistic.

ANNETTE POWER v PANASONIC (UK) LIMITED

UKEAT/0439/04/RN

The Claimant won the battle, in that her complaints of direct discrimination, disability discrimination, unfair dismissal and breach of contract were upheld by the Reading Employment Tribunal and she was awarded compensation and interest totalling £5,855.11, but 'lost the war' (per HHJ Peter Clark in the EAT) when she was ordered to pay the Respondent's costs in the sum of £10,000. She appealed that order.

At the end of the first hearing the Claimant sought an order for 50% of her costs to be paid by the Respondent but the Employment Tribunal did not consider costs to be appropriate. Subsequently the Respondent made a written application for a contribution to its costs, put at £100,000 overall, limited to £10,000. The basis for the application relied heavily on an offer made by the Respondent to settle the proceedings for £10,000, without admission of liability. It was rejected by the Claimant as totally inadequate. No counter-offer was put forward and the offer lapsed after 21 days. Nearly a year later, before the hearing, they increased the offer to £25,000 and that offer was also rejected.

The Claimant's submissions on appeal were all rejected. One of these was that the Employment Tribunal misapplied the principles in *Kopel* and had looked at the offer of £10,000 in isolation, as if applying the Calderbank principle. They failed to take into account, on the other side of the scales, relevant factors including the facts that the Claimant had substantially won on liability, that there were issues upon which the Respondent had given no ground as well as her own attempts to initiate negotiations, her entitlement to pursue a declaration as to her rights (in the absence of concessions) to a tribunal hearing and the lack of any warning as to her costs risks from the Employment Tribunal.

The EAT rejected this and held that the tribunal was not in a position to give any warning to the Claimant as to costs. They were unaware of the earlier offers before the costs hearing. They had reminded themselves that she had been successful in principle in her claims but took the view that she had simply failed to address the point that the loss of her driving licence and refusal to countenance ➡

> lower paid work for the Respondent fatally undermined her claim for lost earnings, the principal part of her compensation claim. They held that she could not envisage closing the gap with a view to meaningful negotiations and she had failed to engage in realistic negotiations.

The *Panasonic* case was considered in *Jones v Sekisui Alveo Limited.*[12] These cases also highlight the importance of not overstating a Schedule of Loss.

MR R JONES v SEKISUI ALVEO LIMITED
CARDIFF EMPLOYMENT TRIBUNAL

Case No 1600376/2007
Supplied by Gwenno Hughes of Hugh James

After a hearing lasting three days, the Employment Tribunal dismissed the claim of unfair dismissal. The Respondent made a verbal application for costs, and then subsequently a written application, based on their argument that the Claimant had acted unreasonably and/or that the proceedings were misconceived. The Tribunal did not on the facts find this to be a case resting on genuine and live issues as to the fairness of an employer in dismissing an employee. Furthermore, they felt that there was a 'crucial' event in the form of an offer by the Respondent to settle for £18,000 (subsequently increased to £20,000), followed by a costs warning. The tribunal's view was that 'it was the Claimant's profound misjudgement that he continued with his claim ... in the knowledge that he was at serious risk'.

The tribunal considered *Kopel* and *Power* and held that the Claimant's Schedule of Loss was wholly unrealistic in all the circumstances. They felt that this took them beyond the point of a clear warning that the Claimant's conduct and his rejection of settlement were unreasonable, saying that:

> '... not only were the merits of the Claimant's case doubtful and ambiguous but the potential expectation of award to the Claimant was inflated significantly; having regard, not only to the arithmetical calculations of the Schedule of Loss but also the prospect at least of a significant finding of contribution. To have proceeded beyond that point was we think sheer folly and misjudgement.'

The tribunal also took into account the fact that the Claimant had been supported throughout by legal advisors and felt that this➡

---

12   Case No 1600376/2007.

meant that he should not bear the same extent of culpability for his conduct in refusing the offer – 'we feel that there is abatement in terms of his culpability'.

On these bases and the basis that he should have accepted the offer, they made an award of 80% of the costs claimed ie £8,000.

PLANNER v 21st CENTURY LIFTS
LONDON SOUTH EMPLOYMENT TRIBUNAL

Case No 2306270/2007
Supplied by Stefan Hagan of Clarkson Wright & Jakes

The Claimant was unsuccessful and a costs award of £2,500 was made against him on the basis that he had turned down a reasonable offer of settlement, pre-issue, of £2,600 and continued with his claim despite being warned that it had little prospect of success. No formal Calderbank offer was made but the Employment Tribunal considered costs once the Claimant had sought to introduce the pre-issue Without Prejudice discussions through ACAS.

Each case will be considered on its own facts and the EAT has made it clear that there can be no standard practice. In *Monaghan v Close Thornton Solicitors*.[13] Lindsay P observed:

> '... whilst we would not want to deter the making and the acceptance of sensible offers, if it became a practice such that a claimant who recovered no more than two thirds of the sum offered in a rejected Calderbank offer was, without more, then to be visited with the costs of the remedies hearing or some part of them, Calderbank offers would be so frequently used that one would soon be in a regime in which costs would not uncommonly be treated as they are in the High Court and other Courts. Yet it is plain that throughout the life of the employment tribunals the legislature has never so provided. It can only be that that was deliberate.'

Some solicitors have indicated that they always write a letter before action inviting discussions so that they have a platform for claiming costs – see *Johnson v Robert Monk*[14] on p 85.

---

[13] EAT/3/01.
[14] 1100943/2007.

CHAPTER 6

DELAY, POSTPONEMENTS AND ADJOURNMENTS

6.1 FAILURE TO ENGAGE

The tribunal has no power to make an award against an employer who entirely fails to respond or engage with the proceedings. The wording in r 38(4) is that a costs order may be made against or in favour of a respondent who has 'not had a response accepted ...' The question arises whether this refers only to a respondent who has not filed a response or includes a respondent who has filed a response but has not had it accepted, for example if it was filed out of time and no extension of time was granted.

Rule 38(4)

(4) A costs order may be made against or in favour of a respondent who has not had a response accepted in the proceedings in relation to the conduct of any part which he has taken in the proceedings.

In these circumstances, r 38 has to be considered in conjunction with r 9.

9.—A respondent who has not presented a response to a claim or whose response has not been accepted shall not be entitled to take any part in the proceedings except to –

(a)   make an application under rule 33 (review of default judgments);
(b)   make an application under rule 35 (preliminary consideration of application for review) in respect or rule 34(a), (b) or (e)];
(c)   be called as a witness by another person; or
(d)   be sent a copy of a document of corrected entry in accordance with rule 8(4);

and in these rules the word "party" or "respondent" included a respondent only in relation to his entitlement to take such a part in the proceedings, and in relation to any such part which he takes.

Both a Respondent who has not put in a response and a Respondent who has done so but whose response has not been accepted, fall within the words, 'a respondent who has not had a response accepted' – see *Sutton v The Ranch Ltd*.[1] So when a Respondent fails to file a response at all, and so has not had a response 'accepted' as envisaged by r 38, can an order for

---

[1]   UKEAT/0072/06/ZT.

costs be made? Yes, but only in so far as they have played a part in proceedings in a manner prescribed under r 9.

SUTTON v THE RANCH LTD

UKEAT/0072/06/ZT

The Respondent filed no response to the various claims. The tribunal awarded the employee a sum of £14,000 and £5,500 costs. At a review hearing the tribunal revoked the costs order and the employee appealed that decision.

The EAT held that the tribunal had correctly applied r 38(4) of the 2004 Rules on review; an order for costs could only be made against a Respondent who had not put in a response and had, therefore, not had a response accepted in relation to any part he had taken in the proceedings. The employers had not taken any part in the proceedings within r 9, and as a failure to put in a response cannot be taking any point in proceedings (as required by r 9), the appeal was dismissed.

HHJ Burke confirmed that r 38(4) is intended to include both the case of the Respondent who puts in a response which is not accepted and also the case of the Respondent who does not put in any response at all. The Rule has the effect of providing that, in both cases, an order for costs can only be made against or in favour of a Respondent in relation to his conduct of a part which he has played in the proceedings, which part must fall within one or more of the exceptions to r 9.

BRITISH SCHOOL OF MOTORING v MR C FOWLER

UKEAT/0059/06/ZT
Supplied by Andrew Midgley of Old Square Chambers

The Respondent failed to submit an ET3 within the prescribed period. It applied for a review under r 33 of the decision to preclude it from taking any further part in the proceedings on the grounds that it had not received the ET1 or ET2 (and by making that application it thereby 'took part' in the proceedings under r 9(a)). The tribunal invited the Claimant to comment on the application. The Claimant's solicitors wrote to the tribunal enclosing copies of the letters they had sent to the Respondent which referred to the fact that proceedings had been issued and to which the details of the complaint had been attached. The tribunal rejected the Respondent's application. ➡

The Respondent applied for a further review, citing an administrative error. The tribunal did not convene a hearing, but again rejected the application on paper. The Respondent appealed. It produced the appeal bundle. In the Bundle was a copy of the ET1 with a fax number which demonstrated that the ET1 had been faxed by the Respondent to its representatives (Croner) within the prescribed period.

While HHJ Peter Clark allowed the appeal on the basis that the chairman should have allowed the Respondent the opportunity to respond in writing or to make representations at a hearing in relation to the review itself, he found that given that the Respondent had had the ET1 all along (and/or even on the assumption that it should have done because the tribunal's file showed that it had been posted to the correct address), the entire appeal was unnecessary. The Claimant was awarded his costs of defending the appeal (approximately £5,500) on the basis that the Respondent had caused such costs to be spent unnecessarily.

However, even if a Respondent fails to submit an ET3, if the Claimant has made an unsuccessful attempt to enter into discussions – in other words, the Respondent fails completely to engage – a costs order may sometimes be obtained.

MR F JOHNSON v ROBERT MONK (1) RICHARD CARTIES (2) TRADING AS FRENCH CONNEXION WORLDWIDE TRAVEL
ASHFORD EMPLOYMENT TRIBUNAL

Case No 1100943/2007
Supplied by Tony Bertin of Employment Relations Solicitors

No response was entered by the Respondent in the claim for unfair dismissal and judgment was entered. At the hearing relating to compensation before the Judge alone, the Judge awarded compensation and an uplift of 30% in respect of the Respondent's failure to follow the statutory dismissal procedures. An application for costs was made by the Claimant, the ground being that the Respondent had acted unreasonably by failing to resist the claim and not responding to an invitation from the Claimant's solicitor to enter into discussions with a view to settling the claim. As a result the Claimant had gone to the expense of incurring legal fees for his representation at the hearing.

The Judge considered that the Respondents had acted unreasonably and that it was an appropriate case for an order for costs, and he allowed costs of five chargeable hours to cover preparation for and ➡

attendance at the hearing. Based on an hourly rate of £190 the amount ordered (inclusive of VAT) was £1,116.25.

6.2   FAILURE TO ATTEND BY A PARTY

If a party fails to attend a hearing, r 25(5) and (6) will apply:

> **25.**—(5) If a party fails to attend or to be represented (for the purpose of conducting the party's case at the Hearing) at the time and place fixed for the Hearing, the tribunal may dismiss or dispose of the proceedings in the absence of that party or may adjourn the Hearing to a later date.

> (6) If the tribunal wishes to dismiss or dispose of proceedings in the circumstances described in paragraph (5), it shall first consider any information in its possession which has been made available to it by the parties.

The tribunal may then consider the issue of costs under r 38.

IRVING v JOHN W HANNAY & CO
GLASGOW EMPLOYMENT TRIBUNAL

S/118789/06
Supplied by Mel Sangster of Dundas and Wilson

The Claimant failed to appear at a PHR to determine whether he had submitted his claim on time. His claim was dismissed pursuant to r 25(5). Costs were awarded for the Respondent in the sum of £230 per hour for four hours, totalling £1,081. The Tribunal ordered costs on the basis that the Claimant had known about the hearing, the onus was on the Claimant to explain why his claim had not been presented on time and the Respondent had been put to unnecessary expense.

6.3   FAILURE TO ATTEND BY A WITNESS

BUTLER & KENDRICK v DONNELLEY UK DIRECTORY LIMITED
LEEDS EMPLOYMENT TRIBUNAL

Supplied by Christopher Newman, barrister, Littleton Chambers

Both Claimants claimed unfair dismissal following a redundancy exercise and both claims failed on the facts. One of the Claimants did not give evidence in support of his own case despite the fact that he was present at the back of the Tribunal. The Tribunal made an order that he pay a contribution towards the Respondent's costs on ➡

the basis that he had conducted the proceedings unreasonably. He was asked how much he had in savings but refused to disclose that to the Tribunal. The Tribunal said that in those circumstances it would have to make assumptions against him as to his means. He was ordered to pay £1,000.

6.4 ADJOURNMENTS

Depending on the reason for an application for an adjournment of a hearing, the Employment Tribunal may consider costs under r 40(1).

> **40.**—(1) A tribunal or chairman may make a costs order when on the application of a party it has postponed the day or time fixed for or adjourned a Hearing or pre-hearing review. The costs order may be against or, as the case may require, in favour of that party as respects any costs incurred or any allowances paid as a result of the postponement or adjournment.

In an early case, *Rajguru v Top Order Ltd*,[2] the EAT held that costs should only be awarded if the paying party is at fault in applying for an adjournment or postponement.

RAJGURU v TOP ORDERS LTD

[1978] ICR 565

At the hearing of a complaint for unfair dismissal, the employee alleged that the employer's reason for dismissal was inadequate. As a result, the employer made five specific allegations against the employee, two of which were new. An adjournment was then requested by the employee in order that the new matters should be considered. The tribunal granted the adjournment, but ordered the employee to pay the employer's costs of the day under the Industrial Tribunals (Labour Relations) Regulations 1974, r 10(2)(a), on the ground that there should have been a request for further and better particulars of the employer's case at an earlier stage. The employee appealed against the order as to costs.

The EAT held that it was not reasonable to have expected further and better particulars to be asked for at an earlier stage, as there was no need to resort to procedural process in such litigation. Further, the failure to ask for further and better particulars was more relevant to the question of whether an adjournment should have been granted than to the question of costs. The tribunal was wrong to subject the adjournment to an award of costs and accordingly, the order would be ineffective.

---

2   [1978] ICR 565.

Does a party have to act vexatiously, abusively, disruptively or otherwise unreasonably etc in causing the circumstances that gives rise to the adjournment? It seems not – the discretion in r 40 is wider than that.

LADBROKE RACING LTD v HICKEY

[1979] IRLR 273

Mr Hickey claimed that he had been unfairly dismissed by the appellants. Some 45 minutes before his hearing was due to be called on, the employers' representative handed some 66 documents to counsel for Mr Hickey. Counsel requested an adjournment of the tribunal hearing so that he could digest the documents and receive instructions. The tribunal granted the adjournment and ordered that the employers should pay £150 costs in respect of the adjournment.

The employer appealed and the EAT dismissed the appeal. The EAT contrasted r 10(1), which gave the power to the tribunal to award costs where in its opinion a party had acted frivolously or vexatiously, with r 10(2) which gave it the power to award costs incurred as a result of a postponement or adjournment (the equivalent 2004 Rules being rr 40(3) and 40(1)). In their judgment the power in subparagraph (2) was deliberately kept distinct from the power in subparagraph (1) – the power relating to costs of the substantive hearing — which was 'deliberately and very tightly restricted'. They held that r 10(2) specifically widens that type of limitation and enables a tribunal which is granting some form of adjournment, or amendments to proceedings, in an appropriate case to make orders against the party who has compelled an adjournment or caused a delay

Thus, in the present case, the tribunal was empowered to make an order charging the employers with the costs of the adjournment, notwithstanding that the employers could not be held to have acted frivolously or vexatiously.

The EAT commented that if a party has a large bundle of documents on which they wish to rely, it is essential, in order that the other side can have the opportunity of appreciating what is involved in the documents and taking instructions, that they should be passed over a sufficiently long time beforehand to make it possible. To deliver such documents only 45 minutes before the case is due to be called on, is not giving the other side a chance. On that basis, the tribunal did not exercise its discretion wrongly.

AYOBIOJO v LONDON BOROUGH OF CAMDEN

EAT/0510/02 ZT

The Claimant did not attend the hearing on 25 January, which had been set down on 29 November. Parts of her claim in ET1 had been struck out on the basis that they were made out of time and she had appealed that decision. She therefore applied in writing for an adjournment of the hearing of the parts of her claim that remained. The Employment Tribunal ordered that she should make the application on the morning of the first day of her hearing. She failed to attend, and instructed her solicitor to make the application for an adjournment. He was not instructed to present her case should the application fail (which it did) and the tribunal then struck out her Originating Application in its entirety. They also ordered costs of £2,180 on the basis that she had acted unreasonably in not attending the hearing.

On appeal Mrs Ayobiojo claimed that it was perfectly reasonable for her not to wish to attend the hearing, given the way her proceedings had, in her view, been decimated by the tribunal and the fact that her appeal was pending. She said that she believed that her cry for true justice had been denied. The EAT's view was that it is not for the litigant to dictate the terms upon which he or she is prepared to attend the tribunal, in other words, to litigate on their own terms. It is for the tribunal to decide what aspects are within its jurisdiction and which are capable of being adjudicated upon. They therefore had no difficulty in finding that the tribunal was correct in finding that there was unreasonable behaviour.

As to the amount, this represented the cost of the full day – the brief fee of the Respondent's barrister and three hours preparation for their solicitor. This was challenged on the basis that the Respondent had prepared for the hearing on the basis that there was going to be a full hearing, when in the end the only contentious hearing was on the adjournment application (which did not take a full day). The EAT took the view that this is a very broad discretion given to the Employment Tribunal and they could only interfere with it if they were satisfied either that the tribunal took into account some important factor which it should not have done, or left out some important factor that it should have included, or that its discretion was in some other way vitiated in such a way as to make its decision plainly wrong in law. The Claimant had behaved unreasonably. The consequence was that Camden prepared for a five-day hearing and in the EAT's judgment when the tribunal decided that that was what ➡

they were entitled to recover, this was a proper exercise of discretion with which they did not think they could interfere.

LINDSAY v GRAMPIAN FOODS LIMITED
GLASGOW EMPLOYMENT TRIBUNAL

Case No S/108738/07
Supplied by Gina Wilson of MacRoberts

The Claimant maintained that he had only learned of the date fixed for the hearing the day before the hearing on 3 August and so sought an adjournment, as the solicitor he had contacted on the day before could not represent him the following day. He said his union had only learned about the hearing the day before, but evidence before the Employment Tribunal showed that they had been aware on 23 July. The tribunal concluded that by maintaining that he had only become aware on 2 August and in seeking the adjournment, the Claimant had acted unreasonably and had further acted unreasonably in failing to ensure that he had legal representation at the hearing, so an award was made for £250 for expenses.

MISS LA PERRINS v ELLISONS HOLDINGS LTD (1) SUPREME ORGANICS LTD (2)
BIRMINGHAM EMPLOYMENT TRIBUNAL

1307816/2006
Supplied by Christopher Nott, Employment Judge

The Respondent's advocate had failed to understand the requirement to make a formal application prior to the hearing for the purpose of allowing them to resist the claim, the claim having been struck out due to non compliance with an unless order relating to service of documents. As she had failed to appreciate that an application should have been made, she was unprepared to deal with the issue, giving rise to an adjournment of the hearing. The Respondent was ordered to pay the full amount requested by the Claimant of the additional costs resulting from the adjournment, which amounted to £3,750 plus VAT. The Tribunal noted that the representative, 'would not be the first representative to misunderstand the meaning and effect of the rules and she certainly would not be the last'.

MS A DUTT v KINGSTON UNIVERSITY, EAT

UKEAT/0351/06/DA

The Employment Tribunal dismissed an application by the Claimant to postpone the (first) hearing, heard the case in her absence and dismissed the claims. She applied for a review, was successful and the case was reinstated The review decision was obtained in June and it was not until September that the final hearing took place and the claims were dismissed. On reinstatement in June, the Claimant was ordered to pay a contribution of £950 to the Respondent's costs incurred at the first hearing.

The Claimant appealed the costs decision, arguing that since she was successful in shifting the dismissal of her case at the first hearing, she should not be liable to pay any costs. She claimed that as a matter of language, r 40(1) does not apply where the order made was to dismiss the claim but applies only where there has been an adjournment or a postponement. She was not at fault herself because, as she proved in due course, she was at the time of the first hearing incapable of attending by reason of her illness.

HHJ Burke pointed out that the rules are deliberately drafted in different terms. The pejorative language for four situations appears in r 40(3) but is conspicuously absent in r 40(1). In this case, there had been in reality a postponement of the hearing from February to September 2005 so r 40(1) was permissibly applied. The Respondent has turned up for three hearings when it was necessary only for it to turn up for one. The costs order was upheld.

MR SAQUIB ALI v WHS RETAIL TRAVEL LTD
LONDON SOUTH EMPLOYMENT TRIBUNAL

Case No 2306024/2004
Supplied by Paul Manson of WH Smith

On the morning of the two day hearing (27 April) when the Respondent, four witnesses and legal advisors had turned up, the Claimant applied for a postponement, claiming not to have received the bundle of documents or witness statements. It was established that the failure to receive this was entirely due to his own fault. The Claimant's solicitors had ceased acting five days before the hearing but the Respondents had tried (unsuccessfully) to exchange with the Claimant. There was in any event no reason why the hearing could not have proceeded because the documents had been with the ➡

Claimant since 15 February and he had not raised any concerns about the bundle when he had spoken to the Respondent's advisors the day before the hearing.

Rule 40(1) was applied. The postponement was entirely due to the actions of the Claimant in failing to act reasonably in ensuring that he made himself available to receive the bundle when it was dispatched. Costs were awarded in respect of the postponement of the first hearing and also in respect of the final hearing, as there was sufficient evidence to show that the Claimant had acted unreasonably in pursuing the proceedings. In the light of findings of fact, the evidence of the Claimant was held to be unreliable. There was no evidence of fundamental breach entitling him to resign or evidence to substantiate his claim that he raised grievances about any issue during his employment, nor were there any issues outstanding at termination which led to his decision to resign. As there was no breach by the employer fundamental or otherwise, the whole basis of the claim was unreasonable.

Costs were worked out on the basis of hours spent in preparation and attendance at the hearing at the hourly rate of £155 for the cost of a solicitor and £95 for an unqualified assistant.

MR IAN LINDSAY v GRAMPIAN FOODS LIMITED
GLASGOW EMPLOYMENT TRIBUNAL

Case No S/108738/07
Supplied by Gina Wilson of MacRoberts

The Claimant maintained that he had only learned of the date fixed for the hearing the day before the hearing on 3 August 2007 and so sought an adjournment, as the solicitor he had contacted on the day before could not represent him the following day. He said his union had only learned about the hearing the day before, but evidence before the Tribunal showed that they had been aware on 23 July. The Tribunal allowed the application on the basis that one of the overriding objectives was, as far as practicable, to ensure that parties were on an equal footing and as the Claimant sought to be legally represented it was just to adjourn the hearing. However the Tribunal concluded that by maintaining that he had only become aware of the hearing on 2 August and in seeking the adjournment, the Claimant had acted unreasonably and had further acted unreasonably in failing to ensure that he had legal representation at the hearing. An award was made for £250 for expenses, although there was no explanation in the judgment of how that sum was reached.

6.5 ALLOCATING COSTS

MR D WALKER v HEATHROW REFUELLING SERVICES COMPANY LTD & ORS

UKEAT/0366/04/TM

The adjournment in this case was the result of late joinder by Mr Walker of six new Respondents and because he sought to add a claim for disability discrimination. The EAT could see no conceivable justification for considering joining the Respondents. In the judgment of the EAT, the adjournment was the consequence of the late joinder and the late addition of the disability discrimination claim, and they believed that he must pay for that. However, they did not believe that there was any question of payment for the entirety of the case or anything of that kind. Burton J said,

> 'It is the cost arising out of the adjournment of the hearing, which was attended by and prepared for by a solicitor and attended by a witness of the Respondent. Plainly the nature of the preparations of the case were not wasted, because eventually the case came on for hearing. But there were plainly wasted costs. (The Respondent's representative) has put his claim at some £1,500. We are satisfied that the appropriate sum is £500 by way of contribution towards the wasted costs by the Appellant.'

In the *Walker* case, the Employment Tribunal had reserved the costs and the EAT were not happy about that:

> 'We must begin by saying in the plainest possible terms that we very much regret that the Employment Tribunal on that occasion reserved the costs rather than deciding it themselves.'

BUCHANAN v ROSEHILL HOUSING COOPERATIVE GLASGOW EMPLOYMENT TRIBUNAL

Case No S/105366/04
Supplied by Karen Harvie of TC Young

The Claimant applied for the two day hearing of her claim for constructive dismissal to be postponed because her solicitors were no longer instructed. The hearing was adjourned and the Respondent's agents applied for £400 expenses incurred by the adjournment. At the adjourned hearing the Claimant wanted to give evidence about an incident which had not been included in the claim form. The Employment Tribunal decided to hear the evidence and then decide whether it should be included in the claim. A date was ➡

fixed to hear the evidence but the day before, the Claimant applied to adjourn it on the basis that she had a viral infection which affected her voice. She also stated in writing that due to a change in her personal circumstances she wished to pursue her claims through other avenues, although it was unclear whether this was a withdrawal of her claim or whether she sought an adjournment. The Claimant did not respond to enquiry about her intentions or a request for medical evidence, and her claim was struck out under r 18(7)(d).

The Respondent applied for the £400 expenses of the adjourned hearing and £2,400 plus VAT for the second hearing. The award for £400 was made; the Claimant had provided no reason why the solicitors instructed were no longer prepared to represent her, although she had been given the opportunity to do so. A further sum of £400 was ordered in respect of the second adjourned hearing as the Claimant had failed to provide any evidence of her viral infection and no explanation was provided for the late postponement request.

The Employment Tribunal considered whether she had acted unreasonably in her conduct of the proceedings and not whether the withdrawal itself is unreasonable. The tribunal was never told by the Claimant why she withdrew and they believed that there was nothing in her conduct which would permit them to conclude that one or more of the circumstances in r 40(3) applied, so they did not make an order for the whole of the costs.

VAT point – the Respondent was a housing association and they could not recover VAT paid to their solicitors so they asked for an order for £470. The Tribunal was not prepared to make an award of expenses including VAT on the basis that the Respondent could not recover it. They said that they would expect that an organisation carrying out business would be registered for VAT purposes and therefore able to set their liability for VAT against any VAT they may have to pay on their expenses.

MRS MARY PIERRE-HARVEY v UNISON (1), MR STUART BAKER (2), MR CHRIS REMINGTON (3)
LONDON SOUTH EMPLOYMENT TRIBUNAL

Case No 2301265/2006
Supplied by Alex Colson of Taylor Walton LLP

The hearing to determine the merits of the Claimant's three separate claims for race and sex discrimination were postponed repeatedly in response to her applications that she was unfit to attend due to →

continued poor health. A year after the first date, a consultant psychiatrist confirmed that she was fit to proceed, whereupon she withdrew all her claims.

The Tribunal did not accept the Respondent's argument that the Claimant had, in bringing her complaint at all, acted vexatiously, abusively and unreasonably. They rejected the fact that the Claimant had failed to heed clear guidance given to her by another tribunal in another case about being realistic in her assessment of claims in the future as an indication of unreasonableness; despite the fact that she had ignored previous guidance, she had not been declared a vexatious litigant and remained entitled to bring claims to the tribunal.

However, it was noted that the Claimant had a duty to assist the tribunal to further the overriding objective, which includes ensuring that the case is dealt with expeditiously and fairly and in ways which are proportionate to the complexity or importance of the issues. The tribunal believed that the Claimant had not acted in ways which would ensure that the case was dealt with fairly, in particular, she had failed to comply with the order to provide a medical report by a specified date and delayed on two occasions in providing the Respondent with medical reports in time for them to prepare any adequate response. The first of those failures had prevented there being an effective hearing in March 2007. She blamed her solicitors for the failure to provide the medical report on time but on assessing the conflicting evidence of the Claimant and her solicitors (who had ceased to act), the Tribunal concluded that the failure was her sole responsibility.

The Tribunal decided that the Claimant's conduct after March 2007 was unreasonable in that she had ensured that hearings were delayed or rendered ineffective. Had she intended to withdraw because of her ill health, she could have done so far earlier than she did and it appeared that it was only when her opportunities to delay any further came to an end that she withdrew her claims. She was ordered to pay the Respondent's costs incurred after March 2007, to be taxed if not agreed.

6.6   SPECIAL CASE – RULE 39

Rule 39 – failure to reinstate or re-engage

39.—(1) Subject to rule 38(2), a tribunal must make a costs order against a respondent where in proceedings for unfair dismissal a Hearing has been postponed or adjourned and –

(a)   the claimant has expressed a wish to be reinstated or re-engaged which has been communicated to the respondent not less than 7 days before the Hearing; and

(b)   the postponement or adjournment of that Hearing has been caused by the respondent's failure, without a special reason, to adduce reasonable evidence as to the availability of the job from which the claimant was dismissed, or of comparable or suitable employment.

(2) A costs order made under paragraph (1) shall relate to any costs incurred as a result of the postponement or adjournment of the Hearing.

Thus, a tribunal has no discretion in cases caught by r 39, where there has been a postponement or an adjournment of a hearing resulting from the failure of an employer to adduce evidence about the availability of the claimant's former job or of comparable or suitable employment, the claimant having expressed a wish to be reinstated or reengaged at least seven days before that hearing. NB the wish to be reinstated or reengaged may have been communicated in the ET1, in which case an employer should give some thought to that evidence as a matter of course in their preparation for the hearing.

CHAPTER 7

MISCONCEIVED CLAIMS AND ARGUMENTS

7.1 THE LEGAL BASIS FOR COSTS

The legal basis for obtaining costs on this basis lies in r 40(2) and (3):

> **40.**—(2) A tribunal or chairman shall consider making a costs order against a paying party where, in the opinion of the tribunal or chairman (as the case may be), any of the circumstances in paragraph (3) apply. Having so considered, the tribunal or chairman may make a costs order against the paying party if it or he considers it appropriate to do so.

> (3) The circumstances referred to in paragraph (2) are where the paying party has in bringing the proceedings, or he or his representative has in conducting the proceedings, acted vexatiously, abusively, disruptively or otherwise unreasonably, or the bringing or conducting of the proceedings by the paying party has been misconceived.

In *Scott v Commissioners of Inland Revenue*,[1] CA Sedley LJ clarified that the key question with regard to the misconceived ground, is not whether the party *thought* he was in the right, but whether he had *reasonable grounds* for doing so.

There is no exhaustive definition of 'misconceived' for the purposes of the 2004 Regulations, but reg 2 (definitions) states that 'misconceived' includes 'having no reasonable prospect of success). The EAT in *Kew College Ltd v Mrs Parsley*[2] confirmed that the definition includes having no reasonable prospect of success but is not limited to this.

7.2 WHAT TEST SHOULD BE APPLIED?

Sir Hugh Griffiths' observation in *Marler v Robertson*[3] is often quoted in costs judgments. He said, 'the ordinary experience of life frequently teaches us that which is plain for all to see once the dust of battle has subsided was far from clear to the competent once they took up arms'.

---

[1]   [2004] IRLR 713.
[2]   UKEAT/0565/06/DA.
[3]   [1974] ICR 72.

KEW COLLEGE LTD v MRS PARSLEY

UKEAT/0565/06/DA

Costs were awarded costs in favour of the Claimant on the ground that the Respondent's response to her unfair constructive dismissal claim was misconceived and that they had acted unreasonably in resisting the claim. In deciding whether the response was misconceived, the tribunal considered the College Governors' failure to deal properly with the Claimant's grievance and a 'secret letter' from the Head to the Governors in which she made it clear that she was determined that the Claimant should no longer be at the school for the next term. They stated:

> '... on that basis and with all of that knowledge we ask ourselves should the Respondent have considered having received the claim that any response would have little prospect of success. The overwhelming answer is yes ... In the knowledge that this information would be before a Tribunal, the Tribunal finds that it is inconceivable that the Respondent could have thought that they would have had any prospect of being successful in resisting a claim for constructive dismissal.'

The EAT dismissed the College's appeal. They confirmed that the word 'misconceived' includes having no reasonable prospect of success. It is not limited only to those cases which in the Employment Tribunal's view have no reasonable prospect of success. The EAT agreed with the Employment Tribunal that pursuing a misconceived claim or defence may also be regarded as unreasonable conduct but the latter may be found to have occurred without the claim or defence being misconceived.

The EAT upheld the tribunal's approach of looking at the *conduct* of the proceedings and found on the facts that the *defence* of the proceedings was misconceived and/or unreasonable. This limb of r 40(3) requires the Employment Tribunal to ask whether the conducting of the proceedings was reasonable ie whether it was unreasonable to defend, or to continue defending past a certain point.

It was submitted on behalf of the College that the Employment Tribunal had erred in law in applying a subjective test to the question of whether or not they should have appreciated that their defence to the claim would have no reasonable prospect of success and whether the response was misconceived. The EAT considered the wording of r 40(3) ie 'the ... conducting of the proceedings by the paying party *has been* misconceived'. They considered that this➡

required the Employment Tribunal to look back at the paying party's acts and decisions in bringing or defending the claim. It required them to decide whether, in any respects, those acts/decisions have been 'misconceived' and this could be for any number of reasons, depending on the facts. The Employment Tribunal correctly applied r 40(3) in considering whether the College's conduct in defending the proceedings was misconceived because the defence was misconceived, ie it had no reasonable prospect of success.

In *Kew* the whole of the costs incurred by the Claimant were ordered, to be taxed on the higher County Court scale on an indemnity basis. This was the whole of the costs excluding any deduction for any amount received by the Claimant via her insurers.

In *Salinas v Bear Stearns*[4] the observation was made that allegations that emerge over time and allegations that are not particularised, evidence of a shifting and expanding case and a propensity for developing arguments as a matter progresses are normally good indicators of a misconceived case and unreasonable behaviour and it is proper to look back at the end of a case and decide whether a party should have appreciated the flaws in his case. The gravity of the paying party's conduct is also relevant.

7.3 FACTUALLY MISCONCEIVED CLAIMS

In cases where a claim is believed to be based on factually hopeless allegations, Respondents should consider applying at an early stage for an order that there is no case to answer (at a PHR or, at a hearing, after hearing the Claimant's evidence). If successful, this naturally leads to a consequent application for costs, but even if it is unsuccessful and having heard both parties the tribunal then dismisses the claims, it can strengthen an application for costs under r 40(3).

Of course, even if a claim transpires to be factually misconceived, it does not follow the Claimant *should have known* it was factually misconceived – for example, where facts are just known to the Respondent. In those circumstances, a Claimant is unlikely to be held to have acted unreasonably in bringing or conducting the proceedings, and likewise a tribunal is unlikely to exercise its discretion to order costs even if decides that the claim lacked any reasonable prospect of success.

When a party sets out to mislead the tribunal or the other side, however, the position is quite different. We consider this situation in the next chapter.

---

4   UKEAT/0596/04/DM.

HAZELEY v ST JOSEPH HOSPICE
STRATFORD EMPLOYMENT TRIBUNAL

Case No 3204306/2001
Supplied by Lynden Lever of Stone King LLP

The Claimant brought claims for disability discrimination (although that claim was subsequently withdrawn) and race discrimination. The Tribunal did not accept her comparators as such, nor that she had been penalised. They could find no direct evidence of racial discrimination whatsoever ('indeed there was evidence of a high degree of racial harmony'), nor could they find any circumstances from which they could draw any inference.

The Employment Tribunal accepted that when she lodged the claim, the Claimant believed that she had a case to put in front of a Tribunal for a decision. However they accepted the Respondent's argument that once the race questionnaire was answered she had all the information necessary to form a view and should have realised from that information, her knowledge about the sickness records of others and her continuing to work at the Hospice that the defence that the Respondents had taken all reasonable practicable steps was likely to succeed. They took the view that the last 'nail in the coffin' was the service of the Notice of Appearance which raised the defence that the Respondent had taken all reasonable practicable steps. They concluded that it was 'disgraceful' for the Claimant to allege institutional racism when her real complaint was that two individuals out of 300 were racist. Costs were awarded against her from the date the Tribunal considered she had had the time to take advice from her solicitor that the case had no reasonable prospect of success, which was six weeks after the Notice of Appearance had been filed. The fact that the Respondents were a charitable organisation was a factor in the decision.

MR J NORTHOVER v PULLMAN PREMIER LEISURE LTD
(1) TRAVEL WEST INNS LTD (2)
SOUTHAMPTON EMPLOYMENT TRIBUNAL

Case No 3100805/2005
Supplied by Simon Martin of Battens Solicitors

The Claimant brought claims of unfair dismissal under ss 98 and 103A of the Employment Rights Act 1996. The Respondents admitted that they had failed to comply with the statutory procedures (s 98) but argued that no compensation should be ➡

awarded on just and equitable grounds and also on the basis that the Claimant had contributed to his dismissal.

The Claimant based his section 103A claim on statements he made during discussions prior to termination about his concerns of a breach of legal obligations amounting to theft by some employees.

The Employment Tribunal held that the crucial elements of reasonable belief and good faith were rendered wholly implausible by reason of some simple questions put to the Claimant, who was an accountant and an intelligent man. The Tribunal did not accept that the failings of the PIDA claim were unknown to him and concluded that, 'the poverty of the PIDA claim would or should have been known to the Claimant had he gone about matters sensibly'.

The Tribunal held that it was not necessary for the proceedings to be capable of a strike out pursuant to r 18(7)(b) for them to be held unreasonable. It is not necessary to establish that the case on behalf of the Claimant falls under its own weight (although it did in this case in any event). It is not necessary to specifically make a finding of fraud or dishonest intent in determining the unreasonableness in bringing or conducting of proceedings. An offer of settlement by the Respondent did not bolster the Claimant's otherwise unmeritorious claims – they believed that the offer was reasonable in the light of the substantial costs and the substantial schedule of loss prepared by the Claimant. This was not a case where the claim was rejected on the basis of a 'near miss'. The Claimant's knowledge of what he was doing meant that the usual argument regarding the 'dust of battle' situation did not apply here.

The Tribunal felt that the proceedings should never have been initiated. The Claimant had made many detailed and unfounded complaints and criticisms. A costs order was made and they stated that, 'we consider that anything short of awarding the costs of resisting the claim in full would not be a proper exercise of our discretion'.

Costs were £65,000 with interest at the rate of 2% above BBR if not paid within nearly four months.

**MR J CHRISTIE v WYSE DRYWALL/WYSE GROUP
EDINBURGH EMPLOYMENT TRIBUNAL**

**Case No 112014/2007
Supplied by Gina Wilson of MacRoberts LLP**

The Claimant's employer had gone into administration and some
contracts were purchased by the Respondent. The Claimant had
resigned before the business had been sold and he was therefore not
an employee of the Respondents. The Employment Tribunal found
that there was no prospect of success against the Respondents; the
Claimant should have been put on notice of this by the contents of
a letter from the Joint Administrator and the terms of the ET3, but
he persisted with the claim nonetheless.

The Employment Tribunal took into account the fact that the
Claimant was in paid employment, was single with no dependents,
and had a mortgage and the usual living expenses. The Respondent
asked for £1,000 as they had had to instruct a solicitor at short
notice and the Tribunal took the view that although it was arguable
that in such a case it was necessary to instruct a solicitor
nevertheless it was 'open to a prudent respondent to do so'.
However, they thought that £500 should be sufficient to cover the
costs.

**MRS D P WAYNE v KENT AND MEDWAY NHS AND SOCIAL
CARE PARTNERSHIP TRUST
ASHFORD EMPLOYMENT TRIBUNAL**

**Case No 1100806/2007
Supplied by Catherine Daw of Brachers**

The Tribunal concluded that the Claimant had been unreasonable in
bringing the proceedings for unfair constructive dismissal and
discrimination on the ground of religion or belief. They considered
the finding in *Sake v Fitzroy Robinson Limited*[5] in which the EAT
said that in a case of discrimination, direct evidence was rare and it
may be difficult for a Claimant to know whether or not she had any
prospect of success until the evidence is heard and therefore costs
orders in discrimination claims are rare. However, the Tribunal
concluded that this was not a case where the evidence had to be
tested. They were satisfied that the Claimant was 'aware at all
material times that the truth of the matter lay within the evidence of
the Respondent, but that she had deliberately manipulated the ➡

---

[5]   EAT0241/00.

evidence to suit her case'. For that reason, the Claimant had been unreasonable in bringing the proceedings.

Applying the test for misconceived claims in *Scott* the Tribunal was satisfied that she had no reasonable grounds for thinking she was right about her claims. The Tribunal believed that she had decided to leave her job when she found another one and not because of the Respondent's alleged breach of contract. She had been unable to produce evidence of religious discrimination and she would have known that when she instituted proceedings.

Having considered the Claimant's ability to pay, the Tribunal decided to make an order for costs of £10,000, to compensate the Respondent for costs incurred. This was despite a reluctance on the part of the Tribunal to make an award; the judgment notes that the two members, who had been sitting since 1995 and 1996 respectively, had only ever acceded to one costs application between them and the third member who had sat since 1993 had heard more costs applications but had only ever granted six in that time.

FRANCIS v ESW MAINTENANCE AND LIGHTING LTD
LONDON CENTRAL EMPLOYMENT TRIBUNAL

Case No 2200350/2001
Supplied by Daniel Barnett

The Claimant's claims for unlawful deduction of wages and breach of contract were both dismissed. The Tribunal found that the Claimant did not actually incur any expenses and there could be no unlawful deduction by the Respondent's failure to pay expense which were not incurred. Furthermore, there was no breach of any existing contracts.

An application for costs was made on hearing the judgment on the ground of r 40(3). This was resisted on the ground that there had been no bad faith on the part of the applicant in bringing the claim and that in order to show that a claim was misconceived the Respondent would have to show that there was no reasonable prospect of success. The Respondent had not made an application for PHR and the claim had been allowed to proceed to a full hearing.

The Employment Tribunal were satisfied that the Claimant did act in good faith and honestly believed that he had a claim. They had had to hear both parties' evidence to reach the conclusion they did, and no application had been made by the Respondent at the end of the Claimant's evidence that there was no case to answer. On these ➡

bases, the Tribunal did not believe that the Claimant had acted frivolously or vexatiously or that the claim was misconceived.

7.4 LEGALLY MISCONCEIVED CLAIMS

DATHI v S LONDON AND MAUDSLEY NHS TRUST & GOSNELL
ASHFORD EMPLOYMENT TRIBUNAL

Case No 06 1100002/2006
Supplied by Nadim Dathi of Sternberg Reed

The issue was whether the Respondent had been unreasonable in its conduct of the proceedings and whether the conducting of the proceedings had been misconceived. There had been a failure by the First Respondent to deal with the Claimant's grievance and, knowing this, they continued to defend the claim in a robust manner, even though it was apparent that no explanation could be offered for their failure and there was no real defence to the claim that the grievance had not been properly dealt with. Their conduct of the proceedings had to some extent been unreasonable, particularly in which, without any substantial evidence, the Claimant's conduct had been attacked. Also the defence was misconceived in view of the lack of explanation about the way the grievance had been handled. The First Respondent was ordered to pay 50% of the Claimant's costs to be assessed pursuant to r 41(1)(c).

DURMAN AND SMITH v BARCHESTER HEALTHCARE LTD
EXETER EMPLOYMENT TRIUBNAL

Case No 1701873/2005 AND 1701874/2005
Supplied by Paul Housego, fee-paid employment judge and partner at Beers Solicitors

The Claimants succeeded in their discrimination claims and made a claim for costs of £10,000 as they did not wish the costs to be assessed. The Tribunal commented that it is always open to a Respondent to defend a discrimination claim and arguments raised by the Claimants about the Respondent's failings in so far as documents and statements were concerned did not assist them because the case finished in the time allowed. However they believed that it was clear that the defences to the Claimants' unfair dismissal ➡

claim were misconceived. Had it just been a discrimination claim it would not have taken so long so a total of £5,000 was ordered (£2,500 for each Claimant).

MR O MITCHELL v OPCS LIMITED
READING EMPLOYMENT TRIBUNAL

Case No 2700967/07
Supplied by Gareth Rosser-Davies of BrookeStreet des Roches

The Claimant's claim of unfair dismissal was misconceived as he did not have the necessary qualifying service to bring the claim, and his breach of contract and discrimination claims were out of time. He had brought a first set of proceedings which were identical and which were dismissed. The Employment Tribunal dismissed his claims and held that his continued pursuit of the claims was unreasonable. They awarded preparation costs of a day and a half and costs of attending the hearing at a daily rate of £500, having taken into account that the Claimant earned £750 per month.

P HALPIN v BELLBARON LTD
BEDFORD EMPLOYMENT TRIBUNAL

Case No 1200289/2007
Supplied by Rob Whitaker of Stanley Tee

The claims for unfair dismissal and failure to provide a statement of terms were dismissed as the Claimant was not an employee of the Respondent, but a self employed contractor. The Claimant was ordered to pay costs of £1,250 to the Respondent.

YOLANDA STEARN v ORCHID PUBS OPERATIONS LTD T/A
THE MUDDLE GO NOWHERE
NOTTINGHAM EMPLOYMENT TRIBUNAL

Supplied by Jayne Harrison of Chattertons

The Claimant applied for the costs of a PHR, requested by the Respondent in order to clarify whether or not the Claimant had one year's continuous service with which to bring a claim of unfair dismissal. The Respondent's representatives were put on notice of costs, on the basis that the application for the PHR was misconceived and had no reasonable prospect of success. Although the start date and the effective date of termination were unclear, the Claimant was able to present three alternative dates to show she had ➡

been employed for one year and at the worst scenario, the application of ERA, s 86(1) took her over the year's service. The Judge accepted this and granted the costs of the preparation and attendance at the PHR.

MR R S GREWAL v LONDON BOROUGH OF BARNET
WATFORD EMPLOYMENT TRIBUNAL

Case Nos 3318116/2006, 3300167/2007
Supplied by Shaman Kapoor, Barrister, Temple Garden Chambers

The Claimant's claims of race discrimination and victimisation were dismissed. The Respondent made an application for costs on the basis that the claims were misconceived. The Claimant argued that he had at all times genuinely believed that he had been the subject of race discrimination. The Respondent argued that the Claimant could not get the claims past the first stage – he was not able to point at any fact other than his race and that of the others involved in the case as a reason for saying that his treatment was on the grounds of race – and by the stage where the disclosure of documents had taken place he must be taken to have known that an essential element of the case could not be sustained. The Employment Tribunal accepted that the pursuit of the case beyond that point was properly to be described as pursuing a claim which has no reasonable prospect of success. The Tribunal noted specifically that he had in his conduct of the hearing behaved with complete courtesy towards both the Tribunal and the witnesses, but this did 'not stop the Tribunal from coming to the view ... that the proceedings had been misconceived'.

Having taken into account the Claimant's 'parlous' means, an award of costs was made in the sum of £2,500.

MISS I HAYES v THE BRITISH VAN HEUSEN CO LTD T/A
MORRISON MCCONNELL (1) ELITE GROUP LOGISTICS
LTD (2)
NOTTINGHAM EMPLOYMENT TRIBUNAL

Case No 2602482/2007
Supplied by Diarmuid Deeney of Halliwells LLP

The Second Respondent made an application for costs against the Claimant after she failed in her claims against it for unfair dismissal and failure to consult in connection with a TUPE transfer, the Second Respondent being the transferee. This was on the ground that the claim had no reasonable prospect of success. She had not ➡

disputed that there was an 'ETO', she had accepted that she had been consulted with and she had objected to the transfer. The Claimant argued that there had been a TUPE transfer and therefore it was normal for the claim to be pursued against both the transferor and transferee.

The Tribunal concluded that the Claimant's continued pursuit of her claims against the Second Respondent having regard to the facts found by the Tribunal was unreasonable and it was appropriate to make a costs order of £1,250.

MR K DOE v SQUAD SECURITY
WATFORD EMPLOYMENT TRIBUNAL

Case No 3302044
Supplied by Rebecca Fox of MAB Law

The Claimant's claims for disability discrimination and unfair dismissal were dismissed. He was found not to have a disability, nor did he have the qualifying service required to bring the claim for unfair dismissal. He was ordered to pay a contribution of £2,500 towards the costs of the Respondents.

MISS R NICKLIN v VICKY MARTIN CONCESSIONS LTD
MANCHESTER EMPLOYMENT TRIBUNAL

Case No 2406032

Where an employer contested disability, a costs award was made against him at the PHR, limited to the sum of £450. The employer should not have contested disability as it was clear that the Claimant was disabled.

MR R J MORGAN v SAINT GOBAIN BUILDING
DISTRIBUTION LIMITED

Case No 1306491/2007
Supplied by Clive Thomas of Watkins & Gunn Solicitors

The Claimant succeeded on the first issue that he was entitled to a statutory redundancy payment but lost on the second issue, which was that he was entitled to an enhanced redundancy payment. The Respondent subsequently made an application for costs by letter, based on their contention that the Claimant had conducted the proceedings in an unreasonable and misconceived fashion. ➡

The Judge's opinion was that the Respondent's application was misconceived. He noted that (i) the Claimant had been partially successful and (ii) that the Respondent had offered to make a payment of the amount of the statutory redundancy payment to the Claimant and he considered the Respondent's tactics to be 'unattractive', namely while choosing to deny that the Claimant was due a redundancy payment they made an offer which indicated that they accepted that it was in fact due. The application for costs would have had more force had they paid the statutory redundancy amount and won on the only outstanding issue of the right to an enhanced payment, in other words, that they had won outright. Finally, (iii) the Tribunal noted that on the issue where the Claimant lost, there were arguments to put forward and in fact the Respondent had engaged in correspondence which gave rise to an impression that the Claimant was entitled to an enhanced redundancy payment. Therefore the Claimant had not acted unreasonably in pursuing the claim.

PHIL JEWER v A ONE INSURANCE SERVICES (BTH) LTD
SOUTHAMPTON EMPLOYMENT TRIBUNAL

Case No 3101345/2006
Supplied by Kate Palka of Palka Downton Solicitors

The substantive claim for disability discrimination was dismissed. The Respondent applied for an order that the Claimant pay costs on the basis that the bringing of the claims was misconceived and that the Claimant acted unreasonably. The Tribunal had found that it had no jurisdiction to hear the claims and had declined to extend time on a just and equitable basis. It had indicated that were this not the case, it would still not have found for the Claimant in any event. The Tribunal had found that there were inconsistencies and difficulties in the evidence and that the Claimant had a negative attitude in relation to reasonable adjustments; despite the fact that adjustments had been made, these did not include the specific adjustment he required.

On the issue of costs, the Tribunal did not consider that it could be said that the Claimant had other than reasonable grounds for believing that his claim had some prospect of success in relation to the extension of time limits. The jurisdiction to extend time is an equitable one depending on the facts and it is not necessarily clear at the institution of proceedings or indeed at the commencement of the hearing how matters are going to turn out. In addition it found that in relation to his conduct in the hearing, the Claimant had not acted unreasonably, even though the conclusions of the Tribunal was at times that he was misguided about his application.

7.5 RELEVANCE OF LEGAL ADVICE

In *Cartier Superfoods Ltd v Laws*[6] Phillips J observed that when dealing with a litigant in person, it is for the tribunal to have regard to what a party knew or ought to have known if he had gone about the matter sensibly.

In the *Kew* case, the fact that the Respondent was advised by First Assist and by a solicitor who appeared at the tribunal was taken into account when considering the issue of costs. The panel stated:

> 'As a Tribunal we would expect that a Respondent legally represented and properly advised would be able to make a more informed judgment and be able to take a more informed view of the likely prospects of success in the event a claim went before a Tribunal than an unrepresented lay respondent.'

MR J M CLIFFE v KSS LTD
MANCHESTER EMPLOYMENT TRIBUNAL

Case No 2409994/2003
Supplied by Guy Guinan of Halliwells LLP

Mr Cliffe's Equal Pay claim was dismissed. The claim had been brought because the Claimant felt that he had not been rewarded equally to his colleagues generally rather than colleagues of the other gender. He thought that 'equal pay' meant 'fair pay' and that equal meant equality.

The Employment Tribunal recognised that the introduction of the misconceived concept in 2004 had lowered the threshold for awarding costs. They considered that when dealing with a litigant in person, it is for the Tribunal to have regard to what a party knew or ought to have known if he had gone about the matter sensibly. If the Tribunal did not think the claim was misconceived at inception, it could consider whether the Claimant's state of knowledge changed along the way such that from a particular point it became misconceived or unreasonable to continue to pursue the claim.

In this case, the claim was clearly misconceived from the outset and so all the costs were awarded. The costs exceeded £10,000 and so were to be assessed in the County Court, if not agreed.

A party's representative can also be liable for costs where factually hopeless allegations are made (see also section ten on wasted costs).

---

[6]   [1978] IRLR.

MR V OYEWOLE v DYNAMIQUE LIMITED
LONDON SOUTH EMPLOYMENT TRIBUNAL

Case No 2305547/2006
Supplied by Natalie Roach of Brethertons

The unfair dismissal claim failed; it was very weak. The Employment Tribunal concluded that:

> '... it was difficult to disagree with the ... submission that the Claimant believed he was blameless simply because he had got away with it for so long.'

The Employment Tribunal noted that the Claimant had not disputed the basis for his (misconduct) dismissal and had repeatedly and significantly changed his story from suspension right up to the hearing.

The Respondent applied for costs under r 40(3), as well as for a wasted costs order. The costs applications were heard separately and although the representative turned up, the Claimant did not. Any initial issue of conflict was resolved because the representative said that the Claimant had given specific instructions for him to appear.

With regard to the wasted costs application, it was accepted that the Claimant's representative had not acted in pursuit of profit – there was no CFA or agreement to be paid and therefore the Tribunal had no jurisdiction.

The Claimant's representative argued in defence of the application for costs against the Claimant that the Respondent had been irresponsible during the litigation by disclosing documents late and by failing to point out to the (represented) Claimant the weaknesses of his claim. In fact the late documents were peripheral ones (two) and there were reasons for not making a costs warning. This was a case where costs were entirely appropriate – it must have been plain to both the Claimant and his representative that the claim had no reasonable prospect of success, given the Claimant's own admissions. Some of the explanations for his actions were completely at odds with unchallenged documentary evidence, the claim form was misleading and the Claimant's version of events changed significantly at different stages. So the bringing of the proceedings was misconceived and the conduct unreasonable. No evidence on ability to pay was given. The costs incurred were £13,000 and an order was made for £10,000.

MR G ADAM v LOMOND MOTORS LIMITED
GLASGOW EMPLOYMENT TRIBUNAL

Case No S/113607/07
Supplied by Lindsay Anderson of Morton Fraser LLP

The Claimant complained of unfair dismissal on grounds related to trade union activities and he made an application under s 161 of the TULR(C)A. This resulted in a hearing and during the second day of his evidence the Claimant informed the Tribunal that he did not wish the Respondents to either reinstate or re-engage him, but sought only his pay from the date of dismissal until the full determination of his claim. The Tribunal dismissed the application and the Respondent then made an application for the costs of the preparation and conduct of the hearing on the grounds that the application had been vexatious, unreasonable and misconceived in circumstances where the Claimant was not seeking reinstatement. The Respondent sought £2,500 for preparation and £3,000 for Counsel's fees for representation at the hearing.

The Tribunal did not find any evidence to support the Respondent's submission that the Claimant had acted vexatiously. It found that he had not acted unreasonably because he had taken legal advice throughout the proceedings. It did, however, conclude that the application had been misconceived. The purpose of the application for interim relief is to return the Claimant to the workplace pending the determination of the substantive claim and not to require the respondent to continue paying the Claimant his salary regardless of whether or not he returned to work.

The Tribunal was not asked to take into account the Claimant's ability to pay and no evidence was given on this. The Tribunal considered it appropriate to make a costs order and considered it appropriate that the Claimant pay the costs of preparation for the hearing (£2,500). The Tribunal was not satisfied that it would be appropriate to grant Counsel's fees, as the issue was not sufficiently complex to justify the employment of Counsel

CHAPTER 8

DISHONEST ALLEGATIONS AND VEXATIOUSNESS

8.1   LEGAL BASIS FOR COSTS

Where a tribunal believes that a party in proceedings has told lies or made false allegations, it is open to them to award costs on the basis that in bringing or in conducting the proceedings he or his representative has acted vexatiously, abusively, disruptively or otherwise unreasonably, or the bringing or conducting of the proceedings has been misconceived.

Examples are allegations of conspiracy or fraud (the latter being introduced to pressure the other side into settling, for example going into various irrelevant business practices which are said to be crooked) or where a litigant has fabricated documents to try to prove their case. Some litigants may introduce a cause of action to try to escape the compensation cap or avoid qualifying periods (for example where they have falsely alleged whistle blowing simply to circumvent the qualifying period).

If a party believes that another party has brought up issues in their witness evidence which has nothing to do with the claim but is an attempt to pressure them into a settlement (for example, that a director is having an affair), they should consider applications to exclude parts of witness statements or – if the circumstances are right – for a restricted reporting order.

8.2   FRAUDULENT ALLEGATIONS/DELIBERATE LIES

Recent years have seen a considerable hardening of tribunals' approaches to parties which simply set out to deceive. The first two cases set out below are the leading cases in this area, setting out the view of the Employment Appeal Tribunal. The cases which are a series of first-instance decisions demonstrating how tribunals have approached this question in practice (note: the tribunal cases pre-date the EAT guidance, although they seem to be decided broadly in line with it).

DALESIDE NURSING HOME LTD v MATHEW

EAT/0519/08

The EAT held that where there is a clear-cut finding that the central allegation in a discrimination claim is a lie, it is perverse for the tribunal to conclude that the making of such a false allegation does not constitute unreasonable behaviour for the purposes of costs.

At the heart of the direct race discrimination claim was the allegation that the Claimant had been called 'a black bitch' by her manager. After hearing evidence, the tribunal concluded that this was untrue. However, when the discrimination claim subsequently failed, the tribunal declined to make a costs order on the basis that the Claimant had a genuine belief in her claim, and had not acted unreasonably.

The EAT held that the tribunal, in light of the findings of fact which had been made, should have come to the conclusion that the Claimant had acted unreasonably in bringing and conducting the proceedings, and was therefore wrong in law to reject the claim for costs on that basis.

(Thanks to Paul Lewis of St John's Chambers for writing this case summary.)

DUNEDIN CANMORE HOUSING ASSOCIATION v DONALDSON

EAT/0014/09

This case followed the EAT's earlier judgment in *Daleside Nursing Home Ltd v Mathew*.[1] Here, the EAT held that it was perverse for the tribunal to have refused to award costs where the Claimant's assertions that she had not disclosed details of her compromise agreement in breach of a confidentiality clause were false.

The Claimant brought proceedings for breach of a compromise agreement, claiming she had not been in breach of a confidentiality clause. The tribunal rejected her evidence and found she had made disclosures to two people. Nonetheless, it declined to award costs against her as it took the view that it was necessary for her to bring proceedings as the employer had alleged that the Claimant had breached the clause.

➡

---

[1]   EAT/0519/08.

The EAT disagreed and observed there was no basis for the view that proceedings were 'necessary' or that the Claimant had no other alternative but bring proceedings where she knew her assertions were false. It also stated that the fact that the Claimant was a lay person was irrelevant – what mattered was whether she had or had not, in simple human terms, approached the essential factual matters that lay at the heart of her case honestly and reasonably

Because she had not approached the case honestly and reasonably, the EAT reversed the tribunal's decision on costs and ordered the Claimant to pay her ex-employer's legal costs.

(Thanks to Will Dobson of Cloisters who prepared this case summary.)

MR S E JEFFERY v WYRE DISTRICT CAB
MANCHESTER EMPLOYMENT TRIBUNAL

Case No 2406533/2004
Supplied by Kathryn Lloyd of Bates Wells & Braithwaite

The Employment Tribunal noted in this claim for unfair dismissal that:

> '... the Chairman and members have been sitting on Tribunal cases for over 20 years in total and none of us have had the misfortune to encounter such a dishonest witness.'

In addition they found that the Claimant had bombarded the Respondent with correspondence about largely irrelevant matters and had thus greatly added to the costs. The Tribunal were satisfied that the Claimant either knew, or certainly ought to have known, that his claim was wholly misconceived but by focusing on irrelevant issues and telling lies he could possibly succeed in his claim and, even if he did not, he could cause the Respondent to incur substantial legal costs in defending it. In those circumstances they held that in bringing and conducting his case the Claimant had acted unreasonably, and that the bringing and conducting of the proceedings was misconceived.

Although the Claimant was unemployed he had stated in evidence that he had been assured that he would be given a position as soon as one became available and so the Tribunal did not consider that his current lack of employment should be an overriding consideration, although they did give some discount upon the award they would otherwise have made. Costs were awarded in the sum of £7,500.

**MISS A HAMEED v KNIGHTSBRIDGE BUSINESS SALES
MANCHESTER EMPLOYMENT TRIBUNAL**

Case No 2403596/2007
Supplied by Simon Whitehead of Brabners Chaffe Street

The claims for unfair dismissal and breach of contract centered upon a meeting between the Claimant and the MD of the Respondent. The Claimant claimed that she was dismissed at that meeting and the Respondent claimed that she had resigned – there were two clearly conflicting accounts. The Tribunal rejected the Claimant's version in its entirety. In its application for costs the Respondent relied on this to argue that the claim was false and where there were two entirely different and mutually exclusive factual accounts advanced, acceptance of one account necessarily meant the rejection of the other account as untrue. It could not be reasonable to bring or conduct proceedings on the basis of a false factual account and therefore the proceedings must be misconceived.

The Employment Tribunal agreed and held that the Claimant had from the outset been advancing a case (that she was dismissed and did not resign) that she knew to be untrue. The Respondent had been put to considerable costs in defending the case and the MD had faced allegations under cross examination that he had lied and falsified evidence. The Tribunal found that as the Claimant's conduct in bringing her claim, in its entirety, was unreasonable, so all the Respondent's costs incurred in defending the claim flowed from that unreasonable conduct. The Claimant was therefore ordered to pay costs of £7,500.

**MRS E MILLER v DR V NAMMALWAR
MANCHESTER EMPLOYMENT TRIBUNAL**

Case No 2400761/2004
Supplied by Guy Guinan of Halliwells LLP

The Claimant decided to withdraw one of her claims (for unfair dismissal) but then at a preliminary hearing she reinstated her claim and amended her original witness statement. At the final hearing, she conceded that a number of statements in that witness statement had been untrue and accepted that a number of documents destined for the bundle had in fact been forgeries. The Employment Tribunal held that she had acted unreasonably and vexatiously and a costs order was made, arising out of the dismissal of her claims as they were tainted by illegality (tax evasion).

➡

She had been put on notice at the preliminary hearing by the Respondent that they would seek costs if she persisted with her claim and the Employment Tribunal thought it only fair that she should be ordered to pay the costs from that date. These amounted to over £10,000 so they were referred for detailed assessment under r 41(3).

MR T CHILD v DUMFRIES AND GALLOWAY COUNCIL
GLASGOW TRIBUNAL

Case No S/105806/06 F585/221
Supplied by Jessel Gair of Biggart Baillie LLP

In what is thought to be the first maximum costs award in Scotland, Mr Child claimed that he had been unfairly dismissed for whistle-blowing. During the course of the proceedings he made a series of allegations including assertions that the Council Social Work Department failed to supervise 17 known paedophiles due to lack of qualified staff, failed to police-check certain education staff with access to children, engaged a Schedule One offender in a disability team, permitted unqualified staff to do work which should be carried out by qualified staff, detained two older clients inappropriately and forcibly in a secure unit at Crichton Hospital, alleged a carer obtained money by deception from clients, inappropriately controlled finances and money of clients and failed to respond to safety concerns. There were no records of these protected disclosures during any meetings, including his disciplinary or appeal hearings or in his original complaint to the Tribunal.

Mr Child then withdrew his claim on the fifth day of the hearing, prior to giving his own evidence. He told the Judge that he had lost his job and his reputation, and offered his 'humble apologies' to the Tribunal. He offered as a gesture of goodwill towards the Council to publish a letter in the local papers stating that, on reflection, his claim against them was misguided.

The Claimant was ordered to pay £10,000 expenses, following the Judge's conclusion that he had acted vexatiously and unreasonably and that his conduct of the proceedings had been misconceived.

WAYNE v KENT AND MEDWAY NHS AND SOCIAL CARE PARTNERSHIP TRUST
ASHFORD EMPLOYMENT TRIBUNAL

Case No 1100806/2007
Supplied by Catherine Daw of Brachers Law

The Claimant's claims for constructive unfair dismissal and religious discrimination were dismissed. The case was based on allegations of bullying and harassment and alleged comments made by a team leader of 'being uncomfortable around religious people'. The Claimant was an apostolic Christian who could not work between sunset on Friday and sunset on Saturday. The Trust did not require her to work between these times.

An award was made of £10,000 against the Claimant. The Tribunal indicated it was making the award on the basis of the Claimant's unreasonable conduct in that she knew the allegations she made were untrue at the point at which she issued her complaint, her evidence was exaggerated and in some instances fabricated. The Tribunal indicated its belief she made her complaints to enable her to leave her employment early in order to take up a new job and so as to avoid her own performance being brought into question. They stressed that a costs award was exceptional and indicated one member of the Tribunal had never made a costs award and another only on one other occasion.

8.3 SCANDALOUS ALLEGATIONS MADE AGAINST LEGAL REPRESENTATIVES AND THE TRIBUNAL

MR G H ZAKARI DEHVASATI v SOUTH LANARKSHIRE COUNCIL
EDINBURGH EMPLOYMENT TRIBUNAL

Case No 104636/2003

At a first application to strike out his claim, the Claimant was warned that his conduct of the proceedings had been scandalous and unacceptable and that he any repetition of ill founded allegations of Nazism, racism, victimisation, abuse of power or conspiracy made against the Respondent's representative or the Tribunal would be treated as grounds for further consideration of striking out the original application. The Claimant persisted in such behaviour, including claims that the Chairman had put his life at risk, that the Respondent's representative had engaged in criminal➡

activities through 'conspiracies and collaborations', references to his living in 'this brutal country' and 'among the barbarians who abuse Law and Legal Procedures for legalisation of the most brutal crimes' and to the Chairman's order having no credibility and being a standard mass production judgment.

A second application to strike out the claim was successful, on the basis that the Claimant had disregarded the Tribunal's order. Costs were awarded also on the basis that the Claimant had wilfully disregarded the Tribunal's order not to repeat any of his allegations about the Tribunal, the Respondent's solicitors or the Justice System and indeed, had escalated the level of allegations made.

The Claimant told the Tribunal that he received jobseekers allowance and had debts of £12,856.63 so this was taken into account and costs were set at £100.

8.4 PROCEEDINGS TAINTED WITH ILLEGALITY

Where a claim is tainted with illegality, the tribunal will not have jurisdiction to hear it. If costs have been incurred in defending such a claim and a costs application is made, the Claimant's knowledge and collusion in the illegality will be taken into account when considering whether r 40(3) applies.

HUMPHREYS v SUPPLY LANE HOLDINGS
READING EMPLOYMENT TRIBUNAL

Case No 2701115/2006
Supplied by Guy Hollebon of Bevans

The Employment Tribunal found that the claim related to an obligation which had illegality at its heart (payment in cash on which no tax was paid, known to the Claimant and the former employer) and so the Tribunal either had no jurisdiction to hear the claim or that it should be struck out as having no reasonable prospect of success. The Respondent had purchased the business employing the Claimant and had no knowledge of the way the company had worked prior to the purchase. The evidence of the cash arrangement only became clear during the hearing.

On the subsequent costs application by the Respondent (at which the Claimant did not appear and gave no indication of his means to pay), in considering whether the illegality issue as it emerged at the hearing brought it within the scope of r 40(3) the Tribunal attached weight to the evidence of the Claimant's collusion with the former employers in accepting cash, his knowledge of their inadequate ➡

financial records and controls and his knowledge of the lack of documentary evidence to refute his claim, knowing that the reason there was no documentation was an essential part of the collusive scheme to which he was party. In the exercise of their discretion and having regard to those factors they considered this an appropriate case for the award of costs.

The Tribunal found that the Claimant knew from well before the commencement of the proceedings that his purpose was to recover a sum which was unlawful. As such, the totality of the Respondent's costs, start to finish, was attributable to the unreasonable conduct of the Claimant, the proceedings should never have been brought and the Tribunal therefore considered it appropriate for the maximum award of £10,000.

The Claimant was funded by the Union and so would not bear the costs ordered, but the Tribunal specifically disregarded the involvement of the Union in its reasoning on the amount to be ordered.

The Tribunal stated:

> 'Access to the tribunal should remain free access generally unhindered by the risk of legal costs but that right must be weighed in the balance against the rights of a respondent not to have to defend unreasonable proceedings, and the rights of other members of the public whose cases are delayed by the devotion of public resources to this case ...'

8.5   VEXATIOUS CLAIMS

The benchmark definition for vexatious claims is found in *ET Marler Ltd v Robertson*,[2] that:

> '... if an employee brings a hopeless claim not with any expectation of recovering compensation but out of spite to harass his employers or for some other improper motive, he acts vexatiously.'

Examples are where an employee had carried out 'deliberate campaign calculated to cause the maximum of distress and inconvenience to the Respondents' in *Mach v BT*[3] and *Meghani v Clark Pixley*,[4] in which the employee was found to have lied and made false allegations in respect of race discrimination claim and costs of £1,250 were awarded against him. The vexatious complaint was compounded by a vexatious appeal where

---

2   (1974) ICR 72 NIRC.
3   847/83.
4   EAT 639/79.

further false allegations made, some of which contradicted the notes made by the Employment Tribunal, resulting in a further costs award of £1,000.

MR A CHOUDRY v STAGECOACH MANCHESTER EMPLOYMENT TRIBUNAL

Case No 2405726/2003

The claim for racial harassment failed and the Employment Tribunal found that the evidence of the Claimant was unreliable and that he did not always tell the truth if the truth did not suit him. They thought the Respondent's evidence was consistent and there was no evidence of harassment. The case was referred to a fresh tribunal to do full justice to the case once a witness had been traced. The Claimant placed reliance on the witness to vindicate his version of events but the witness did not do so.

Despite the fact that the Claimant did not persuade the first Tribunal of the veracity of his allegations, he chose to revisit them all against the fresh tribunal and added some new ones in as well. The second Employment Tribunal's view was:

'... that the Claimant should persist with such allegations ... having had them roundly rejected by (the first) tribunal simply beggars belief. The situation must be aggravated by the somewhat incredible allegations ... which were simply without any evidential foundation whatsoever and bordered on the outlandish.'

The Tribunal followed *Towu v Lewisham NHS Hospital Trust*[5] (para 24) and noted that the correct test was whether the Claimant had reasonable grounds for believing that he was right. In this case, there was no reasonable prospect of the witness supporting the Claimant's version of events (according to police interviews) and his evidence was insufficient to carry the day, objectively. In addition, there was no evidence of the Respondent tampering with a video of an alleged incident, as claimed by the Claimant. The Tribunal believed that Mr Choudry had brought a vexatious case out of spite for one of the Respondent's employees, in that he had pursued the allegation of racial harassment with the intention of getting back at him for whatever perceived slight he had suffered at his hands.

As the case was governed by the 2001 Rules, the Tribunal was constrained by Kovacs from considering the Claimant's means to pay but costs were awarded against him to be assessed by the County Court and they were estimated in the region of £45,000.

---

[5]   EAT 0314/05.

Where allegations are made that are irrelevant to the way the claim is being put forward and are designed to embarrass or distress the other party, this may be considered to be vexatious or abusive.

MISS E EDGE v HERTFORDSHIRE CENTRE FOR DENTISTRY
BEDFORD EMPLOYMENT TRIBUNAL

Case No 1200305/2008
Supplied by Alec Colson of Taylor Walton LLP

The Claimant's claims of sex discrimination and constructive unfair dismissal were rejected on their merits and on jurisdiction. The Respondent made an application for costs, divided between costs wasted by reason of the Claimant's non attendance on the first day of the hearing and costs generally for all three days. As to the Claimant's non appearance, her representative had thought that the time would be used dealing with points of law. The Tribunal considered it unreasonable to take that 'gamble' and in the light of the absence of any medical evidence to support non-attendance, it was unreasonable not to attend.

In considering the whole claim, the Tribunal held that the allegations were without foundation and that the Claimant knew this to be the case. They also considered that certain aspects of the allegations were not relevant to the claim (health issues, cash discrepancies and financial impropriety) and their inclusion was designed to cause embarrassment or distress to the Respondent.

Although the Claimant's means were slender, she had brought a costs order upon herself by her conduct within the proceedings, which were brought unreasonably and were conducted in a manner which was unreasonable and at times, in relation to specific allegations pursued in cross examination and which caused distress to one of the Respondent's witnesses, was vexatious and abusive. She was ordered to pay £2,600, being Counsel's fees without the VAT.

In *Telephone Information Services Ltd v Wilkinson*[6] it was held that it is not frivolous or vexatious for a Claimant to pursue an unfair dismissal claim even though the employer has offered to pay the maximum statutory compensation, as he is entitled to pursue his claim to obtain the declaration of unfair dismissal. This was decided under the old Rules and the authors believe it would probably be decided differently now, unless there was a compelling reason for the employee to hold out for the declaration of unfair dismissal (or unless the employee had a reasonable

---

[6]   [1991] IRLR 148.

prospect of obtaining reinstatement or reengagement). In the absence of those factors, it would possibly be distinguished now, on the basis either that it would be unreasonable to continue with the proceedings once the maximum compensation is offered, or that *Telephone Information Services v Wilkinson* was decided at a time when the parties were not under a duty to follow the overriding objective (ie cooperating, and acting in a way to save tribunal time).

CHAPTER 9

CONDUCT OF PROCEEDINGS

9.1 In *Khan v Kirklees Metropolitan Borough Council*,[1] Mummery LJ stated that the reason that costs orders are the exception rather than the norm in Employment Tribunals is that most people bringing and resisting cases in the Employment Tribunals behave in a reasonable way:

> 'If you behave in a reasonable way and you lose your case you do not have to pay the costs, but if you behave in an unreasonable way ...'

An example of the conduct an Employment Tribunal will consider unreasonable is in *Kelly v Patrons of Cowane's Hospital*.[2]

KELLY v PATRONS OF COWANE'S HOSPITAL
EDINBURGH EMPLOYIMENT TRIBUNAL

Case Nos S/113027/06 and S/118841/06
Supplied by Elizabeth Williams of Turcan Connell

The Employment Tribunal believed that the Claimant's vexatious and separately unreasonable conduct had not assisted the tribunal to further the overriding objective but rather had frustrated the objective on a number of occasions, had put the Respondents to unnecessary and avoidable expense, had resulted in the Respondent not being on an equal footing through the withholding of information and had resulted in the case not being dealt with expeditiously or fairly (due to absence of fair notice and breach of the rules of Natural Justice). On these grounds they struck out the claim.

The Claimant's conduct included failure to obtemper various tribunal orders, delayed in provision of information and giving fair notice of positions and documents he intended to advance (placing the Respondent at a tactical disadvantage), failing to appear at a hearing in direct contravention of the tribunal's order that he do so, absenting himself from the jurisdiction in the knowledge of a ➡

---

[1] [2007] EWCA Civ 1342.
[2] Case Nos S/113027/06 and S/118841/06.

hearing date fixed in consultation with him and delaying communication of intention not to attend until the morning of the hearing.

The costs awarded related to the Respondent's costs of preparation for and conduct of the PHR and the second PHR, in the sum of £534.18.

Other examples of unreasonable conduct throughout a hearing is in *Khan v Kirklees*[3] *Metropolitan Borough Council* and *Wyhed Muhammed Gill v Homefirst Community Trust & ors*.[4]

KHAN v KIRKLEES METROPOLITAN BOROUGH COUNCIL

[2007] EWCA Civ 1342
Supplied by Edward Brown of Bar Pro Bono Unit

In the tribunal made orders for costs against Mr Khan consequent on the striking out of his race and disability claims, after hearings that had taken place over a period of 49 days over three years, interrupted by numerous adjournments. The tribunal referred to Mr Khan's unreasonable conduct throughout and formed the view that the exceptional length of time taken to hear the case was almost entirely attributable to his conduct and the unreasonable manner in which he had conducted himself throughout the hearing. They accepted that a period of up to ten days would have been a reasonable period for him to have presented his case without incurring any unnecessary costs, and for that reason they only awarded a sum equal to 80% of the costs of an estimated £100,000 bill for the Kirklees Council's costs, as well as another order for £3,000 costs.

The EAT upheld the orders and Mr Khan applied to the Court of Appeal. Mummery J stated that:

> '... it must be, in the vast majority of cases, the normal rule that costs will not be ordered against a party because he fails. This was no ordinary failure. The case was struck out after a long hearing in which the applicant's conduct gave adequate grounds for the tribunal concluding that he had behaved unreasonably, and taking into account all the discretionary matters, he ought to bear a large percentage of the costs.'

---

[3]   [2007] EWCA Civ 1342.
[4]   Case No 279/00FET: 1214/00:243/00; 1414/01.

WYHED MUHAMMED GILL v HOMEFIRST COMMUNITY TRUST & ORS
BELFAST EMPLOYMENT TRIBUNAL

Case No 279/00FET: 1214/00:243/00; 1414/01
Supplied by Claire Tiffney of Directorate of Legal Services, Central Services Agency

The Claimant issued three sets of proceedings in relation to his dismissal, against 12 Respondents. The claims were dismissed in their entirety. The Tribunal felt that an award of costs was appropriate due to his conduct, which included:

- Naming three Respondents even though the problem he had with them were well outside the time limit for presentation of the complaints.

- Naming the Chief Executive as a Respondent in relation to alleged wrongdoing in respect of references, none of which were produced or referred to.

- Withdrawing claims against three Respondents more than six years after lodgement and four years after making serious allegations about them in his Particulars.

- Accusing a Respondent of being a racist when he had acknowledged that she was not during internal procedures.

- Displaying a 'level of vitriol and animosity' to one Respondent that was wholly unreasonable.

- Obtaining witness orders for persons whose evidence was not relevant to the issues;

- Wasting a great deal of hearing time on matters which the Tribunal told him were not an issue for determination;

- Making derogatory and contemptuous remarks about the law, the legal process, the Tribunal system, the Tribunal itself and counsel for the Respondent during the hearing. In a letter to the Tribunal he claimed that he had been 'driven ill by your God forsaken racist filthy country and all the morally dissolute liars that it is infested with'.

- Making references to 'the friendly Irish' although he was told this was offensive. ➡

The Respondent's solicitor had written at an early stage to the Claimant putting him on notice that his claims were without foundation and invited him to withdraw them, failing which they would proceed to defend it and would seek costs. The Tribunal also took into account the level of the Claimant's knowledge and experience of the law and legal system, which was fairly considerable, and concluded that he must have been able to assess the merits of his claim and understand the implications of a lengthy and unsuccessful hearing of his claims.

The Claimant was ordered to pay £10,000 towards the costs of the Respondents.

9.2 INADEQUATE/EXCESSIVE DISCLOSURE

LEE v LONDON ATHLETIC RAIDERS SOCCER ACADEMY STRATFORD EMPLOYMENT TRIBUNAL

Case No 320188/03
Supplied by Neil Russell of BD Laddie

Costs of £350 were allowed to cover costs incurred by the Respondent as a result of the Claimant's failure to provide adequate disclosure resulting in the necessity for chaser letters and the job of counsel being more difficult (although this did not affect the refresher fee). The Employment Tribunal believed that this was acting unreasonably and that this had caused some additional expenditure but there was no clear basis upon which to assess the exact amount of that expenditure and it was disproportionate to attempt the task.

The unreasonableness the tribunal can look at can only be conduct during the course of the proceedings and not conduct by the employer during the employment. It will consider, in some circumstances that either late or excessive disclosure falls within r 40(3).

LOBO v LONDON UNDERGROUND LIMITED WATFORD EMPLOYMENT TRIBUNAL

Case No 3300654/05
Supplied by Kiran Daurka of Russell Jones and Walker

Every day but one of the liability hearing the Respondent produced new documents that had not been disclosed before (almost 100 of them), some of them detrimental to the defence. Documents also came to light during a witness giving evidence and the Tribunal ➡

asked for them but they were not produced. Most of the evidence was hearsay, despite the fact that witnesses were available, which the Employment Tribunal said was an entirely inappropriate way to deal with matters. The Tribunal also believed that the defence of some of the complaints was indefensible because on the same day the ET3 was lodged, an independent body upheld the Claimant's complaints but the Respondent nevertheless persisted in its defence.

As a result the Tribunal found that the matter was conducted unreasonably. They noted that:

> '... the Tribunal must have regard to the nature, gravity and effect of the unreasonable conduct as they are factors relevant to the exercise of the discretion. We have had regard to the fact the liability hearing lasted ten days and to the Respondent's unreasonable conduct on non disclosure (and) ... we consider this to be an appropriate case to make an order'.

The costs were to be taxed by the County Court if not agreed.

WOODLAND v MPI

UKEAT/0042/07/RN

There was a preliminary hearing on the application of the Claimant's appeal against an order for costs of £2,000 against him in respect of the Respondent's wasted costs of an adjourned remedies hearing. The EAT held that there were no reasonable prospects of a successful appeal; the Employment Tribunal had been entitled to adjourn to ensure proper earnings disclosure by the Claimant, albeit that such disclosure when eventually made showed little by way of unknown earnings.

The Claimant also argued that the amount involved was disproportionate to the amount involved; the Respondent used very senior and expensive counsel on the costs application when counsel of less experience could have been instructed. The EAT disagreed; MPI were entitled to use the same counsel as the counsel who had appeared throughout the liability trial and who had at his fingertips all the issues canvassed.

MR V SHARMA v TILDA LTD
STRATFORD EMPLOYMENT TRIBUNAL

Case No 3200672/07
Supplied by Marc Jones of Turbervilles

A Case Management Conference was held by reason of delays by the Respondent in dealing with requests for specific disclosure and failure to provide written answers. Costs of £640.38 were allowed.

MRS M MUNU v GREAT ORMOND STREET TRUST NHS TRUST & ORS
LONDON CENTRAL EMPLOYMENT TRIBUNAL

Case No 2202864/2005
Supplied by Claire McCann, barrister, Cloisters Chambers

The Claimant's claims were dismissed and the Respondent made an application for costs on the grounds that:

(a)   in bringing the proceedings, the Claimant acted vexatiously, abusively, disruptively or otherwise unreasonably and the bringing of the proceedings were misconceived. The Tribunal accepted this; the Claimant did not have the continuous service required to bring two of her claims. Moreover, she had relied on a statement of terms and conditions when it was not previously disclosed to the Respondent or disclosed in accordance with the Tribunal's order for disclosure;

(b)   in conducting the proceedings the Claimant had acted vexatiously, abusively, disruptively or otherwise unreasonably and the conducting of the proceedings were misconceived. The Tribunal accepted this; the Claimant's evidence lacked credibility and she had at first denied that she had been given a copy of a document, which she later conceded she had received. The Tribunal also believed that she had fabricated eivdence;

(c)   in conducting the proceedings the Claimant's representative had acted vexatiously, abusively, disruptively or otherwise unreasonably. The Tribunal believed this to be the case. The Claimant's representative had withdrawn from the proceedings, necessitating an adjournment but when the case was resumed, he was again acting, having used the adjournment to apply to the EAT to appeal the Tribunal direction that a witness be allowed to give evidence by video link. His conduct with the➡

Respondent's witnesses was inappropriate and he had to be reminded not to lose his temper with one of them. He repeatedly suggested that the Respondent's legal representatives were conducting the case in a manner bordering on professional misconduct and suggested that the Tribunal was biased, but when pressed he would draw back from these suggestions. The Tribunal's conclusion was that, 'in our collective experience, we have never encountered a representative who acted in such an unreasonable manner';

(d)   the Claimant had failed to comply with orders of the Tribunal; the Claimant had served her witness statements late and as a result forced the Respondents to apply for an adjournment to take instructions, leading to a waste of time and to difficulties for the individual Respondents as the witness statement raised new and serious allegations. She had also failed to comply with orders for disclosure.

Having held that the grounds for a costs order were made out, the Tribunal went on to say that they had:

> '... seldom, if ever witnessed such deplorable conduct on the part of a claimant or her representative. We ... have no qualms in making the order requested, that is the claimant pay the Respondents' costs in the sum of £10,000.'

In the absence of any evidence of her means and the fact that the Respondents were seeking only a small proportion of their costs (which totalled approximately £120,000), they were satisfied that it was appropriate to make the order.

9.3   LATE WITHDRAWAL OF CLAIMS

The Rules of Procedure make provision for the withdrawal of claims in Rule. A Claimant may withdraw all or part of his claim at any time and this may be done either orally at a hearing or in writing (r 25(1)). However, the costs consequences are governed by the general power in r 40.

In many cases, Respondents will be faced with a withdrawal of their claim by the Claimant prior (sometimes immediately prior) to the hearing. The Respondent may have incurred significant legal costs in the preparation for the hearing, but without a decision on the substantive merits, there will be limited opportunity for them to recover these.

The Rules of Procedure do not replicate the general rule laid down in CPR Part 38, r 38.6(1) that a Claimant who discontinues proceedings is liable for the costs which a defendant has incurred before notice of discontinuance was served on him. The CPR treats discontinuance as a concession by the Claimant of defeat or likely defeat.

Withdrawal on its own is not necessarily unreasonable behaviour for the purposes of r 40.

MCPHERSON v BNP PARIBAS

[2004] IRLR 558, CA

The Claimant withdrew his case several weeks before the hearing so there was no decision on the substantive merits, but the tribunal nevertheless made an order for costs in favour of the Respondent for £90,747.82.

Mummery J set out the conflicting considerations. On the one hand, it is important for Claimants not to be deterred from making a sensible litigation decision ('the dawn of sanity' – Thorpe LJ) and dropping claims by the prospect of an order for costs on withdrawal, which might well not be made against them if they fought on to a full hearing and failed. In most cases, the withdrawal will result in a saving of costs. On the other hand, a practice of never making costs orders on withdrawal might encourage speculative claims, by allowing applicants to start cases and to pursue them down to the last week or two before the hearing in the hope of receiving an offer to settle, and then, failing an offer, dropping the case without any risk of a costs sanction. He concluded:

> 'The solution lies in the proper construction and sensible application of r 14 [*now r 38*]. The crucial question is whether, in all the circumstances of the case, the claimant withdrawing the claim has conducted the proceedings unreasonably. It is not whether the withdrawal of the claim is in itself unreasonable.'

In *McPhearson* the EAT held that the tribunal was entitled to conclude that there was unreasonable conduct of the proceedings on the part of the Claimant. He had not, for example, complied with orders of the tribunal, he had been asked for documentation which he was obviously loathe to supply; and he had given the impression right up the date of withdrawal on 9 May 2002 that he was pursuing the complaint and allowed BNP Paribas to incur considerable expense in preparing the case on that basis, while, on his own evidence and unknown to the tribunal and BNP Paribas, he had been seriously considering with his GP in December 2001 the question of abandoning the proceedings on health grounds.

MR A C UNEGBU v NEWMAN STONE LIMITED

UKEAT/0157/08/ZT

The Claimant withdrew his race discrimination claim on 8 November, 3 days after the ET3 had been filed, citing health problems. The Respondent had claimed that the health reasons given were not genuine and that in fact the Claimant was what they described as a serial litigator trying to obtain compensation from recruitment firms by setting up claims of discrimination. Also, it alleged that an inference could be drawn that his motivation in bringing proceedings was out of resentment of not being forwarded, rather than having a legitimate claim for discrimination. The Employment Tribunal made an order for £500 costs against him.

The EAT upheld his appeal on the basis that the Employment Judge had declined expressly to make findings on the allegations that were made on either side and the single decision was the act of withdrawal. Following *McPherson,* an award of costs cannot be made simply on the basis of the act of withdrawing proceedings and no inference could be made that withdrawal meant that the Claimant was a speculator, or had a spurious claim.

DENNIS LAW v NORTHERN IRELAND SEAFOODS LIMITED
NORTHERN IRELAND

Case No 1018/05
Supplied by Harry Coll of EDG Legal

As a general proposition a party who withdraws their complaint (or as the case may be, their defence) should not be in a worse position than a party who has run and lost their case. However it may be appropriate to consider what a party knew or ought to have known if he had gone about the matter sensibly.

Relying on *McPherson* the tribunal held that the mere fact of withdrawal cannot be equated with unreasonableness. The issue is whether the Claimant has acted reasonably in the conduct of the proceedings which is determined by looking at his conduct overall. In this case, the tribunal declined to infer unreasonableness simply from the non attendance of the Claimant at the costs hearing.

However, there are a number of examples in which Claimants who have withdrawn have been ordered to pay costs and those advising Claimants who intend to withdraw their claims should ensure that as soon as it becomes obvious that a withdrawal is going to occur, the Claimant should be advised of the costs risk in delaying the decision to do so.

MISS M KUSI v ALPHA PLUS SECURITY
LONDON CENTRAL EMPLOYMENT TRIBUNAL

Case No 2200302/06
Supplied by Andrew Knorpel of ASB Law

The Claimant brought a claim for discrimination under the DDA, as well as claims for unfair dismissal, wrongful dismissal and unpaid wages. A report was received on 19 May showing normal vision and no adverse effect on her ability to carry out day to day activities and she withdrew the DDA claim on 22 June. The Employment Tribunal believed that it should have been clear to her once she had read the report that there was no reasonable prospect of success so her continued conduct of the claim until withdrawal was misconceived and costs were ordered.

The Claimant's means were considered and as she had been awarded £14,000 region of the Tribunal thought she would have sufficient means to be able to satisfy any costs order. Costs were limited to the work carried out by the Respondent on the DDA claim, in the sum of £2,274.

MRS J BARRINGTON BOYCE v J MEDDIS
READING EMPLOYMENT TRIBUNAL

Case No 2702596/2006
Supplied by Andrea Bateman of BPE Solicitors

The Claimant withdrew his claim for constructive dismissal ten days before the two day hearing was fixed to take place. There had been settlement discussions and a compromise agreement had been agreed in principle but the Claimant decided not to sign this. The Respondents applied for a costs order and the application was heard by a Chairman sitting alone. The Respondent claimed that the claim was misconceived at the outset because the Claimant had been looking for a job four months before he left. The Claimant said that there had been an arguable case about whether the employer's actions had amounted to a breach of contract (confirmed at the PHR stage when the Respondent claimed that there was no reasonable prospect of success) and what was the real reason for the resignation. He argued that by withdrawing, he had saved the Respondent costs and therefore not acted unreasonably. ➡

The Chairman considered that there were factual matters to be addressed but that the Claimant had conducted the proceedings in an unreasonable manner in delaying either signing the compromise agreement or indicating in terms his intention to withdraw. He had known at the time the compromise agreement had been discussed that he intended to withdraw but the Respondent did not and had incurred costs. Failing to take action in a reasonable time was unreasonable conduct under r 40(3). The Claimant was ordered to pay the Respondent £1,500 towards their costs incurred from the time he knew he would be taking the claim no further.

SAJEED KHAN v HEYWOOD & MIDDLETON PCT

UKEAT/0581/05/ZT

The Claimant had changed his mind following an application to withdraw and he applied to set aside the Notice of Withdrawal. The Employment Tribunal refused the application and awarded the Respondent £1,294.79 in respect of their costs of his failed application to have the withdrawal notice set aside, holding that the Claimant's change of mind following his decision to withdraw his claim on day one, then changing his mind on day two, causing a hearing to take place on day three which would not have been necessary at all but for his change of mind, had caused unnecessary expense to the Respondent.

Rimer J said:

> 'Dr Khan had, in effect, been messing them about. No-one is suggesting that a claimant cannot have a change of mind about how to conduct his litigation; but the respondent is likely to regard it as nerve of a high order for the claimant to expect the respondent to bear his own costs of the consequences of the claimant's indecisiveness.'

The Chairman's conclusion that this was unreasonable was an exercise of judgment about which there could be reasonable scope for disagreement but there was nothing perverse about his decision and the appeal was dismissed.

Withdrawal of weak elements of a claim should always be a consideration if a party intends to apply for costs. A party may be more likely to succeed with their application if they have withdrawn weak elements of their claim (in the case of a Claimant, see *Sweetman v Mitie Security (London)*

Limited (1), Danielle White (2))[5] or concede elements of a claim (in the case of a Respondent, see *Morgan v Saint Gobain Building Distribution Limited).*[6]

MR D SCOTT v BRITISH ENERGY GROUP PLC
ASHFORD EMPLOYMENT TRIBUNAL

Case No 1101005/07/EB
Supplied by Alison Peat of MacRoberts LLP

The Claimant withdrew his public interest disclosure claim upon terms that the Respondent would not apply for costs and then sought to withdraw his constructive unfair dismissal claim nearly eight weeks later (but without the Respondent agreeing not to apply for costs). During that period the Respondent incurred over £10,000 in costs, most of which related to dealing with disclosure and the preparation of witness statements. The Claimant had sought orders for extensive disclosure of documents. The Respondent made a written application to the Tribunal for disclosure of the application form completed by the Claimant for his new job. When the Claimant received the application, he withdrew his claim for unfair dismissal.

The Tribunal accepted that withdrawal of a claim is not unreasonable conduct but it considered the circumstances of the withdrawal and they were persuaded that the Claimant's reason for withdrawing was that he did not wish his application form to be disclosed because it would seriously damage his case that he had resigned because of the Respondent's conduct rather than because he had by then applied for the position with his new employer. The Tribunal made an order for a costs contribution of £3,000 be paid to the Respondent.

(The Claimant applied for a review of this decision based on documentary evidence not in existence at the time of the hearing, but this was refused.)

---

[5] 2301897/2007.
[6] 1306491/2007.

MS B CLARKE v THE COMMISSIONER OF POLICE FOR THE CITY OF LONDON

Case No 2202461/2007
Supplied by Rashmi Chopra of Comptroller and City Solicitor's Office

All of the Claimant's complaints of sex discrimination were out of time and jurisdiction was only extended in respect of one of her complaints arising out of allegations made against her in respect of criminal and disciplinary proceedings. She subsequently withdrew her claim and was ordered to pay a contribution of £10,000 towards the Respondent's costs.

9.4 LATE AMENDMENTS

MR A J LARWOOD v EARTH TRONICS INC LTD

EAT/0558/03

The appeal by the Applicant was of an order by a Judge that his failure to instruct solicitors earlier, which resulted in a late application for permission to amend being made, was unreasonable conduct of the proceedings within the meaning of the Rules.

This was set aside by the EAT. There is no obligation upon a party before the Employment Tribunal to instruct solicitors and so it could not be unreasonable conduct of itself to instruct solicitors after proceedings have been instituted.

BRETT v A J INNS LTD
LEEDS EMPLOYMENT TRIBUNAL

Case No 1802940/06
Supplied by Simon Price of Chadwick Lawrence

The Claimant made an application to amend his claim form, which was granted but a costs award was made against him on the basis that had his application been made earlier, it was likely that the hearing would not have been necessary and the PHR costs could have been avoided. The Employment Tribunal allowed two hours preparation and three hours attendance. They accepted that it was appropriate for a solicitor to attend on behalf of the Respondent and allowed the hourly rate of £139 per hour.

MR L RANDALL v SOUTHAMPTON CITY COLLEGE
SOUTHAMPTON EMPLOYMENT TRIBUNAL

Case No 3102705/03
Supplied by James Humphrey of Trethowans

The Respondent changed or modified its position on seven occasions (as to whether or not they acceded that the Claimant was disabled and had Dysphonia). The Tribunal could find no justifiable reason for the Respondent's behaviour and made an order for costs, although the costs of the Claimant were discounted to take account of the work that would have been carried out in any event (eg outline statement supporting the Claimant's contention that he was disabled). The award was therefore reduced from £2,652.56 to £2,000.

MRS A COOPER v THE CHIEF CONSTABLE OF WEST YORKSHIRE POLICE (1) WAKEFIELD METROPOLITAN DISTRICT COUNCIL (2)

UKEAT/0035/06/RN & UKEAT/0036/06/RN

The Claimant made an application to amend her case against the Police Force on an entirely different basis to that on which it had previously been put; in her ET1 she alleged specific acts of discrimination by the Police Force directly and not through the agency of the Council. On the day of the hearing she applied to amend the claim to add the claim that the Police Force was vicariously liable for the acts of the Council. The first news that the Tribunal had of the proposed amendment was when counsel for the Police Force told the Tribunal he had been informed of the proposed intention to seek an amendment.

The Tribunal found that the most telling point was that there was no explanation why allegations were made against the Police Force in the Appellant's ET1 and her witness statement which she did not personally believe. It described the claim as 'unique in the experience of the Members of the Tribunal' in that the Appellant on advice took proceedings against two Respondents. In the context this is clearly a reference to the proceedings as they were brought, ie making separate allegations against each Respondent rather as opposed to making a claim that one Respondent was vicariously liable for the acts of another. The Claimant, the Tribunal found, had become engaged on the advice of her solicitors in a speculative piece of litigation, unsupported by evidence from the Claimant or from any other source.   ➡

The Tribunal held that there should be an order for costs on the basis that the Claimant had no reasonable prospect of success when the claim was issued and noted that her evidence in cross-examination which 'was in no sense forced from her' revealed the hopelessness of the claim which had been pursued.

The Tribunal awarded the Police Force costs against the Claimant in the sum of £10,000 and made it clear in their reasons that they anticipated that the costs awarded would be paid by the Appellant's legal advisers and not by her personally. This decision was upheld by the EAT.

MISS L WILKINSON v SPRINGWELL ENGINEERING LTD
NEWCASTLE UPON TYNE EMPLOYMENT TRIBUNAL

Case No 25047420/07
Supplied by Jamie Anderson of Counsel

The Claimant succeeded in her claim of age discrimination. The Tribunal found that the Respondent had caused an adjournment by seeking to bring evidence on the first day of hearing that had not been previously disclosed, and thereafter by seeking to change the basis upon which they sought to rely on that evidence, they had acted unreasonably and should be penalised in costs in respect of necessitating a second, unplanned day of hearing. An award of £400 was made.

In the absence of being able to assess the merits of a claim at a substantive hearing, how do tribunals approach the issue where they believe a costs award is appropriate?

MR BARRY CUNNINGHAM v HUNTER & CURRIE
(SCOTLAND) LTD (1) AND RASHID AHMED
GLASGOW EMPLOYMENT TRIBUNAL

Case No S/1014898/05
Supplied by Gina Wilson of MacRoberts

The claims of sexual orientation discrimination and sex discrimination never reached the stage of a full hearing but they had a substantial procedural history. Victimisation was subsequently added and then an amended application was presented for race discrimination. This latter claim was eventually withdrawn as was the associated claim under the Religion or Belief regulations. Subsequently, separate proceedings for unfair dismissal were lodged. Preparations for the remaining sex discrimination and unfair ➡

dismissal claims then proceeded and the hearing was fixed. Three days prior to the hearing the Claimant dropped these as his partner and baby were seriously ill in hospital. The legal expenses of the Respondent incurred by that date amounted to over £12,000.

Having considered the procedural history the Employment Tribunal considered that there had been an ex facie case to answer in relation to the sex discrimination and unfair dismissal claims. As to the unreasonableness of the late withdrawal the Tribunal understood that, '... the Claimant may well have reached the point at which he could not cope with any more emotional stress' and to withdraw in those circumstances was not unreasonable. However, in relation to the race discrimination claim there appeared to be nothing in the pleadings to justify it and it seemed to be founded on little more than the fact that the Second Respondent was of different ethnic origin to the Claimant. To describe this as a 'potential' race relations claim was, the Tribunal's view, misconceived. The Respondents had treated the claim seriously and had spent a great deal of time on it, even though it had been withdrawn at an early stage.

The Tribunal accepted that it would serve no useful purpose to investigate the merits of the case simply to establish liability for expenses. They noted that the Claimant had little in the way of resources and awarded costs restricted to the misconceived race relations claim and made an award of £500.

9.5　FLOUTING ORDERS

The fact that a Claimant does not understand the requirements of tribunal orders will not prevent a costs award being made against them.

MRS J GASCOIGNE – BECKER v AGE CONCERN SUTTON BOROUGH LONDON SOUTH EMPLOYMENT TRIBUNAL

Case No 2328231/2008
Supplied by Malcolm Lawrence of Copley Clark & Bennett

The Claimant complied with the Employment Tribunal's order to serve witness statements, but failed to serve a statement of her own evidence. When challenged in writing, she claimed that her statement was contained in Section 5 of her claim form, although she had indicated that she wished to give evidence of harassment over a period of time and this evidence was clearly not contained in Section 5. Once the Respondent had served its statements, she applied for an adjournment which was granted on the basis that she had not yet prepared a witness statement. The Respondent then ➡

applied for costs, being £2,880 costs occasioned by the adjournment and £5,834.55 in respect of Counsel's fees and witness statements.

The Employment Judge concluded that the Claimant had brought herself in jeopardy of costs because she had conducted the proceedings in such a manner than an adjournment was inevitable due to her failure to prepare a witness statement. The situation had come about because of her failure to understand what was required of her, despite letters from the Respondent's solicitor and the Tribunal.

The Respondent was a small charity dependent on local authority funding and donations and its Schedule showed costs amounting to £5,834.45. However, the Judge took into account her ability to pay and noted that her income did not meet her outgoings and a substantial award would eat into her saving, upon which she relied to meet her living expenses. He applied the overriding objective that he should deal justly with the case in a way that is proportionate with the complexity of the case and the importance of the issues. He held that the level claimed in respect of the costs incurred between the date of the adjournment and the hearing was not proportionate and so he made no award of costs in respect of that category of costs. With regard to Counsel's costs he felt that £500 was a proportionate amount to award but in view of the Claimant's means, made an order for £385.

A representative's administrative 'internal problems' will not prevent costs being ordered where these problems have resulted in non compliance with a tribunal order.

MS A KALUZA v VANDA COERULEA LTD (1) ANSHU MOORJANI (2)
LONDON CENTRAL EMPLOYMENT TRIBUNAL

Case No 2203254/2007
Supplied by Louise Taft of J R Jones Solicitors

The Claimant made an application for her costs, on the ground that the Respondents had conducted the defence unreasonably. The Tribunal found that the only matter that had caused problems for the Claimant was the Respondent's failure to comply with a Case Management Order to exchange witness statements by a certain date. They had served them 33 days late due to the fact that the Respondent's representative had been ill. The Tribunal did not accept this as a reason for the delay saying, 'the internal difficulties within the legal service provider is not an excuse for non-compliance with orders of the Employment Tribunal'. The Claimant's solicitors' ➡

costs in chasing service and writing to the Tribunal to seek an unless order were justified and so the costs of the extra work was ordered, at a rate of £180 per hour (£423 in total).

MOORSE v NTL GROUP LTD

UKEAT/0258/07/LA

Although the EAT overturned the strike out of the Claimant's claim by the tribunal, it refused to interfere with the order for costs limited to Counsel's fees of £2,173.75. It accepted the tribunal's finding that the proceedings had been conducted unreasonably by the Claimant's solicitors after it reached the view that orders had been flouted and that the conduct of the Claimant's case had been 'appalling'.

MR J BARBER v SALFORD ROYAL NHS FOUNDATION TRUST
MANCHESTER EMPLOYMENT TRIBUNAL

Case No 2401475/08
Supplied by Saira Ali of Hill Dickinson LLP

The Claimant repeatedly failed to serve a detailed schedule of loss, despite the Tribunal's order that he do so. The Tribunal made an unless order requiring him to serve his schedule failing which his claim would be struck out. In the same order, the Tribunal ordered him to pay £750 costs to the Respondent on the basis that he had conducted the proceedings unreasonably.

PAYNE v ATLANTIC COMPUTING
GLASGOW EMPLOYMENT TRIBUNAL

S/105404/01
Supplied by Lindsey Cartwright of Maclay Murray & Spens

At a preliminary hearing to decide length of qualifying service the Respondent's solicitor made a successful application for a strike out as a result of the Claimant's failure to comply with a further particulars order.

Costs were awarded on the basis of the Claimant's failure to comply with the Tribunal's order. The Tribunal accepted that the Respondent's solicitor was required to do a number of hours work as a consequence of the Claimant's conduct and her wasted ➡

professional fees were £500. This was ordered, along with the Respondent's witness's air fare from London to Glasgow of £97.50 and his B&B cost of £49.

In 2001 the Employment Appeal Tribunal laid down recommended guidelines for appointment of expert witnesses in tribunal cases. The EAT suggested that if these guidelines are not followed it may be appropriate for a tribunal to consider awarding costs against the defaulting party (*De Keyser Ltd v Wilson*[7]).

9.6   FAILURE TO ATTEND

IAN IRVINE v JOHN W HANNAY & CO
GLASGOW EMPLOYMENT TRIBUNAL

Case No S/118789/06
Supplied by Mel Sangster of Dundas and Wilson

The Claimant failed to appear at a PHR to determine whether he had submitted his claim on time and his claim was dismissed pursuant to r 27(5) of the 2004 Rules. He had known about the hearing and the Employment Tribunal felt that dismissal was a proper disposal of the matter and ordered costs on the basis that onus was on the Claimant to explain why his claim had not been presented on time. The Respondent had been put to unnecessary expense and so the award was £230 per hour for four hours (including travelling time) totalling £1,081.

KHAN v KIRKLEES

[2007] EWCA Civ 1342

The Claimant was ordered by the Employment Tribunal to pay 80% of the Respondent's costs, estimated in the region of £100,000. One of the aspects of the Claimant's unreasonable behaviour taken into account by the tribunal in this case was the non attendance of the Claimant at a number of hearings. The tribunal concluded that the Claimant had not established that either he or his wife were unable to attend the hearings listed as opposed to expressing a preference to attend only on dates of his own choosing and that he had not advanced any medical or other evidence to show that he was unable to attend any hearing without the assistance of his wife or to establish that no other person would be able to assist him in presenting the case. The tribunal found that the Claimant had ➡

---

[7]   [2001] IRLR 324, EAT.

deliberately chosen not to attend hearings on three separate dates in an attempt to force the tribunal to abandon those dates. They also noted that he had been inconsistent in his stated objections to the hearing dates, having initially relied solely on the issue of his wife's employment and then having changed his ground to state that he could not attend because of his own disability, race and religion. He had been given warnings about the consequences of non attendance and a number of opportunities to attend a hearing to explain the situation. The tribunal noted that in conclusion in his letter of 30 December, he had indicated that he was not prepared to attend any further hearings before the present tribunal and they concluded:

'He therefore removed any doubt that he was acting unreasonably and engaging by this time in a calculated and wilful refusal to attend and complete the hearing of the case.

Mr Khan is by some distance the most obdurate, recalcitrant and openly contemptuous party that any of us have ever had to deal with. His stubborn refusal to accept any guidance or direction from the Tribunal and his repeated complaints and accusations of bias against the Tribunal were the cause of a substantial waste of Tribunal time from more or less the outset of the hearing and every effort of the Chairman to bring some objectivity and proportionality to the Claimant's presentation of his case, was rebuffed by the Claimant, usually with an accusation of bias or some other complaint in relation to the conduct of the Chairman of his lay colleagues, which then occupied even more time within the hearing.'

The EAT and the Court of Appeal rejected the subsequent appeals.

MRS A W AYOBIOJO v LONDON BOROUGH OF CAMDEN

EAT/0510/02 ZT

The Claimant did not attend the hearing, which had been set down two months earlier. Parts of her claim in IT1 had been struck out on the basis that they were made out of time and she had appealed that decision. She therefore applied in writing for an adjournment of the hearing of the parts of her claim that remained. The Employment Tribunal ordered that she should make the application on the morning of the first day of her hearing. She failed to attend, and instructed her solicitor to make the application for an adjournment. He was not instructed to present her case should it fail (which it did) and the tribunal then struck out her originating application in its entirety. They also ordered costs of £2,180 on the basis that she had acted unreasonably in not attending the hearing. ➡

On appeal Mrs Ayobiojo claimed that it was perfectly reasonable for her not to wish to attend the hearing, given the way her proceedings had, in her view, been decimated by the tribunal and the fact that her appeal was pending. She believed that her cry for true justice had been denied. The EAT's view was that it is not for the litigant to dictate the terms upon which he or she is prepared to attend the tribunal, in other words, to litigate on their own terms. It is for the tribunal to decide what aspects are within its jurisdiction and which are capable of being adjudicated upon. They therefore had no difficulty in finding that the tribunal was correct under the first limb of the Rule in finding that there was unreasonable behaviour.

As to the amount, this represented the cost of the full day (the brief fee of the Respondent's barrister and 3 hours preparation for their solicitor). This was challenged on the basis that the Respondent had prepared for the hearing on the basis that there was going to be a full hearing, when in the end the only contentious hearing was on the adjournment application. The EAT took the view that this is a very broad discretion given to the tribunal and they could only interfere with it if they are satisfied either that the tribunal took into account some important factor which it should not have done, or left out some important factor that it should have included, or that its discretion was in some other way vitiated in such a way as to make its decision plainly wrong in law. The Claimant had behaved unreasonably. The consequence was that Camden prepared for a five-day hearing and in the EAT's judgment when the tribunal decided that that was what they were entitled to recover this was a proper exercise of discretion with which they did not think they could interfere.

MR JOHN JEFFREY v RESOURCE DATA MANAGEMENT GLASGOW EMPLOYMENT TRIBUNAL

Case No S/1111045/2006
Supplied by Claire Brattey of SJ Berwin

The Claimant failed to appear at the hearing of his claims for unfair dismissal, wages, holiday pay and notice. He had instructed solicitors but they had ceased to act, although they were able to confirm, on enquiry by the Clerk on the morning of the hearing, that the Claimant was aware of the date of the hearing and intended to represent himself. The Tribunal accepted that it did not appear that he was unaware of the date and time of the hearing, and he had made no attempt to explain why he had not attended. His applications were dismissed and he was ordered to pay £300 towards the Respondent's costs.

9.7   CONDUCT DURING THE HEARING

Harvey on Industrial Relations and Employment Law (para 1053) states that factors that might induce the Tribunal to award costs on the basis of unreasonable conduct are excessive procrastination and time wasting, unduly lengthy cross examination of witnesses, calling unnecessary witnesses and making outrageous and unsubstantiated allegations.

MR S DEMAN v VICTORIA UNIVERSITY OF MANCHESTER (1), PROFESSOR ANDREW STARK (2), PROFESSOR STUART TURLEY (3)

UKEAT/0211/06/RN

The Employment Tribunal made a number of findings critical of the Claimant's conduct of the case: he had constantly made what they described as loud and aggressive interventions and applications, through the hearing, taking up a few minutes short of 20 hours; and they found that, accordingly, on the basis of 5 hours a day for sitting, 4 days of tribunal hearing time had been wasted. They referred to a person who had accompanied the Claimant for the first two weeks of the hearing, who never gave evidence and it seems was never likely to, who made at least two interjections during the hearing which troubled the tribunal and who conducted a picket outside. They concluded that the Claimant's whole approach to the conduct of the case was to be disruptive and, perversely so as to avoid the tribunal being able to conclude the hearing. They were in no doubt that the conduct which they expressly found the Claimant to have been guilty of amounted to vexatious, abusive and disruptive conduct; at times it was scandalous and at all times it was unreasonable.

The tribunal concluded that they must consider making an order for costs against him and awarded costs of £8,000. The award was upheld by the EAT.

MS F HAQUE v GREEN & CO

UKEAT/0616/06/LA, UKEAT/0202/07/LA, UKEAT/0284/07/LA

The Claimant appealed against a costs order made following the successful application by the Respondent to strike out her case. The chairman concluded that all the requirements of r 40(3) had been met. The manner in which the Claimant and her representative had conducted proceedings was unreasonable and they had conducted ➡

proceedings disruptively. In addition the Claimant had acted vexatiously and abusively in the manner in which she conducted proceedings.

Some examples recorded of the behaviour giving rise to the order were:

- Shouting while the judgment was being recorded by the chairman.

- Disobeying the order that neither the Claimant nor her representative should correspond with the tribunal following the first part of the strike out hearing by sending a letter headed 'Consumer Einsatzgrupen Sword Investigations' and captioned, 'Defenders of Truth & Justice', accusing the tribunal of 'scandalous, vexatious and racist behaviour'.

- Disregarding warnings by Judges in the proceedings about bringing allegations of bias which failed by a long way, having no substance whatever, and continuing to refuse to believe that there was no bias.

- Making highly inflammatory allegations against the Judge and other Judges.

- Writing to the Respondent's solicitor, who was Jewish, attacking her professionalism and indicating that her concern was, 'that when we met with racist Jews we automatically have to suspect that the part of your religion which preaches racism will have influenced such behaviour, hence it became inseparable from a race discrimination case where the employer and British judiciary, or rather British Jewdiciary is concerned'.

HHJ McMullen upheld the condemnation of the Claimant's abusive, disruptive, vexatious and unreasonable conduct as correct and saw no error in the decision to award costs of £7,500 against a costs schedule of £20,000.

WYHED MUHAMMED GILL v HOMEFIRST COMMUNITY TRUST & ORS
BELFAST EMPLOYMENT TRIBUNAL

Case No 279/00FET: 1214/00:243/00; 1414/01
Supplied by Claire Tiffney of Directorate of Legal Services, Central Services Agency

The Claimant issued three sets of proceedings in relation to his dismissal against 12 Respondents. The claims were dismissed in their entirety. The Tribunal felt that an award of costs was appropriate due to his conduct, which included:

- Naming three Respondents even though the problem he had with them were well outside the time limit for presentation of the complaints.

- Naming the Chief Executive as a Respondent in relation to alleged wrongdoing in respect of references, none of which were produced or referred to.

- Withdrawing claims against three Respondents more than six years after lodgement and four years after making serious allegations about them in his Particulars.

- Accusing a Respondent of being a racist when he had acknowledged that she was not during internal procedures.

- Displaying a 'level of vitriol and animosity' to one Respondent that was wholly unreasonable.

- Obtaining witness orders for persons whose evidence was not relevant to the issues.

- Wasting a great deal of hearing time on matters which the Tribunal told him were not an issue for determination.

- Making derogatory and contemptuous remarks about the law, the legal process, the Tribunal system, the Tribunal itself and counsel for the Respondent during the hearing. In a letter to the Tribunal he claimed that he had been 'driven ill by your God forsaken racist filthy country and all the morally dissolute liars that it is infested with'.

- Making references to 'the friendly Irish' although he was told this was offensive.   ➡

The Respondent's solicitor had written at an early stage to the Claimant putting him on notice that his claims were without foundation and invited him to withdraw them, failing which they would proceed to defend it and would seek costs. The Tribunal also took into account the level of the Claimant's knowledge and experience of the law and legal system, which was fairly considerable, and concluded that he must have been able to assess the merits of his claim and understand the implications of a lengthy and unsuccessful hearing of his claims.

The Claimant was ordered to pay £10,000 towards the Respondents' costs.

MISS K FLETCHER v MINISTRY OF DEFENCE
LEEDS EMPLOYMENT TRIBUNAL

Case Nos 1804324/2005 – 1802882/2006 & 1804001/2006
Supplied by John MacKenzie, Solicitor Advocate

Miss Fletcher was successful in her claims of sexual harassment, discrimination and victimisation. Her application for costs was successful and one reason given was that the conduct of the Respondent in seeking to lead the evidence of witnesses who were present at the time the Claimant had been sexually harassed, despite an internal finding in her favour, had effectively doubled the length of the liability hearing. The hearing had lasted twelve days and could have, in the Tribunal's view, been dealt with in six days and so the saving in preparation and attendance time for six days was calculated at the level of £1,666 per day.

MR P R MARTIN v GLASGOW CITY COUNCIL
GLASGOW EMPLOYMENT TRIBUNAL

Case No S/124561/2006
Supplied by Alison Peat of MacRoberts LLP

The Respondent applied for costs purely on the basis that the Claimant had conducted an inordinately lengthy and occasionally repetitive cross-examination, which unnecessarily and unreasonably extended the time of the hearing (his estimate was by one day). The Respondent's solicitor has periodically objected to the Claimant covering old ground in his cross examination and the Judge had had to encourage the Claimant from time to time to stay on a relevant path regarding his questions. ➡

The Tribunal accepted that there was no rule of thumb regarding how long examination in chief and cross examination should relate to each other. They noted that the Claimant had proposed to call three of the Respondent's witnesses as his own witnesses, and therefore had he done so then his questioning of those witnesses would have consisted not merely of cross examination but also of examination in chief. They could not say that lengthy cross examination can be described as unreasonable conduct since they accepted the Claimant's contention that in cross examination he was also attempting to take evidence from witnesses he would have called and from whom he would have taken in chief. They noted that he was a litigant in person with no professional legal training and as a result it was harder for him to avoid repetition or extensive and lengthy cross examination than a professional representative.

They did not believe that the Claimant had acted unreasonably in conducting his own costs and therefore declined to make a costs award.

9.8   UNTRUTHFUL EVIDENCE

The Employment Tribunal rarely specifically states that a party has been lying but they will sometimes 'prefer' one party's evidence to another's. To what extent will the tribunal's preference of one party's evidence over the other's affect their decision to make an award of costs?

MS S RAMSEY v GOVERNING BODY OF MORNINGSID PRIMARY SCHOOL (1), THE LEARNING TRUST (2), THE LONDON BOROUGH OF HACKNEY (3)
STRATFORD EMPLOYMENT TRIBUNAL

Case No 3202992/2007
Supplied by Kym Beeston of The Learning Trust

The Claimant's complaints for race discrimination were stated by the Employment Tribunal to have no merit and they were dismissed. The Respondent then made an application for costs on the basis that it was clear from the Tribunal's decision that the Claimant's claim had been misconceived that it had no reasonable prospect of success. The Tribunal noted that it was concerned at the way in which the Claimant changed her case throughout the procedures, which had made them find that her evidence was difficult to accept and although they did not find that the Claimant had been untruthful they stated that the only alternative to such a finding was that she had been able to elaborate and persuade herself that the events happened in the way she claimed, against the weight of the evidence. There was 'a total failure' to provide any evidence that the➡

treatment she had received occurred because of her race. As a result of her pursuing the case, the Respondents had been caused a great deal of expense and the Tribunal decided that a costs order should be made.

As to the amount, the Respondent claimed £7,500 but the Claimant's likely level of income in the future (she was in receipt of Income Support) made the figure excessive and they ordered that the sum of £2,500 be paid.

DR E M EL-MANSI v NAPIER UNIVERSITY
EDINBURGH EMPLOYMENT TRIBUNAL

Case No S/106063/08
Supplied by Andrew Brown of Anderson Strathern LLP

The Claimant's claims were dismissed and the Employment Tribunal accepted the Respondent's criticism that there was not one piece of evidence which might go towards establishing a prima facie claim of race discrimination. Moreover, on at least two occasions Dr El-Mansi had received costs warnings from the Tribunal to the effect that if he was to lose his claim then an award of expenses could possibly be made against him. Despite that, he persisted although it was not clear why he did so when he made no serious attempt to support it either in evidence or in submissions. Furthermore, the Claimant's attempts to explain away the 'substantial body' of evidence against him 'stretched credulity to breaking point'.

The Tribunal commented, 'naturally, parties to a claim have a vested interest in the outcome of it. No doubt, it is part of human nature to embellish or dissemble. Nevertheless, the Claimant gave his evidence on oath and we are satisfied that his evidence was less than truthful from beginning to end'. All of these factors resulted in a finding that the Claimant's conduct was unreasonable.

On those bases the Claimant was ordered to pay all of the Respondent's costs.

CHAPTER 10

WASTED COSTS ORDERS

10.1   THE LEGAL BASIS

Prior to the 2004 Rules, it was not possible to obtain costs against a party's representatives, and where that representative conducted proceedings abusively or disruptively or required costly adjournments to suit his or her convenience, any costs orders would have to have been made against the party themselves. Rule 48 now provides for the personal liability of representatives in such situations.

Personal liability of representatives for costs

48.—(1) A tribunal or chairman may make a wasted costs order against a party's representative.

(2) In a wasted costs order the tribunal or chairman may: –

(a)   disallow, or order the representative of a party to meet the whole or part of any wasted costs of any party, including an order that the representative repay to his client any costs which have already been paid; and

(b)   order the representative to pay to the Secretary of State, in whole or in part, any allowances (other than allowances paid to members of tribunals) paid by the Secretary of State under section 5(2) or (3) of the Employment Tribunals Act to any person for the purposes of, or in connection with, that person's attendance at the tribunal by reason of the representative's conduct of the proceedings.

(3) "Wasted costs" means any costs incurred by a party –

(a)   as a result of any improper, unreasonable or negligent act or omission on the part of any representative; or

(b)   which, in the light of any such act or omission occurring after they were incurred, the tribunal considers it unreasonable to expect that party to pay.

(4) In this rule "representative" means a party's legal or other representative or any employee of such representative, but it does not include a representative who is not acting in pursuit of profit with regard to those proceedings. A person is considered to be acting in pursuit of profit if he is acting on a conditional fee arrangement

(5) A wasted costs order may be made in favour of a party whether or not that party is legally represented and such an order may also be made in favour of a representative's own client. A wasted costs order may not be made against a representative where that representative is an employee of a party.

(6) Before making a wasted costs order, the tribunal or chairman shall give the representative a reasonable opportunity to make oral or written representations as to reasons why such an order should not be made. The tribunal or chairman shall also have regard to the representative's ability to pay when considering whether it shall make a wasted costs order or how much that order should be.

(7) When a tribunal or chairman makes a wasted costs order, it must specify in the order the amount to be disallowed or paid.

(8) The Secretary shall inform the representative's client in writing –

    (a)   of any proceedings under this rule; or

    (b)   of any order made under this rule against the party's representative.

(9) Where a tribunal or chairman makes a wasted costs order it or he shall provide written reasons for doing so if a request is made for written reasons within 14 days of the date of the wasted costs order. This 14 day time limit may not be extended under rule 10. The Secretary shall send a copy of the written reasons to all parties to the proceedings.

10.2 WHO IS ELIGIBLE?

Any party can apply for a wasted costs order, whether or not they are legally represented, and they may apply for such an order against the other party's representative or indeed their own (r 48(5)).

Any party can apply for an order against a party's legal representative or any employee of that representative (including paralegals and legal executives) or any other representative, including employment consultants. This can result in a representative having to repay to their own client any costs that their client has already paid them.

The exception to this rule is where a representative is not acting in pursuit of profit *with regard to those proceedings*. A human resources officer employed by a respondent employer would not be liable, although an employment or human resources consultant engaged under a commercial contract to assist a party may do. A representative acting on a conditional fee arrangement would be considered to be acting in pursuit of profit.

MR A VEKARIA v VIPIN GUDKA INSURANCE SERVICES LIMITED
WATFORD EMPLOYMENT TRIBUNAL

Case No 3301387/2007
Supplied by Lee Xavier of Bevans Solicitors

The tribunal was satisfied that the claimant's claims for constructive dismissal and unpaid wages were misconceived and that both the claimant had acted unreasonably in pursuing the claim when an offer for settlement had been made which was in excess of an amount which could have been ordered by the Tribunal. It was not clear why he had done so and his failure to accept the offer led to the Respondent having to continue to defend the claim, including a two-day hearing.

The Tribunal also considered that a wasted costs order should be made against the representative because of his unreasonable and improper attitude to the litigation, including the fact that he was acting for profit, was not registered under the Compensation Act 2006 and was involved in the claimant's rejection of the offer for a sum which exceeded what he could possibly have received. The representative claimed not to be acting in pursuit of profit, despite the fact that a letter of authority quoting a retainer fee was disclosed and he had attempted to negotiate a settlement to include £1,500 towards the claimant's legal costs. The tribunal held that he had acted improperly in not registering under the Compensation Act and in being involved in advising the claimant to turn down the offer.

The claimant was ordered to pay £3,000 and the representative £4,000 towards the respondent's costs.

10.3 WHEN AND HOW SHOULD AN APPLICATION BE MADE?

The Rules do not specify when an application can or should be made but it would not normally become appropriate or apparent until the conclusion of a preliminary or substantive hearing.

Applications can be made orally at the hearing or in writing, and Rule 48(6) provides that before making a wasted costs order, the representative must be given a reasonable opportunity to make oral or written representations as to reasons why such an order should not be made.

The tribunal or chairman 'shall' take the representative's ability to pay into consideration when deciding whether to make the order or how much the order should be. Written reasons must be provided by the tribunal or chairman if requested to do so, within 14 days of that request (r 48(9)).

10.4 WHEN WILL A WASTED COSTS ORDER BE MADE – THE THREE STAGE TEST

Rule 48(3) provides for costs incurred as a result of any improper, unreasonable or negligent act or omission on the part of any representative.

The Employment Tribunal should give the representative a reasonable opportunity to make oral or written submissions as to why the order should not be made (r 48(7)).

The principal authorities on this issue are *Ridehalgh v Horsefield*[1] and *Metcalfe v Wotherill*,[2] which make it clear that before a wasted costs order can be made against a legal representative on the grounds that he has presented a hopeless case, the representative must be shown not only to have acted improperly, unreasonably or negligently, but also to have lent assistance to proceedings which amounts to an abuse of the court.

In *Ridehalgh* at p 861(A)-(C) the Court of Appeal stated that a three-stage test is required when a wasted costs order is contemplated, namely:

(1)   has the legal representative of whom the complaint is made acted improperly, unreasonably or negligently;

(2)   if so, did such conduct cause the applicant to incur unnecessary costs?;

(3)   if so, is it in all the circumstances just to order the legal representative to compensate the applicant for the whole or any part of the relevant costs?

RIDEHALGH v HORSEFIELD

[1994] CH 205, [1994] 3 WLR 462, [1994] 2 FLR 194

Following the determination of four actions, the Judge in each case made an order under s 51(6) of the Supreme Court Act 1981[3] (as substituted by s 4 of the Courts and Legal Services Act 1990) against the other party's solicitors requiring him personally to pay ➡

---

[1]   [1994] Ch 205.
[2]   [2002] UKHL 27.
[3]   Now referred to as 'Senior Courts Act 1981' (see Constitutional Reform Act 2005).

the costs thrown away in the proceedings as a result of 'improper, unreasonable or negligent' conduct on his part. The conduct complained of included:

(i)   failure to discover that the plaintiff's workplace was not dangerously noisy at an earlier stage in proceedings seeking damages for noise-induced hearing loss;

(ii) failure to notify the defendants of the grant of legal aid to the plaintiff where such notification could have resulted in early settlement of the action;

(iii) use of an implied threat of a winding-up petition in a negotiating offer as an inducement to the debtor to compromise a claim relating to a disputed debt; and

(iv) failure to respond to issues raised by the other party's solicitors and, in consequence, failure to negotiate the terms of a trust deed and avoid the need to apply to the court for directions.

The solicitors appealed in each case, contending that their conduct had not been improper, unreasonable or negligent within the meaning of s 51(7) of the 1981 Act and had not resulted in wasted costs. In the fifth action, the Judge made a wasted costs order against the unsuccessful party's counsel on the ground that her failure to conduct the trial with proper expedition (despite the inadequacy of her instructions) arose as the direct consequence of her improper and unreasonable acceptance of the brief at short notice, since it was obvious that she would be unable to achieve an adequate grasp of the matters at issue within the available time and that she had thereby unnecessarily prolonged the proceedings by one full day.

Counsel appealed on the basis that s 62 of the 1990 Act preserved the immunity from suit enjoyed by an advocate in relation to the conduct of litigation.

It was held:

(1)   In exercising its jurisdiction to ensure that litigants should not be financially prejudiced by the unjustifiable conduct of litigation by their or their opponent's legal representatives, the court would only make an order under s 51(6) of the 1981 Act if it was satisfied that the conduct characterised as 'improper, unreasonable or negligent' directly caused the wasted costs complained of, and it would be astute to safeguard against→

wasted costs orders becoming a back-door means of recovering costs not otherwise recoverable against a legally aided or impoverished litigant.

The meaning of the words 'improper, unreasonable or negligent' was well-established and not open to serious doubt. 'Improper' covered any significant breach of a substantial duty imposed by the relevant code of professional conduct, as well as conduct which would be improper according to the consensus of professional opinion, whether it violated the letter of a professional code or not. 'Unreasonable' described conduct which was vexatious, designed to harass the other side rather than advance the resolution of the case, and it made no difference that the conduct was the product of excessive zeal and not improper motive, since the acid test was whether the conduct permitted of a reasonable explanation. 'Negligent' was to be understood in an untechnical way to denote failure to act with the competence reasonably expected of ordinary members of the profession.

The conduct complained of in the first four cases and the sixth case was not 'improper, unreasonable or negligent' and had not resulted in wasted costs, with the result that none of the s 51 orders should have been made. The four appeals were allowed.

(2)　Although s 62 of the 1990 Act preserved an advocate's immunity in relation to his conduct of court proceedings, that section was to be read subject to ss 4, 111 and 112 of the Act so that if an advocate's conduct in court was improper, unreasonable or negligent he would be liable to a wasted costs order. However, a legal representative would not be held to have acted improperly, unreasonably or negligently for the purposes of s 51 of the 1981 Act simply because he acted for a party who pursued a claim or defence which was doomed to fail, having regard to the cab-rank rule imposed on barristers by their Code of Professional Conduct and the underlying public policy that representation should be afforded to the unpopular and unmeritorious. On the other hand, a barrister would be liable to a wasted costs order if he lent his assistance to proceedings which were an abuse of the process of the court. On the facts, counsel's conduct in court could not be described as improper, unreasonable or negligent nor as wasteful of costs, since she had been professionally obliged under the code to accept the brief at short notice and was then prevented from withdrawing once the inadequacy of her instructions became apparent because to do so would prejudice her clients. It followed that the Judge should not have made a wasted costs order against counsel and that her appeal would be allowed.

When a party pursues a hopeless case, what is their representative's potential liability under r 48?

In *Rondel v Worsely*[4] at 1029 and at 275 Lord Pearce stated:

> 'It is easier, pleasanter and more advantageous professionally for barristers to advise, represent or defend those who are decent and reasonable and likely to succeed in their action or their defence than those who are unpleasant, unreasonable, disreputable, and have an apparently hopeless case. Yet it would be tragic if our legal system came to provide no reputable defenders, or representatives or advisors for the latter.'

Sir Thomas Bingham MR, as he was, in the *Ridehalgh* case (p 863) made it clear that a legal representative is not to be held to have acted improperly, unreasonably or negligently simply because he acts for a party who pursues a claim or a defence which is plainly doomed to fail.

> 'It is, however. .quite another (thing) to lend his assistance to proceedings which are an abuse of the process of the court ... Whether instructed or not, a legal representative is not entitled to use litigious procedures for purposes for which they were not intended, as by issuing or pursuing proceedings for reasons unconnected with success in the litigation or pursuing a case known to be dishonest, nor is he entitled to evade rules intended to safeguard the interests of justice, as by knowingly failing to make full disclosure on ex parte application or knowingly conniving at incomplete disclosure of documents ...'

The distinction therefore is between conduct which is an abuse of process and conduct falling short of that.

It was made clear in *Medcalfe* by Lord Hobhouse that a representative owes no duty to his opponent.

A good example of the application of the rules is *Williams & ors v Wessex Stores Ltd.*[5]

MS M WILLIAMS & ORS v WESSEX STORES LTD
BRISTOL EMPLOYMENT TRIBUNAL

Case Nos 1401151/08, 1401152/08, 1401153/08, 1401154/08
Supplied by Philip Cameron of CMS Cameron McKenna LLP

The Respondent made a claim for a wasted costs order against the Claimants' solicitors, who had issued claims for unfair dismissal. The Respondent took legal advice and before time had expired for entering a response the Claimants withdrew their claims, having indicated that they had not given instructions to anyone to ➡

---

4   [1967] 3 All ER 993, [1969] 1 AC 191.
5   Case Nos 1401151/08, 1401152/08, 1401153/08, 1401154/08.

commence proceedings on their behalf. The Respondent's costs application was dealt with by a Judge alone on written representations. He ordered that the Solicitors pay £876 plus VAT in respect of the Respondent's costs.

The solicitors named as acting for the Claimants on the ET1 had issued the claims on the instructions of the Communication Workers Union, three days before the expiry of the limitation period. They issued without contacting the four Claimants. The details of one of the Claimants were provided by the Union in error and she had no connection with the Respondent. Rule 2.01(1)(c) of the Solicitor's Code of Conduct requires that where instructions are given by someone other than the client, a solicitor must not proceed without checking that all clients agree with the instructions given.

The Judge noted that the wasted costs jurisdiction should only be exercised with great caution and as a last resort, where the Tribunal is satisfied that the conduct of the representative was properly to be characterised as improper, unreasonable or negligent. He applied the three stage test set out in *Ridehalgh* and first considered the definitions of improper and negligent given in *Harvey* in paras 1072-1077. The Judge held that failure to comply with the Code of Conduct is both improper and negligent. That conduct resulted in the Respondent incurring unnecessary costs, as the claims had been served on the company which then took legal advice. Finally he considered whether it was just to order payment of the whole or part of the relevant costs, referring to the Summary Assessment of Costs 2008 published by HM Courts Service and considered the complexity of what the Respondent's solicitors had had to do. There had been no requirement to draft a Response as shortly after the Respondent was served with the claims it was informed that they were to be withdrawn. In his opinion, four hours attendance time was more than adequate to draft the application for costs, prepare submissions and correspond with the Tribunal and he held that it was disproportionate to allow the hourly rate claimed by the Respondent's solicitor, on the basis that a case of this nature could be adequately dealt with by a junior assistant solicitor. He therefore adopted the guideline rate for City of London solicitors at grade C, namely £219 per hour.

MITCHELLS v FUNKWERK
EAT 2008

Appeal No UKEAT/0541/07/MAA

W brought claims for sex discrimination and unfair dismissal arising from her resignation in the face of disciplinary hearings. She was ➡

represented by Mitchells. The claim was heard over five days in two sets of hearings. The tribunal dismissed her claims, holding that the discriminatory acts alleged had occurred well before the period of three months prior to the presentation of the claim and were out of time and that, in any event, the allegations were without substance. The Respondent subsequently sought a wasted costs order on the basis that W's claims had never had any prospect of success. Alternatively, it was submitted that it had become clear after W had given her evidence that she could not win. The tribunal made the wasted costs order against Mitchells, effectively finding that, following the third day of the action, a competent solicitor would have advised W that her claim was bound to fail.

The Employment Tribunal's decision was challenged on the ground, inter alia, that the tribunal had erred in failing to consider and properly apply the guiding principles laid down in the authorities. This succeeded, in that the EAT held that the tribunal had erred in failing to consider and apply the guidance laid down in *Ridehalgh v Horsefield* and *Medcalf v Mardell*. In particular it had failed to consider whether the pursuit of a hopeless case had not only been very negligent but had amounted to an abuse of the court; whether an assessment of the merits of W's case had been made between the third and fourth days of the hearing and, if so, how that assessment had been reached; and whether the Appellant's failure had caused the costs of the final two days of the proceedings.

Accordingly, the wasted costs order was quashed. It was held that a legal representative is not to be held to have acted improperly, unreasonably or negligently simply because he acts for a party who pursues a claim or a defence which is plainly doomed to fail.

In *Persaud v Persaud*[6] a wasted costs application against counsel was based on alleged failure on his part to give his clients accurate advice as to the prospects of success. In his judgment Peter Gibson LJ said, 'it is clear from what was said in both *Ridehalgh* and *Medcalf* that it is necessary for a duty to the court to be breached by the legal representative if he is to be made liable for wasted costs. An example of such a breach is *Highvogue Ltd v Morris*.[7]

HIGHVOGUE LTD v MORRIS

EAT/0093/07

The EAT upheld a wasted costs order against solicitors arising from their conduct of an Employment Tribunal claim. However the order ➡

---

6   [2003] EWCA Civ 394.

7   EAT/0093/07.

there was not based on negligence but on improper or unreasonable conduct. The tribunal considered that there were inadequate witness statements, non-disclosure of relevant documents and refusal to desist from repetitive, unnecessarily lengthy and irrelevant cross-examination. Contentions and lines of defence were put forward which had no reasonable prospect of success, there were attacks on the Claimant's character and conduct and the statutory defence was put forward with no supporting evidence and very late in the day. Although they acknowledged that the defence was not misconceived, it was this conduct of the Respondent's solicitors that resulted in the wasted costs order.

Beatson J acknowledged that:

> '... it is true that many hopeless cases are litigated because the litigants are persistent rather than because of their representatives. We consider this Tribunal had positive evidence in respect of the particular failures that it found which enabled it to conclude that those failures were the responsibility of the Respondent's solicitors.'

MAIR v MARTIN PIPELINE INDUSTRIAL (1) AND ENVIRONMENTAL CLEANSING LTD (2) S106315/03 GLASGOW EMPLOYMENT TRIBUNAL

Case No S/106315/2003

A COT3 settlement was agreed between the parties and the Respondent's had given their solicitor a cheque for the settlement sum, so the Claimant agreed to a discharge of the hearing. The Respondent then instructed their bank to stop the cheque but their solicitor told the Claimant's agent that he was in funds and allowed a process of adjustment of the COT3 knowing that his client had stopped the cheque. That fact was concealed for nearly three weeks.

The Claimant's applied for a wasted costs order on the ground that the Respondent's solicitor had acted improperly, and unreasonably in not indicating that there was a problem with the settlement funds, and that he had been negligent in his conduct. The Tribunal agreed and held it entirely reasonable that wasted costs should be awarded from the period the agent had said he was in funds to the date of (and including) the hearing and these costs were ordered on an indemnity basis. The Respondent was ordered to pay the costs of the whole proceedings but the wasted costs were ordered to reduce the liability of the Respondent.

10.5 PRIVILEGE

In answering an allegation that they have acted unreasonably, improperly or negligently, the difficulty many legal representatives will face is that their communications with clients are covered by legal professional privilege, and it is for their client to decide whether or not privilege should be waived. At this point a legal representative would have to consider advising their client to take independent advice.

This difficulty was recognised by Sir Thomas Bingham MR (as he then was) in *Ridehalgh*. He said:

> 'Judges who are invited to make or contemplate making a wasted costs order must make full allowance for the inability of the ... lawyers to tell the whole story. Where there is room for doubt the ... lawyers are entitled to the benefit of it. It is again only when, with all allowances made, the lawyers' conduct of proceedings is quite plainly unjustifiable that it can be appropriate to make a wasted costs order ... It is rarely if ever safe for a court to assume that a hopeless case is being litigated on the advice of the lawyers involved. They are there to present the case, it is as Samuel Johnson unforgettably pointed for the judge and not the lawyers to judge it.'

In *Medcalf v Mardell & ors*[8] the circumstances were considered in which a court may make wasted costs orders where barristers are precluded by legal professional privilege from answering complaints made against them.

MEDCALF v MARDELL & ORS

[2002] UKHL 27

The Appellant barristers acted as advocates for two defendants in an appeal to the Court of Appeal against a judgment in the Claimant's favour. The first day-and-a-half of the four day hearing was taken up by an application by the defendants to amend their notice of appeal in order to make serious allegations of fraud and other impropriety against the Claimant. Those allegations had been set out in a draft amended notice of appeal, bearing the names of both barristers, and a skeleton argument in support of the application to amend, signed by both barristers. The court rejected the application to amend in respect of the allegations of fraud and impropriety, and also dismissed the appeal. The Claimant then sought wasted costs orders against the barristers, seeking to recover the costs said to have been incurred in investigating and rebutting the allegations of fraud and impropriety.   ➡

---

8   [2002] UKHL 27.

On this point the House of Lords held that where a wasted costs order was sought against a practitioner precluded by legal professional privilege from giving his full answer to the application, the court should not make an order unless, proceeding with extreme care, it was: (a) satisfied that there was nothing the practitioner could say, if unconstrained, to resist the order; and (b) that it was in all the circumstances fair to make the order. Even if the court were able properly to be sure that the practitioner could have no answer to the substantive complaint, it could not fairly make an order unless satisfied that nothing could be said to influence the exercise of its discretion. In the instant case, the court did not know, and could not be told, whether the barristers, when signing the draft amended notice of appeal and the skeleton argument, had had before them material of any kind which justified the making of the allegations. Hunch and suspicion were not enough, and the barristers had to be given the benefit of the doubt. Accordingly, the appeal was allowed.

SALLY THORNLEY NASH v OPTIMA HEALTH LTD
CARDIFF EMPLOYMENT TRIBUNAL

Case No 1602631/2004
Supplied by Kate Palka of Palka Downton solicitors

Following an order for £400 costs to be paid to the Respondent, the Respondent's solicitors wrote to the Claimant to persuade her to cooperate with the Respondent in suing her solicitors for negligence. They argued that it was against the public interest for the Respondent to have to bear the significant costs of defending her claims because the means of the Claimant had resulted in a costs order of £400. They wished the Claimant to waive privilege so that the Respondent could gain access to the privileged communication between the Claimant and her solicitor.

The Claimant refused to cooperate with the Respondent or to waive privilege. The Respondent then applied for a review of the decision to limit the award to £400 and for a wasted costs order against the Claimant's solicitors. The wasted costs application was quickly dismissed, as there was no evidence before the Tribunal that could give rise to or enable the Judge to consider the application. In relation to the review, the Judge held it did not follow from the fact that an order for costs was made against the Claimant that the Claimant's solicitors had given advice that was incorrect or negligent, thus entitling the company to justify an increase of the costs order for £400, or that the Claimant had received correct advice but had continued regardless. There is nothing in law that represented an unreasonable refusal to waive privilege, and even if ➡

there were, this would not apply in this case. Nothing new had occurred since the date of the costs order that could justify a review of that order. Both applications were dismissed and the Claimant and her solicitors then applied for costs against the Respondent in respect of those applications, but this too was refused.

10.6 HOW MUCH?

Under r 48(2)(a) the tribunal may either:

(a)   disallow the whole of part of any wasted costs;

(b)   order the representative to pay the whole or part of any costs; or

(c)   order the representative to repay his client any costs which have already been paid.

The costs will include the cost of the service provided in relation to the proceedings as well as costs payable under ss 5(2) and (3) of the Employment Tribunals Act 1996 (r 42(2)(b)). These include the fees and allowances paid by the Secretary of State to:

(a)   employment tribunal members;

(b)   assessors appointed in relation to employment tribunal proceedings??

(c)   any member of an independent panel of experts who prepares a report on work of equal value for the purposes of the Equal Pay Act 1970;

(d)   anyone in connection with their attendance at tribunals, (such as witness expenses).

In the *Mitchells* case, the wasted costs ordered by the tribunal amounted to £3,325, £2,125 of which were the Respondent's solicitors and counsel's fees for the two last days hearing (part heard) and £900 of the costs on the wasted costs application. The sum was based on the tribunal's conclusion that by the end of the third day, when the hearings were adjourned to late November, the Claimant's solicitor should have told the Claimant that her case was very likely to fail. He had not done so and as a result the costs of the two days in November were wasted.

Where a wasted costs order is made, the actual loss flowing from the misconduct must be calculated.

**RATCLIFFE DUCE AND GAMMER v BINNS
AND McDONALD**

UKEAT/0100/08/CEA

The Employment Tribunal made a wasted costs order against the Claimant's solicitors on the basis that the continued pursuance of the claim was unreasonable and misconceived and that the Claimants should have appreciated that.

The EAT held that the Employment Judge acted on the wrong principles and the costs order was set aside. When a wasted costs order is concerned, the test is more rigorous than whether the party has acted unreasonably. A wasted costs order should not be made merely because a Claimant pursues a hopeless case, and his representative does not dissuade them from doing so.

Even if it was fair to infer that the solicitor should have appreciated that it was hopeless – and in this case the Claimant had maintained that he had relevant evidence to support his case until the last minute – it did not follow that the solicitor could have influenced the Claimant to drop the case. Since there was no evidence that the Claimant would have withdrawn even if advised to do so, there was no basis for inferring that any costs had been incurred as a consequence of any misconduct. Unlike the position where an ordinary costs order is made, where there is no need to fix the amount by reference to the additional costs actually resulting from unreasonable conduct, where a wasted costs order is made, the actual loss flowing from the misconduct must be calculated. If the Claimant would have continued the action in any event, no costs are wasted.

**SINGH JOHAL v ASSOCIATED TRANSPORT SERVICES & ORS
LEEDS EMPLOYMENT TRIBUNAL**

Case No 1802508
Supplied by Simon Shepherd of Schoeys

The Employment Tribunal held that claims for victimisation under the RRA 1976, the Employment (Religion or Belief) Regulations 2003 and on the ground of having made a protected disclosure, a claim under the National Minimum Wage Act 1998 and a contention that the Respondent had failed to comply with the Dispute Resolution Regulations and s 32 of the Employment Act 2002 were all misconceived. Other claims were brought ➡

unreasonably. The Tribunal noted that the Claimant's representatives' conduct had directly caused the claims which were wholly unmeritorious and had been conducted in a thoroughly unreasonable way.

Examples of the representative's behaviour were making inappropriate remarks and comments on witness evidence and inviting the Respondent's witnesses to do so; grossly exaggerating evidence in submissions, asking completely contradictory questions, misleading witnesses as to evidence they had given earlier, regularly interrupting witness answers and causing the Chairman to intervene 50 times during the hearing to prevent him from asking irrelevant questions.

The Tribunal considered the Claimant's means but nonetheless considered that the conduct of the Claimant should be marked by an order for costs which 'should not be ameliorated by his limited means' and therefore the order for costs was made on an indemnity basis. They believed that a large proportion of the costs had been wasted purely as a result of the misguided advice given to the Claimant and the unreasonable conduct of his representatives. The costs incurred by the Respondent from the date the representatives had received full disclosure from the employer were ordered as wasted costs, with the representative being held jointly and severally liable with the Claimant for the costs from that date. The Tribunal declined, however, to divide elements of time up into the proportion which might fairly have been used for parts of the claims that could properly have been brought, as this was a disproportionate waste of resources.

Finally, the argument that the representative was not 'acting in pursuit of profit' rejected as he was employed by a commercial organisation; although not legally qualified he acted in a commercial capacity offering advice and representation in Employment Tribunals.

Examples of refusals by ET of costs applications

MUKARI v READING TRANSPORT
READING EMPLOYMENT TRIBUNAL

Case No 2701538/2007
Supplied by Tanushree Sehmbi of Clarks Legal

The claim for unfair dismissal was unsuccessful because the Employment Tribunal believed that the decision to dismiss the Claimant bus driver for talking on his mobile while driving passengers was well within the range of reasonable responses a➡

reasonable employer may take. The Respondent's claim for costs was unsuccessful, though 'properly made'. The Tribunal accepted that the Claimant had poor prospects of succeeding but accepted that the Claimant genuinely believed another sanction apart from dismissal might have been imposed and therefore his claim was not 'vexatious'.

MISS SUSAN JANE NICOL v MILLS GLOBAL SERVICES OF UK LTD (1), THE MILS CORPORATION (2)
GLASGOW EMPLOYMENT TRIBUNAL

Case No S/125023/06
Supplied by Claire Brattey of SJ Berwin

Both parties made applications for expenses against the other and neither party was successful. Although the Claimant was unsuccessful, the Tribunal did not share the Respondent's view that the matter was so clear that embarking on litigation was an unreasonable course of conduct or that it had been unreasonable to commence or continue the proceedings for breach of contract. The Claimant's request for expenses against both Respondents was made on the basis that she would not have incurred expenses if it had been made clear to her that she was only entitled to a pro rata amount of shares. The Tribunal rejected this argument – as soon as the ET3 had been filed she would have known this and the Tribunal did not believe that the Respondents had acted unreasonably in contesting the claim. Both claims for expenses were therefore rejected.

In *Lake v Acro Grating (UK) Ltd*,[9] the EAT said (para 14):

> 'What employment tribunals usually need to consider ... is whether at the conclusion of the case a party can be said to have had an arguable case in any respect (including for example procedural matters), even if they are ultimately unsuccessful. The reasoning should therefore explain the Tribunal's findings on that issue. Although the Employment Tribunal found against Mr Lake, they did not accuse him of lying. It frequently happens that Employment Tribunals find the totality of the evidence from one side preferable to that from the other side, without triggering a costs order.'

Another example of a claim in which the tribunal found against the Claimant but declined to make a costs order is *Marie Elizabeth Deery v GMB Trade Union*.[10]

---

[9]   UKEAT/0511/04/RN.
[10]   Case No 99/06FET.

MARIE ELIZABETH DEERY v GMB TRADE UNION
FAIR EMPLOYMENT TRIBUNAL, NI

Case No 99/06FET
Supplied by Aoife MacManus of Donnelly & Kinder and by Gerry Daly of Francis Hanna & Co solicitors

The Claimant's claim that she had suffered discrimination on the ground of her political opinion and/or her religious belief failed and the Respondent's sought costs on the basis that the proceedings should not have been initiated in the first place, and having initiated them, the Claimant should have withdrawn them. They contended that the Claimant did not have an arguable case or any reasonable prospect of success from the time of submission of the ET1, and continued to do so when she was warned (by the Respondent) that a costs application would be made.

The Tribunal said that although they had held against the Claimant, there were serious issues that had required to be considered. They did not think she had acted abusively or unreasonably in bringing the proceedings and did not agree that her application had no reasonable prospect of success. For example, the matter of whether a person's association with their trade union brings them within the scope of the relevant legislation was a reasonable one to put before the Tribunal. In any event, the Claimant gave evidence as to her means and in the event of the Tribunal being wrong in finding that the Claimant had not acted in one or more of the ways alleged, they exercised their discretionary power and on the basis of her means (including the fact that her husband was in receipt of sickness benefit), they did not make a costs order.

CHAPTER 11

ENFORCEMENT, REVIEW AND APPEALS OF EMPLOYMENT TRIBUNAL COSTS ORDERS

11.1   ENFORCEMENT

Once an award has been made by an Employment Tribunal, if the paying party fails to pay redress can be sought through the county court procedures.

An order of the tribunal for the payment of costs may be registered in the county court: see s 15(1) of the Employment Tribunals Act 1996, which provides:

15 Enforcement

(1) Any sum payable in pursuance of a decision of an [employment tribunal] in England and Wales which has been registered in accordance with [employment tribunal] procedure regulations shall, if a county court so orders, be recoverable by execution issued from the county court or otherwise as if it were payable under an order of that court.

At the time of enforcement, the County Court has a wide power to take into account the ability of the paying party to pay. Section 71 of the County Courts Act 1984 provides as follows:

71 Satisfaction of judgments and orders for payment of money.

(1) Where a judgment is given or an order is made by a county court under which a sum of money of any amount is payable, whether by way of satisfaction of the claim or counterclaim in the proceedings or by way of costs or otherwise, the court may, as it thinks fit, order the 'money to be paid either –

> (a)   in one sum, whether forthwith or within such period as the court may fix; or
>
> (b)   by such instalments payable at such times as the court may fix.

(2) If at any time it appears to the satisfaction of the court that any party to any proceedings is unable from any cause to pay any sum recovered against him (whether by way of satisfaction of the claim or counterclaim in the proceedings or by way of costs or otherwise) or any instalment of such a sum, the court may, in its discretion, suspend or stay any judgment or order given or made in the proceedings for such time and on such terms as the court thinks fit, and so from time to time until it appears that the cause of

inability has ceased.

An application to enforce the award must be made on Form n322a in the County Court. The normal methods of enforcement apply: attachment of earnings orders, charging orders, garnishee orders, warrants of execution, delivery of goods (or writs of *fieri facias* in the High Court).

In Scotland, the award 'may be enforced in like manner as an extract registered decree arbitral bearing a warrant for execution issued by the Sheriff Court of any Sheriffdom in Scotland' (Employment Tribunals Act 1996, s 15(2)).

For recovery of judgment debts and enforcement of other money claims generally (of up to £99,999) the Government Courts Service provides a useful Money Claim Online

11.2   REVIEW UNDER RULES 33–36

Orders for costs can be reviewed under rr 34-36 of the Rules of Procedure 2004.

> **34.**—(1) Parties may apply to have certain judgments and decisions made by a tribunal or a chairman reviewed under rules 34 to 36. Those judgments and decisions are –
>
> (a)   a decision not to accept a claim, response or counterclaim;
>
> (b)   a judgment (other than a default judgment but including an order for costs, expenses, preparation time or wasted costs); and
>
> (c)   a decision made under rule 6(3) of Schedule 4;
>
> and references to "decision" in rules 34 to 37 are references to the above judgments and decisions only. Other decisions or orders may not be reviewed under these rules.

Under r 28, a 'judgment' is 'a final determination of the proceedings or of a particular issue in those proceedings' and an 'order' is issued in relation to interim matters and it will require a person to do or not to do something.

Thus a judgment in r 34(b) may include an award of compensation, a declaration or recommendation and it may also include orders for costs, preparation time or wasted costs. It also includes a strike out order (*Sodexho v Gibbons*)[1] but not a deposit order under r 20(1), which is an 'order' and not a 'judgment'. As such, a deposit order is not susceptible to review by virtue of r 34(1) but it can be revoked or varied by a chairman under r10(1)(2)(n).

---

[1]   [2005] ICR 1647, EAT.

Either party to the proceedings may apply and a tribunal or Judge may also on their own initiative review a decision they have made (r 34(5). Any review can only be carried out if one or more of the specified grounds set out in r 34(3) apply.

> **34.**—(3) Subject to paragraph (4), decisions may be reviewed on the following grounds only –
>
> (a) the decision was wrongly made as a result of an administrative error;
>
> (b) a party did not receive notice of the proceedings leading to the decision;
>
> (c) the decision was made in the absence of a party;
>
> (d) new evidence has become available since the conclusion of the hearing to which the decision relates, provided that its existence could not have been reasonably known of or foreseen at that time; or
>
> (e) the interests of justice require such a review.

How can an application for a review be made?

Under r 35, an application under r 34 to have a decision reviewed must be made to the Employment Tribunal Office within 14 days of the date on which the decision was sent to the parties. The 14 day time limit may be extended by a chairman if he considers that it is just and equitable to do so.

The application must be in writing and must identify the grounds of the application in accordance with r 34(3), but if the decision to be reviewed was made at a hearing, an application may be made orally at that hearing.

The application to have a decision reviewed shall be considered (without the need to hold a hearing) by the chairman of the tribunal which made the decision or, if that is not practicable, by a Regional Chairman or the Vice President, any chairman nominated by a Regional Chairman or the Vice President; or the President;

A preliminary consideration is carried out and the application shall be refused if it is considered that there are no grounds for the decision to be reviewed under r 34(3) or there is no reasonable prospect of the decision being varied or revoked.

If the application is not refused, the decision is then reviewed under r 36.

11.3 APPEALS PROCEDURE

An appeal is instituted by sending notice of appeal, in (or substantially in) accordance with Forms 1 or 2 of the Schedule, to the Rules to the Employment Appeal Tribunal, together with a copy of the decision being appealed against and (if the appeal is from an Employment Tribunal) a copy of the written reasons for the decision.

The time limit for appeal is 42 days from the day on which the written reasons were sent to the parties or if none, within 42 days from the date on which the written record of the judgment was sent to them. There is a 'sifting' procedure and if the appeal is rejected on the paper sift an appellant has a further 28 days to present a fresh notice of appeal which then goes on for a further consideration (on paper or, if requested, an oral hearing). In *Haritaki v SE England Development Agency*,[2] HHJ McMullen clarified the process and that: (a) this was 'a once and for all' opportunity to have a second go at appealing; (b) the fresh notice of appeal is not an appeal against the first sift decision; and (c) the overall time-limits are generous as in practice a person is given almost three months in which to finalise an appeal against a judgment of an Employment Tribunal.

Once instituted, the appeals will be listed for short Preliminary Hearing Directions, usually no more than half an hour in length. The Notice of Appeal must clearly identify the point of law that is being made (para 2.4 of the 2004 Practice Direction) and appellant is required to satisfy the EAT at the PHR that it is reasonably arguable that the Employment Tribunal made an error of law in their decision.

Where a costs order made by an Employment Tribunal is appealed the prospects of success are substantially reduced by the restriction of the right of appeal to questions of law and by the respect paid by appellate courts to the exercise of discretion by the tribunal below. Unless the discretion has been exercised contrary to principle, in disregard of relevant factors or is just plain wrong, an appeal against a tribunal's costs order will fail.

MR B WOLFF v (1) KINGSTON UPON HULL CITY COUNCIL (2) THE GOVERNORS OF PICKERING HIGH SCHOOL SPORTS COLLEGE

Appeal No UKEAT/0631/06/DA

The Employment Tribunal had made an award of costs where the Claimant persisted unreasonably in pursuing his claim for re-engagement. He had been guided to take advice in a CMD but appeared to have ignored that guidance, and persisted with his claim long after it had become 'blindingly obvious that no such remedy was remotely practicable'. The Respondent had made a settlement offer of £1,000, which was almost twice what he received as a compensatory award.   ➡

---

2   EAT2008 on 22 July 2008, reported at [2008] IRLR 945.

Before the EAT Mr Wolff argued that this was an unlawful exercise by the tribunal of its discretion. He said that as a Claimant who had succeeded in establishing that he had been unfairly constructively dismissed, and who had only ever sought reengagement as a remedy, he was entitled to pursue that remedy to a remedies hearing.

The EAT (per HHJ Wilkie) said that in order for Mr Wolff to establish that the exercise by the Employment Tribunal of their discretion was unlawful, he had to surmount a high hurdle. It was not enough to persuade the EAT that it might have done something different. What he had to do was to establish that the Employment Tribunal was unreasonable in exercising its discretion in the way that it did. They were unable to accede to his argument that the tribunal, in awarding costs against him, acted unlawfully and therefore his appeal fails.

ONEGBU V NEWMAN STONE LTD
EMPLOYMENT APPEAL TRIBUNAL

Appeal No UKEAT/0157/08/ZT

Mummery LJ I McPherson who, at para 24, referred to what was the then r 14 of the 2001 rules, which is in similar terms to the current rules. He continued as follows at para 26:

> 'When a costs order made by an employment tribunal is appealed to the employment appeal tribunal or to this court the prospects of success are substantially reduced by the restriction of the right of appeal to questions of law and by the respect properly paid by appellate courts to the exercise of discretion by lower courts and tribunals in accordance with legal principle and relevant considerations. Unless the discretion has been exercised contrary to principle, in disregard of the principle of relevance or is just plainly wrong, an appeal against a tribunal's costs order will fail. If, however, the appeal succeeds, the appellate body may substitute a different order or, if it is necessary to find further facts, the matter may be remitted to the tribunal for a fresh hearing of the costs application.

If the result of the PHD is that the appeal is allowed to proceed, the EAT office will send the Respondent the Notice of Appeal and 'Form 3' entitled 'Respondent's Answer'. He will have 14 days from the date of the letter accompanying the form to return it if he wishes to contest the appeal.

A Respondent who fails to return the form within the 14 days allowed may be ordered to pay costs and will not be allowed to defend the appeal, raise any cross-appeal or obtain any directions from the EAT 'unless there is good reason for the delay which excuses a failure to comply with the time-limit'

The procedure for the appeal is set out in Practice Directions. The EAT issued a new Practice Direction on 22 May 2008, replacing the 2004 Practice Direction.

CHAPTER 12

COSTS IN OTHER COURTS

12.1 EMPLOYMENT APPEAL TRIBUNAL

12.1.1 Legal tests

The power of the Employment of Appeal Tribunal to award costs is contained in r 34 of the Employment Appeal Tribunal Rules 1993, SI 1993/2854, which follow the same basic line as the 2004 Rules of Procedure in the Employment Tribunals. The Employment Appeal Tribunal (Amendment) Rules 2004 introduced a new r 34A dealing with costs. It also provides for the possibility of a wasted costs order being made against a party's representative.

When a costs or expenses order may be made

34A.—(1) Where it appears to the Appeal Tribunal that any proceedings brought by the paying party were unnecessary, improper, vexatious or misconceived or that there has been unreasonable delay or other unreasonable conduct in the bringing or conducting of proceedings by the paying party, the Appeal Tribunal may make a costs order against the paying party.

(2) The Appeal Tribunal may in particular make a costs order against the paying party when –

    (a)   he has not complied with a direction of the Appeal Tribunal;

    (b)   he has amended its notice of appeal, document provided under rule 3 sub-paragraphs (5) or (6), Respondent's answer or statement of grounds of cross-appeal, or document provided under rule 6 sub-paragraphs (7) or (8); or

    (c)   he has caused an adjournment of proceedings.

(3) Nothing in paragraph (2) shall restrict the Appeal Tribunal's discretion to award costs under paragraph (1).

Therefore costs may be awarded under r 34A(1) if:

- proceedings are unnecessary, improper, vexatious or misconceived;

- there has been unreasonable delay or other unreasonable conduct in bringing or conducting the proceedings.

Rule 34A(2) provides particularly for costs orders to be made in circumstances when a party:

- has not complied with a direction of the EAT;

- has amended a notice of appeal, answer or cross-appeal; or

- has caused adjournment of proceedings.

The statutory provisions as to costs are amplified by the Employment Appeal Tribunal Practice Direction 2008 which came into force on 22 May 2008 and supersedes all previous practice directions.

19. Costs (referred to as Expenses in Scotland)

19.1 In this PD 'costs' includes legal costs, expenses, allowances paid by the Secretary of State and payment in respect of time spent in preparing a case. Such costs may relate to interim applications or hearings or to a PH or FH.

19.2 An application for costs must be made either during or at the end of a relevant hearing, or in writing to the Registrar within 14 days of the seal date of the relevant order of the EAT or, in the case of a reserved judgment, as provided for in paragraph 18.3 above, copied to all parties.

19.3 The party seeking the order must state the legal ground on which the application is based and the facts on which it is based and, by a schedule or otherwise, show how the costs have been incurred. If the application is made in respect of only part of the proceedings, particulars must be given showing how the costs have been incurred on that specific part. If the party against whom the order is sought wishes the EAT to have regard to means and/or an alleged inability to pay, a witness statement giving particulars and exhibiting any documents must be served on the other party(ies) and lodged with the EAT. Further directions may be required to be given by the EAT in such cases.

19.4 Such application may be resolved by the EAT on the papers, provided that the opportunity has been given for representations in writing by all relevant parties, or the EAT may refer the matter for an oral hearing, and may assess the costs either on the papers or at an oral hearing, or refer the matter for detailed assessment.

19.5 Wasted Costs: An application for a wasted costs order must be made in writing, setting out the nature of the case upon which the application is based and the best particulars of the costs sought to be recovered. Such application must be lodged with the EAT and served upon the party(ies) sought to be charged. Further directions may be required to be given by the EAT in such cases.

19.6 Where the EAT makes any costs order it shall provide written reasons for so doing if such order is made by decision on the papers. If such order is made at a hearing, then written reasons will be provided if a request is made at the hearing or within 21 days of the seal date of the costs order. The Registrar shall send a copy of the written reasons to all the parties to the proceedings.

12.1.2 When should an application be made?

An application for costs must be made either during or at the end of a relevant hearing, or in writing to the Registrar within 14 days of the seal date of the relevant order of the EAT or, in the case of a reserved judgment, as provided for in para 2.1.4 above, copied to all parties.

12.1.3 What should be in the application?

- The legal ground on which the application is based.

- The facts upon which it is based.

- How the costs which are being claimed have been incurred (usually by way of a Schedule of costs).

If the party against whom the order is sought wishes the EAT to consider their means, they should serve a witness statement with relevant exhibits on the other party and lodge this with the EAT.

The EAT will then either resolve the matter on the papers or refer it to an oral hearing. In either event, further directions may be given.

12.1.4 Similarities to the employment tribunal

As in the Employment Tribunal, costs are the exception and not the rule – see *Lodwick v London Borough of Southwark*.[1]

Costs can only be awarded to a party to proceedings – *G Baxter Ltd v Quinn* and at time costs occurred – *Lowbey v Lindo*.[2]

Rule 34A(1) is similar in wording to the 2004 Employment Tribunal Rules, in that costs can be ordered if proceedings are unnecessary, improper, vexatious or misconceived, or where there is unreasonable conduct in bringing or conducting proceedings (which is expressed to include unreasonable delay). Examples of the application of these concepts in the EAT are given below.

---

[1] [2004] ICR 884.
[2] [1981] ICR 216.

12.1.5 Unnecessary, improper or vexatious proceedings

MR S EMMS v UCATT

EAT/0105/03 ZT

The hearing was of an appeal from a refusal of an Employment Tribunal chairman sitting alone to grant either a pre-hearing review and/or to strike out a Notice of Appearance.

The appeal was dismissed and an application for costs was made by the Respondent on the grounds that the proceedings fall within the category of unnecessary, improper or vexatious. When the decision was taken to commence these appeal proceedings there was already a final hearing date fixed for the tribunal claim, originally fixed for the week after the appeal hearing. next week. That was against a background where the only effect of such a review would be to require a Union to pay £500 as a deposit of carrying on with proceedings; to HHJ Ansell's mind, 'a fairly pointless exercise in any event'. On that basis, the Appellant was ordered to pay £1,000, although the Schedule of Costs indicated a total sum in excess of £2,000. The Judge added: 'I will order, however, that that sum should not be enforced until the conclusion of any Employment Tribunal proceedings and thus, at the end of the day, if he is successful then there can no doubt be as it were a counting exercise one way or the other in relation to either an award of compensation or costs.'

MR J MAGUIRE v BAE SYSTEMS (DEFENCE SYSTEMS) LTD

Appeal No UKEAT/0605/03/DA

The Employment Tribunal had dismissed claims by the Appellant that he had been constructively dismissed and that the reason for his dismissal was redundancy. The tribunal found that the cause of Mr Maguire's departure was that he had decided to take the job offered to him by Thomson. At the appeal Mr Maguire produced letters which had not been before the tribunal which revealed that Mr Maguire had indeed agreed to take his new job some 4 months before the final event which he asserted entitled him to treat himself as constructively dismissed. In those circumstances Mr Maguire's evidence to the tribunal was plainly untrue.

The Respondent made an application for costs on the grounds that the appeal was improper and vexatious and that Mr Maguire's conduct in pursuing the appeal was unreasonable. In the judgment➡

of the EAT the circumstances were such that Mr Maguire should be ordered to pay BAE's costs of the appeal. As preparation for the appeal was carried out by BAE's trade federation, they sought only counsel's fees amounting to £4,668.33.

12.1.6   Misconceived proceedings

ALLAN MCKENCHNIE OLIVER v JOHN R WEIR LTD [2006]

UKEAT 0042_05_0104

The Appellant was unsuccessful in his appeal. The Respondents subsequently lodged an application for an award of expenses under and in terms of rr 34 and 34A of the Employment Appeal Tribunal Rules 1993 and this was determined on the basis of written submissions.

At the heart of the Respondents' argument is the submission that the Claimant's appeal was bound to fail because he was seeking to interfere with the tribunal's findings in fact. They sought an award of a sum in the order of £4,000.

The view of the EAT was that the exercise of their discretion did not arise since it cannot be said that the appeal was unnecessary or misconceived. They did not agree with the Respondents' approach. The essence of the Claimant's appeal was that he sought the opportunity to seek to persuade the EAT that the tribunal's findings in fact gave rise to the conclusion that the Respondents had indicated an intention to breach the Claimant's contract of employment. He was not seeking to have different findings in fact made. Although the EAT did not, in the event, agree with the Claimant that did not mean that the lodgement and pursuit of his appeal was misconceived.

In relation to the discretion, the EAT said:

> '... the discretion exists against a background of a practice whereby the awarding of expenses is not the rule and there being no rule in the Employment Appeal Tribunal that expenses follows success.'

12.1.7   Unreasonable conduct

HAQUE v GREEN

Appeal No UKEAT/0616/06/LA, UKEAT/0202/07/LA, UKEAT/0284/07/LA

The appeals were about the strike out of proceedings and an award of costs in a case arising from an allegation of race discrimination by the Claimant who was dismissed for her racist abuse of others. She made allegations of bias by 'the Jewdiciary' for upholding the decision of her manager whom she condemned as a 'Coconut – brown but white beneath the skin'. The Claimant had been warned in directions that there would be a cost implication if she pursued a claim of bias and it was unsubstantiated. She pursued it and the claim failed.

The Claimant says she had a genuine belief in her case of discrimination, which has not been heard. She alleged that the EAT showed the same bias as the Employment Tribunal Judges and that they were simply repeating their bias, for there was a history of tribunals killing off merits hearings in race discrimination claims. She also contended that it would be wrong to order costs to be paid by her because the Respondent was at a preliminary hearing and it would not normally attend.

In the judgment of the EAT, the application for costs was properly made. The Claimant had been warned by Judges about bringing allegations of bias which failed, by a long way. They had no substance whatever and did not survive even a Preliminary Hearing. The EAT felt that she should have considered what the chairman in each case said, and taken advice upon it; or alternatively have recognised how hopeless her contention was once warned by EAT Judges. She obviously did not, for she continued to refuse to believe that there was no bias and indeed made the allegation against the EAT to the same extent.

The EAT considered her means and held that it would not be right to award all of the costs which were sought by the Respondent for they related to the preparation of documents for the purposes of responding to Notices of Appeal and to a preliminary hearing. They held that it was right that that counsel attended and awarded his brief fee of £2,000 since it is focussed on the failed allegations of bias.

MONFORT INTERNATIONAL PLC v MR T A MCKENZIE

UKEAT/0155/06/LA

The appeal (by the original Respondent) was on the ground that a member of the original Employment Tribunal panel had fallen ill when the case had gone part heard. The Regional chairman had appointed new member for remedies hearing without consultation but the Employment Judge had given the parties the opportunity to object and none did. As the Judge had given the parties an opportunity to object, it was misconceived to appeal on the basis of the constitution of the tribunal. As an alternative argument, the Respondent claimed that it was unreasonable conduct not to respond to an offer made after the tribunal hearing to settle for the amount of the original tribunal award. The matter could have been settled then and it would have been unnecessary to proceed to the EAT hearing.

The EAT accepted the alternative submission. They did not think it right to say that the appeal was improper, vexatious or misconceived but they did consider that the wording of Rule 34(A)(1) contemplated separate consideration where there had been unreasonable conduct.

They ordered the Appellant to pay the Respondent's costs of Counsel's fees of £1,700, disbursements in the form of solicitor's travel costs for the hearing at £171 and time at five hours at £152 per hour, totalling £2,631.70 plus VAT.

It is not unreasonable conduct to threaten a costs application.

MR G READ v THE MEMBERS OF THE LLANYRAFON COMMUNITY ASSOCIATION

UKEAT/0530/05/CK

The Appeal was allowed and following the judgment of the EAT the Claimant made an application for costs in the appeal. He claimed that the Respondent had been guilty of unreasonable conduct in the conduct of these proceedings. The basis for that proposition was an e-mail which was sent to the Claimant's solicitors from those acting for the Respondent which stated:

> 'Upon reading your skeleton argument, counsel has asked us to write to you inviting you to withdraw the appeal, failing which we will be applying for costs at the hearing ...'

➡

HHJ Peter Clark rejected the submission and said:

> 'It seems to us that it is commonplace for parties to adopt the posture that their case is incontrovertible and, that if the opponent proceeds to trial, then there will be an application for costs, whether it has very much affect I doubt. It certainly did not in this case ... In our judgment the expression 'unreasonable conduct' does not begin to envisage the sort of comment that appeared in that e-mail communication.'

It is also not unreasonable conduct if a party is seeking to uphold a decision of the tribunal below – *Kapadia v London Borough of Lambeth*.[3] In the EAT, the application for costs by the Council was rejected on grounds that 'it cannot be said that in seeking to hold a decision of the tribunal below the [employer] has acted unreasonably in conducting these proceedings'.

The rules also give specific examples when costs orders may be made. Rule 34(2) identifies these as cases where a party:

- has not complied with EAT direction;

- has amended a notice of appeal, answer or cross-appeal;

- has caused an adjournment.

Some examples of cases in which these failures have resulted (or not) in a costs order are set out below.

DR S M VAEZI-NEJAD v UNIVERSITY OF GREENWICH

EAT/1114/02/RN

In the Court's judgment, the manner in which the Appeal had been conducted from the time of its inception until the hearing, and in particular the 'flagrant' failure to get a draft and amended Notice of Appeal to the tribunal for the date fixed was such that a de-barring order should properly be made. The Respondent sought an order for costs.

The EAT judgment was:

> '... in the opinion of the Court, notwithstanding that the EAT does not follow the usual practice in other Courts of costs following event, there had been conduct which, in their judgment does mean that the Appellant should pay some part of the Respondent's costs.'   ➡

---

3   [2000] IRLR 14, CA.

A limited costs order was made on that basis that:

> '... justice would be done in this case if the Appellant is ordered to pay the Respondent's costs of attending today's Hearing, such costs to be subject to detailed assessment if not agreed.'

ASHLEY V CITY HOLDINGS

Appeal No EAT/0129/07/CEA

An application for costs was made against the Respondent. HHJ Burke, sitting alone at the EAT, came to the conclusion that there has been unreasonable conduct in the case on Peninsula's part to a limited extent. There was also a failure to comply with directions, a failure to deal with a request for co-operation in agreeing the bundle and a failure to comply with the direction in relation to a skeleton argument, which were failures to comply with a clear direction.

The explanation for delay was that the person with conduct of the matter was very busy. HHJ Burke said, 'I am afraid will not do' and accordingly, the door to a discretionary costs order, as set out in r 34(a)(1) of the EAT Rules opened.

In relation to the amount, a very detailed schedule had been prepared. HHJ Burke said:

> 'What I do not want is to spend a lot of court time going line-by-line through the schedule. If I have to, I will, but it will not please me very much, as the parties I am sure will readily understand, but I will do what I have to do. It may be that the best course is for (the parties) to sit down and go through the schedule and see what can be worked out. If nothing sensible can be worked then I will have to decide whether to hear some kind of assessment of these costs later today, or whether it should be heard by a district judge in the county court.'

The parties managed to agree a figure.

SMART INTERIORS CONTRACTORS LTD v MR P THOMAS

Appeal No UKEAT/0477/06/JOJ

In the Employment Tribunal, the Chairman refused an application for costs on a strike out application and the Respondent appealed that order. The appeal succeeded in the EAT. The Respondent made an application for the costs of the EAT proceedings. The Claimant had failed to put in a Respondent's answer and was therefore is in breach of the orders made the EAT and the Practice Direction.➡

Nevertheless he had submitted late a letter which was to be taken into account when considering the question of costs. HHJ McMullen refused the application and said:

> 'Simply being in breach of an order to produce a Respondent's Answer puts the Respondent at risk in the EAT proceedings. But as of (the date of his letter) there was a fully constituted answer ... I do not consider the circumstances here cross the threshold for such unreasonable conduct as would justify an award of costs in the EAT.'

WOLVERHAMPTON VOLUNTEER BUREAU SERVICES V MR A P CLARKSON

EAT/0414/02/SMCosts

At the full hearing there was no appearance for the Appellant. The EAT dismissed the appeal for non prosecution and lack of merit. The Respondent applied for the costs of the appeal in the absence of the Appellant and written submissions were ordered. In the judgment of Judge Birtles, the conduct of the case amounted to unreasonable conduct in conducting the proceedings as defined by r 34(1). That unreasonable conduct fell into two parts. First, in relation to the allegations of bias and fair procedure at the Employment Tribunal hearing, no evidence whatsoever had been put forward by the Appellant at any time to support these allegations and the failure to do so suggested that these allegations were made in bad faith. Second, the Appellant had: (1) failed to file a bundle of documents for use; (2) failed to file a skeleton argument at all; and (3) failed to attend or arrange representation at the appeal hearing. The EAT had been only notified the day before the hearing that there would be no representation or presence and the reason given was that the Appellant's witness had a doctor's appointment. The application was made for an adjournment and no alternative representation was obtained if that was refused. The Appellant was a limited company with resources and so it could easily have arranged for legal representation even on short notice. The appeal to be argued were not complex. Therefore an order for the costs of the appeal amounting to £1,292 were ordered to be paid within 28 days.

12.1.8   Differences from the employment tribunal

Only EAT proceedings are considered

Rule 34A(1) refers to 'any proceedings' and it has been argued that this includes prior proceedings in the Employment Tribunal. However, the EAT in *Somjee v North West Regional Health Authority (1) & Sefton*

Health Authority (2)[4] made it clear that only EAT proceedings are to be considered and not those in the Employment Tribunal.

MISS S SOMJEE v NORTH WEST REGIONAL HEALTH AUTHORITY (1) SEFTON HEALTH AUTHORITY (2) [1997] UKEAT 87_90_1804

An application for costs was made by the North West Regional Health Authority, the Respondent to four unsuccessful appeals brought from the Employment Tribunal to the EAT by Somjee. The grounds for seeking costs were that the appeals were unnecessary, improper and/or vexatious and that her conduct was unreasonable in the bringing and conduct of the appeals.

In his judgment Mummery J was of the view that it is only relevant to take into account the proceedings in the Appeal Tribunal and that it is not necessary to repeat the account in the handed down judgments on these appeals of the long history of the matter in the Employment Tribunal. He said:

> '... what happened in the (Employment) Tribunal is a matter for application for costs to that tribunal, not to this tribunal.'

12.1.9 Where appeals are withdrawn, the EAT will not order costs

---

DAVID MACLAINE v AD PARTNERS LTD

Appeal No EAT/447/99

On the morning of the appeal hearing, the Appellant withdrew three of his four grounds of appeal and, the fourth ground having been dismissed, the Respondent applied for costs on the basis that they had been put to unnecessary expense of preparation.

Lord Johnstone said that he had:

> '... it is our opinion that the entitlement to expenses under the Rule should be used very sparingly and normally having regard to the general flavour of the various heads within the Rule, to reflect conduct by a party beyond what might be described as the due process of conducting an appeal, ie the lodging of the grounds of appeal and the subsequent sustaining or abandoning if the case may be. It has never been the practice of this Tribunal to order the expenses when an appeal is withdrawn in favour of the party thus succeeding and it seems to us in the present case that the withdrawal of 3 of the 4 grounds of appeal is merely another example of that same facet. ➡

---

4   UKEAT 87_90_1804.

> Public policy, in our opinion, dictates there should be no impediment to a party seeking to gain access to this Tribunal based on a fear that an unsuccessful appeal *per se* may result in an award of expenses. The Rule is more designed in our opinion to act as a sanction against general unreasonable conduct surrounding the whole circumstances of the case rather than the way in which it is particularly presented.'

12.1.10   The role of the sift/preliminary hearing

In the EAT there is a preliminary process to go through; this used to be a preliminary hearing. Now every appeal that comes forward is sifted by a Judge. Some cases go straight through to a full hearing and some are the subject matter of a preliminary hearing. When there is a preliminary hearing, there is sometimes, depending upon the precise order made, an obligation on the Respondent to put in submissions setting out concisely why the appeal should not go forward, but more usually simply an opportunity for the Respondent to do so; but at least on a preliminary hearing there is now the opportunity for consideration and for knocking out an appeal with the benefit of the Respondent's having put forward a case.

Where case goes straight through to a full hearing on a sift, then there will have been no opportunity for the Respondent to have made any such input. For that reason, the EAT has rejected the suggestion that there ought to be any practice which says that where a case has gone through the sift, (or indeed for that matter gone through an ex parte preliminary hearing) costs would only be awarded in exceptional or extraordinary circumstances.

> **ISTC v ASW LTD (IN LIQUIDATION) EAT**
>
> **UKEAT/0452/04/SM**
>
> Although the claim had no reasonable prospect of success and was dismissed, the Claimant did not act unreasonably in bringing or continuing it. But the suggestion of a practice at the EAT that costs would not be awarded where the appeal survived the sift or a Preliminary Hearing were scotched (and thus dicta by Judge Clark in *Cootes v John Lewis plc*[5] was disapproved. He had said that it is generally not the practice of the Employment Appeal Tribunal to award costs in circumstances where the appeal has survived effectively a preliminary stage. The EAT said that this was no longer the practice, and 'indeed it may well be that that would be an impermissible trammel of the power of the Employment Appeal Tribunal to award costs under Rule 34' (Burton J, para 4).

---

[5]   27 February 2001 (unreported).

12.1.11   Quantifying costs

The amount of a costs or expenses order is set out in r 34B and follows the same wording as in the Employment Tribunal, with the important exception that unlike the limit of £10,000 in r 41.1(a), there is no upper limit in the EAT.

The amount of a costs or expenses order

34B.—(1) Subject to sub-paragraphs (2) and (3) the amount of a costs order against the paying party can be determined in the following ways –

(a)   the Appeal Tribunal may specify the sum which the paying party must pay to the receiving party;

(b)   the parties may agree on a sum to be paid by the paying party to the receiving party and if they do so the costs order shall be for the sum agreed; or

(c)   the Appeal Tribunal may order the paying party to pay the receiving party the whole or a specified part of the costs of the receiving party with the amount to be paid being determined by way of detailed assessment in the High Court in accordance with the Civil Procedure Rules 1998 or in Scotland the Appeal Tribunal may direct that it be taxed by the Auditor of the Court of Session, from whose decision an appeal shall lie to a judge.

(2) The Appeal Tribunal may have regard to the paying party's ability to pay when considering the amount of a costs order.

(3) The costs of an assisted person in England and Wales shall be determined by detailed assessment in accordance with the Civil Procedure Rules.

The EAT can order delay in enforcement of any award – see *Semms v UCATT*.[6]

The EAT may make an order for partial costs. This is provided for in r 34B(1)(c) and also in para 19.3 of the EAT Practice Direction which also provides for an order for partial costs. This position was confirmed by the EAT in *The Home Office v Mrs A Bailey & Ors (1) Mrs J Martin & Others (2) Mrs A Beachcroft & Others (3)*.[7]

12.1.12   Litigants in person

Rule 34D provides for payments to be made in favour of a party who is a litigant in person, in the same way as preparation time orders can be made in the Employment Tribunal. Rule 34D limits the costs ordered (except in the case of a disbursement) two-thirds of the amount which would have been allowed if the litigant in person had been represented by a qualified legal representative.

---

[6]   EAT/0105/03 ZT.
[7]   UKEAT/0706/04/SM & UKEAT/0140/05/SM.

Costs allowed are costs for work and disbursements which would have been allowed had the litigant in person been legally represented, as well as payments reasonably made by him for legal services relating to the proceedings, fees and expenses in relation to experts and other expenses incurred in conducting the proceedings (r 34(3)).

If the litigant in person can prove that they have suffered financial loss as a result of carrying out the work, they can be awarded that amount. If not, they are entitled to an hourly rate (currently £26) for each hour the EAT considers they have reasonably spent on the work.

Litigants in person and party litigants

34D.—(1) This rule applies where the Appeal Tribunal makes a costs order in favour of a party who is a litigant in person.

(2) The costs allowed under this rule must not exceed, except in the case of a disbursement, two-thirds of the amount which would have been allowed if the litigant in person had been represented by a legal representative.

(3) The litigant in person shall be allowed –

    (a)   costs for the same categories of –
        (i)   work; and
        (ii)   disbursements,

which would have been allowed if the work had been done or the disbursements had been made by a legal representative on the litigant in person's behalf;

    (b)   the payments reasonably made by him for legal services relating to the conduct of the proceedings;

    (c)   the costs of obtaining expert assistance in assessing the costs claim; and

    (d)   other expenses incurred by him in relation to the proceedings.

(4) The amount of costs to be allowed to the litigant in person for any item of work claimed shall be –

    (a)   where the litigant in person can prove financial loss, the amount that he can prove he had lost for the time reasonably spent on doing the work; or

    (b)   where the litigant in person cannot prove financial loss, an amount for the time which the Tribunal considers reasonably spent on doing the work at the rate of £25.00 per hour;

(6) A litigant in person who is allowed costs for attending at court to conduct his case is not entitled to a witness allowance in respect of such attendance in addition to those costs.

12.1.13   Effect of legal advice

With legal representation

In *Stannard & Co (1969) Ltd v Wilson*,[8] the EAT held that the fact that legal advice has been taken was a relevant but not decisive factor in considering whether an appellant's conduct was unreasonable but it does not automatically mean that it is reasonable to bring a case.

STANNARD & CO (1969) LTD v WILSON

[1983] ICR 86, EAT

The employers sought legal advice on whether to appeal from an Employment Tribunal's finding of unfair dismissal and were advised that they had an even chance of succeeding. The appeal was dismissed on the ground that it raised no point of law, and the employee applied for an order for costs and was awarded these on the ground that there had been unreasonable conduct in bringing the appeal.

The employers applied for a review on the grounds that the Appeal Tribunal had no discretion under the rules to award costs against the employers and, alternatively, that in exercising their discretion the Appeal Tribunal ought to have taken account of the fact that the appeal had been brought following the advice of solicitors and counsel.

Held, refusing the application, that the fact that legal advice had been taken was a relevant but not decisive factor in considering whether an appellant's conduct was unreasonable, and that, having regard to the nature of the advice and the circumstances of the case, the employers' conduct in bringing the appeal was unreasonable and the order for costs would be confirmed.

12.1.14   *Without legal representation*

MS M JONES v ROTHERHAM METROPOLITAN BOROUGH COUNCIL & OTHERS

UKEAT/0441/04/MAA

The Claimant appealed the decision of the Employment Tribunal in which the tribunal ordered him to pay over £4,000, in costs. His appeal was dismissed and the Respondent sought the costs of this➡

---

8   [1983] ICR 86.

appeal. The EAT did not criticise them for so doing, pointing out that the language used by the Claimant's unqualified representative had been:

> '... intemperate and ill-considered. For the cost of a postage stamp our Tribunal system allows people to make allegations against others. That is a right; but rights can be abused. It can cause great pain ...'

Having said that, they did not attach the criticism they would attach to him if he was acting in a professional capacity rather than acting for a friend. In the 'interests of humanity' the discretion was exercised and they did not award costs.

12.1.15   Wasted costs order

As in the Employment Tribunal, since the 2004 amendment, the EAT has been able to make a wasted costs order against a party's representative. With the exception that r 48(5) is omitted, the wording in r 34C follows that of r 48.

Personal liability of representatives for costs

34C.—(1) The Appeal Tribunal may make a wasted costs order against a party's representative.

(2) In a wasted costs order the Appeal Tribunal may disallow or order the representative of a party to meet the whole or part of any wasted costs of any party, including an order that the representative repay to his client any costs which have already been paid.

(3) "Wasted costs" means any costs incurred by a party (including the representative's own client and any party who does not have a legal representative) –

    (a)   as a result of any improper, unreasonable or negligent act or omission on the part of any representative; or

    (b)   which, in the light of any such act or omission occurring after they were incurred, the Appeal Tribunal considers it reasonable to expect that party to pay.

(4) In this rule "representative" means a party's legal or other representative or any employee of such representative, but it does not include a representative who is not acting in pursuit of profit with regard to the proceedings. A person is considered to be acting in pursuit of profit if he is acting on a conditional fee arrangement.

(5) Before making a wasted costs order, the Appeal Tribunal shall give the representative a reasonable opportunity to make oral or written representations as to reasons why such an order should not be made. The Appeal Tribunal may also have regard to the representative's ability to pay when considering whether it shall make a wasted costs order or how much that order should be.

(6)   When the Appeal Tribunal makes a wasted costs order, it must specify in the order the amount to be disallowed or paid.

(7) The Registrar shall inform the representative's client in writing –

(a)   of any proceedings under this rule; or
(b)   of any order made under this rule against the party's representative.

(8) Where the Appeal Tribunal makes a wasted costs order it shall provide written reasons for doing so if a request is made for written reasons within 21 days of the date of the wasted costs order. The Registrar shall send a copy of the written reasons to all parties to the proceedings.

12.2   COURT OF APPEAL AND SUPREME COURT

We deal with the approach of the civil courts in the following chapter. The principles and method of assessment are considered in detail there and readers are referred to that chapter.

However, one important question arises on appeals from the EAT to the Court of Appeal. Should the Court of Appeal follow its ordinary practice of awarding costs to follow the event, or should it take a more relaxed view, recognising that employment appeals which have worked their way through the (largely) non-costs bearing regime of the Employment Tribunal and EAT fall into a different category.

Until very recently, there was no doubt: if a case is heard in the Court of Appeal, normal civil costs rules applies and the overwhelming likelihood is that the loser will pay the winner's costs.

However, in an intriguing (and, in the authors' experience, one-off) case in November 2009, the Court of Appeal suggested otherwise. In a supplemental four-paragraph judgment in *St Alban's Girls' School v Neary*,[9] Smith LJ stated:

'1.   Following our judgment in which we allowed the appeal of St Albans, there was an application for costs to follow the event. Mr Neary opposed that application, arguing that, in the particular circumstances of the case, there should be no order as to costs. We considered written submissions from both parties. We recognised that, in the Court of Appeal, it is usual for costs to follow the event. Nonetheless, we have decided to make no order for costs in this case for the following reasons.

2.   Mr Neary began proceedings in a cost-free jurisdiction. He lost. On the state of authority in the EAT, he was justified in bringing an appeal. Again, he was in a cost-free jurisdiction. He won. Because St Albans (reasonably) wished to overturn that line of authority, the case came to the Court of Appeal. There Mr Neary was pitched against his will into a cost-bearing jurisdiction. It would have

---

9   [2009] EWCA Civ 1214.

been very hard on him if he had had to cave in so as to avoid the risk
of costs. In the event he lost but only because St Albans was able to
persuade us that the line of EAT authority had developed wrongly.

3.   We accept that conduct can be relevant to an order for costs but we
      consider that it is only conduct which affects costs which should be
      taken into account. Mr Neary's bad conduct has had no effect on
      costs.

4.   We accept that Mr Neary is impecunious. It would be unrealistic to
      make a substantial order against him in that we foresee that a
      disproportionate amount of time and money would have to be
      expended in order to enforce it.'

It is important to note that, in this case, previously binding EAT authority
was overturned and the parties had had no choice but to go to the Court
of Appeal. It will be easy for subsequent divisions of the Court of Appeal
to distinguish the majority of appeals to it on that basis alone. The
authors' view is that this case should be regarded as a one-off and is
unlikely to be followed.

12.3   EUROPEAN COURT OF JUSTICE

The rules on costs in proceedings before the European Court of Justice
(ECJ) are covered in the ECJ Rules of Procedure, Arts 69–75. These are
explained briefly below. The rules for the Court of First Instance are not
set out here but these essentially mirror the ECJ rules and can be found in
the CFI Rules of Procedure, Arts 87–97.

12.3.1   Direct action

The general rules about costs in cases of direct action in the ECJ are
found in Art 69:

Article 69

1.   A decision as to costs shall be given in the final judgment or in the
order which closes the proceedings.

2. The unsuccessful party shall be ordered to pay the costs if they have been
applied for in the successful party's pleadings. Where there are several
unsuccessful parties the Court shall decide how the costs are to be shared.

3. Where each party succeeds on some and fails on other heads, or where
the circumstances are exceptional, the Court may order that the costs be
shared or that the parties bear their own costs. The Court may order a
party, even if successful, to pay costs which the Court considers that party
to have unreasonably or vexatiously caused the opposite party to incur.

4. The Member States and institutions which intervene in the proceedings
shall bear their own costs. The States, other than the Member States, which
are parties to the EEA agreement, and also the EFTA Surveillance
Authority, shall bear their own costs if they intervene in the proceedings.

The Court may order an intervener other than those mentioned in the preceding subparagraphs to bear his own costs.

5. A party who discontinues or withdraws from proceedings shall be ordered to pay the costs if they have been applied for in the other party's observations on the 36 discontinuance. However, upon application by the party who discontinues or withdraws from proceedings, the costs shall be borne by the other party if this appears justified by the conduct of that party.

Where the parties have come to an agreement on costs, the decision as to costs shall be in accordance with that agreement. If costs are not claimed, the parties shall bear their own costs.

6. Where a case does not proceed to judgment the costs shall be in the discretion of the Court.

12.3.1.1   *Where is the order found?*

Article 63 requires a decision to be made about costs in each case and Art 69(1) provides that a decision as to costs shall be given in the final judgment or in the order which closes the proceedings. Where a case does not proceed to judgment the costs shall be in the discretion of the Court. Where the Court omits to give a decision on a specific head of claim or on costs, any party may within a month after service of the judgment apply to the Court to supplement its decision (Art 67).

12.3.1.2   *What costs are recoverable?*

Court fees

Article 72

Proceedings before the Court shall be free of charge, except that:

- (a)   where a party has caused the Court to incur avoidable costs the Court may, after hearing the Advocate General, order that party to refund them;
- (b)   where copying or translation work is carried out at the request of a party, the cost shall, in so far as the Registrar considers it excessive, be paid for by that party on the scale of charges referred to in Article 16(5) of these Rules.

In principle therefore, proceedings before the ECJ are free of charge and there are no court fees for proceedings. However, where there are excessive or avoidable costs incurred by either court (eg excessive translation or copying charges), a party may be ordered to reimburse the Court.

Other fees

Article 73

Without prejudice to the preceding Article, the following shall be regarded as recoverable costs:

(a)   sums payable to witnesses and experts under Article 51 of these Rules;

(b)   expenses necessarily incurred by the parties for the purpose of the proceedings, in particular the travel and subsistence expenses and the remuneration of agents, advisers or lawyers

The type of costs recoverable under Art 73 specifically includes witnesses' expenses, travel and subsistence expenses and the costs of obtaining legal and other advice. The costs must be related to the judicial proceedings and so pre-litigation costs, such as the administrative investigation into a purported infringement of competition law, cannot be recovered. In *Hake v Commission*,[10] the Court confirmed that the word, 'proceedings' used in Art 73 only refers to proceedings before the court and does not include any prior stage.

Article 73(b) refers to costs 'necessarily' incurred. In ECJ, *DEP Mulder and others v Council and Commission*,[11] the parties were required by the Court to agree the amount of damages and the issue was whether or not the legal costs incurred in respect of those negotiations themselves were 'necessary'. They were held to be necessarily incurred and so were recoverable.

VAT paid by a VAT taxable person on lawyers' and experts' fees is not viewed as a cost and so are not recoverable.

The Court is not bound by national scales of lawyers' fees and rates of 210 and 400 Euros per hour have been deemed acceptable in some cases (*Thomae v Commission*[12] and *Schneider Electric v Commission*[13] respectively).

12.3.1.3   *How can costs be recovered?*

Article 74

1. If there is a dispute concerning the costs to be recovered, the formation of the Court to which the case has been referred shall, on application by the party concerned and after hearing the opposite party and the Advocate General, make an order.

2. The parties may, for the purposes of enforcement, apply for an authenticated copy of the order.

If the parties cannot agree the amount of recoverable costs, the interested party can apply to the particular Chamber which has heard the case for an order on the amount of the costs (as opposed to an application for a review of the costs order itself). An order will then be made after the

---

[10]   Case 75/69 (1970) ECR 901.
[11]   Case C-104/89 (2004) ECR 1-1.
[12]   Case T-123/00 DEP.
[13]   Case T-77/02 DEP.

other party and the Advocate General have had the opportunity to make representations. There is no right to appeal that order. If the dispute is about the amount of legal fees, the Court will only rule on the extent to which they are recoverable and to do this, it will take into account the subject matter and character of the proceedings, the importance of the dispute from the point of view of Community law, the volume of work for the lawyer and the economic importance of the case for the parties concerned.

12.3.1.4   *What currency?*

Where costs to be recovered have been incurred in a currency other than the euro or where the steps in respect of which payment is due were taken in a country of which the euro is not the currency, conversions of currency shall be made at the European Central Bank's official rates of exchange on the day of payment (Art 75(2)).

12.3.1.5   *Who pays?*

The general rule is that the unsuccessful party will pay the costs, but only if costs have been applied for in the pleadings. If they are not applied for in the proceedings, then the parties have to bear their own costs – Arts 69(2) and 69(5). This rule is generally applied e g *Commission v Italy*,[14] in which the order which was sought by the Italian Republic was for the Court to declare the Commission's action inadmissible or unfounded 'with the measures which in consequence follow'. That form of order was not regarded as a request that the applicant should be ordered to pay the costs and consequently, it was decided that the Commission and the Italian Republic would bear their own costs.

The claim for costs must be made in the initial stage of the claim – see *CICCE v Commission*,[15] in which a claim for costs made in the rejoinder was considered too late to be admissable.

There have been exceptions to this rule, for example in *NTN Toyo Bearing v Council*,[16] when Advocate General J-P Warner (at 1274) took the view that omission by a party to ask for costs under Art 69(2) does not debar the Court from awarding them under Art 69(1). Any application for costs must be made without ambiguity (*Vlachaki v Commission*[17] (judgment of 8 March 2005).

Article 69(3) gives the Court the discretion to order that costs be shared or that the parties bear their own costs (for example, where each party succeeds on some and fails on other heads of claim).

---

[14]   ECJ Case C-456/03 (2005) ECR 1-5335.
[15]   ECJ C-298/83.
[16]   ECJ Case 113/77(1979) ECR 1185.
[17]   ECJ Case T-277/03.

The Court may decide to order even a successful party to pay costs on the specific grounds under Art 69(3), being costs that the Court considers that party to have 'unreasonably or vexatiously caused the other party to incur. For example *Atlantic Container Line and Others v Commission*[18] (paras 1645-1647), the applicants were held to have substantially and needlessly added to the burden of dealing with the case and to the costs of the Defendant with their 'voluminous' application.

In *Korter v Council*[19] the Court said:

> '... it seems in fact that the occurrence and continuation of the dispute were due in part to the attitude of the council's administration, especially to the legal ambiguity which it maintained in regard to the nature, under the staff regulations, of the possible transfer ... and to its refusal to give the applicant any explanation of the reasons for its action, which were disclosed only during the proceedings before the court. Under those circumstances the applicant cannot be criticized for having brought an action in response to what he had reason to regard as arbitrary conduct on the part of the administration in relation to him.'

Accordingly, the Council were ordered to bear all the costs, including those of the applicant.

12.3.1.6   *Intervenors*

Article 69(4) provides as a general rule that the Member States and institutions which intervene in the proceedings shall bear their own costs. As a general rule, an intervenor which intervened in support of the successful party will recover its costs from the unsuccessful party. However, there is discretion in to order an intervenor to bear their own costs, even if they intervened in support of the successful party.

12.3.1.7   *Settlement and discontinuance*

Article 77

> If, before the Court has given its decision, the parties reach a settlement of their dispute and intimate to the Court the abandonment of their claims, the President shall order the case to be removed from the register and shall give a decision as to costs in accordance with Article 69(5), having regard to any proposals made by the parties on the matter. This provision shall not apply to proceedings under Articles 230 and 232 of the EC Treaty and Articles 146 and 148 of the EAEC Treaty.

---

[18]   ECJ Case T-214/98 (2003) ECR II-3275.
[19]   ECJ Case 148/79(1981) ECR 615.

Article 78

If the applicant informs the Court in writing that he wishes to discontinue the proceedings, the President shall order the case to be removed from the register and shall give a decision as to costs in accordance with Article 69(5).

If parties reach a settlement they must inform the Court and a decision will then be made on costs, taking into account the parties' proposals.

Upon discontinuance or withdrawal, normally the discontinuing or withdrawing party will be ordered to pay the costs (as long as they have been claimed). However the discontinuing or withdrawing party can apply for their costs to be paid by the other party if this appears justified. For example, where the Commission withdraws proceedings against a Member State for failure to fulfil obligations because that Member State has fulfilled the obligation, it is likely that the Member State will have to bear the costs.

12.3.1.8 Enforcement

Article 71

Costs necessarily incurred by a party in enforcing a judgment or order of the Court shall be refunded by the opposite party on the scale in force in the State where the enforcement takes place.

If a party has to enforce a judgment or order and 'necessary' costs are incurred in doing so, the scales and rates of the Member State in which the enforcement takes place will be applied.

12.3.1.9 Legal Aid

Article 76

1. A party who is wholly or in part unable to meet the costs of the proceedings may at any time apply for legal aid. The application shall be accompanied by evidence of the applicant's need of assistance, and in particular by a document from the competent authority certifying his lack of means.

2. If the application is made prior to proceedings which the applicant wishes to commence, it shall briefly state the subject of such proceedings.

The application need not be made through a lawyer.

3. The President shall designate a Judge to act as Rapporteur. The Court, on the Judge-Rapporteur's proposal and after hearing the Advocate General, shall refer the application to a formation of the Court which shall decide whether legal aid should be granted in full or in part, or whether it should be refused. That formation shall consider whether there is manifestly no cause of action. The formation of the Court shall give its decision by

way of order. Where the application for legal aid is refused in whole or in part, the order shall state the reasons for that refusal.

4. The formation of the Court may at any time, either of its own motion or on application, withdraw legal aid if the circumstances which led to its being granted alter during the proceedings.

5. Where legal aid is granted, the cashier of the Court shall advance the funds necessary to meet the expenses.

In its decision as to costs the Court may order the payment to the cashier of the Court of the whole or any part of amounts advanced as legal aid.

The Registrar shall take steps to obtain the recovery of these sums from the party ordered to pay them.

In the UK, legal aid is available if a party fulfils the criteria and this can be extended to cover proceedings before the ECJ. However, a party may also make an application directly to the ECJ for legal aid under Art 76. Any application must be supported by evidence, and it does not have to be made by a lawyer. Once received, the application will be referred to a formation of the Court, which will decide whether legal aid should be granted in full or in part or whether it should be refused. If it is granted, it is likely that the order will either specify an amount to be paid for legal fees (including disbursements), or fix a limit. The Court's cashier will pay the funds, but if an order is eventually made for recovery of costs from the other party, the Court will recover the costs.

12.3.2 Preliminary rulings

Article 104(6)

It shall be for the national court or tribunal to decide as to the costs of the reference.

In special circumstances the Court may grant, by way of legal aid, assistance for the purpose of facilitating the representation or attendance of a party.

If a national court is in any doubt about the interpretation or validity of an EU law it may, and sometimes must, ask the Court of Justice for advice, which is given in the form of a 'preliminary ruling'. Insofar as preliminary rulings are concerned, judgments contain a standard costs clause which essentially leaves the matter of costs to be decided by the referring court. Since these proceedings are a step in the action pending before the national court, the decision on costs is a matter for that court.

12.3.3 Appeals

Article 122

Where the appeal is unfounded or where the appeal is well founded and the Court itself gives final judgment in the case, the Court shall make a decision as to costs.

If the appeal is of a final decision (of the Court of First Instance), Art 122 provides that the ECJ shall make a decision on costs. There is no right to appeal only the amount of costs or the party ordered to pay them.

If an appeal is withdrawn Art 69(5) shall apply.

CHAPTER 13

COSTS IN CIVIL PROCEEDINGS

13.1 INTRODUCTION

Costs in Civil Proceedings are governed by the Senior Courts Act 1981, the Civil Procedure Rules 1998 (in particular CPR Parts 43–48 and the Costs Practice Direction) and the common law. Since the advent of the Civil Procedure Rules 1998, costs litigation has become increasingly an area of specialisation and expertise. This is particularly the case since the introduction of conditional fee agreements, where issues regarding enforceability and the correct level of success fees have taxed the appellate Courts.

Consequently, this chapter on costs in civil proceedings can only serve as an introduction to the relevant general principles, the procedure for summary and detailed assessment, practical guidance regarding the assessment of costs and enforcement of any award. Detailed consideration of the enforceability of Conditional Fee Agreements is necessarily outside the scope of this work, as are the cost implications of offers to settle in civil proceedings made pursuant to CPR Part 36. If practitioners are faced with issues regarding the enforceability of conditional fee agreements, they are well advised to have regard to specialist practitioner texts or seek advice from Counsel.

The development of costs litigation and the upward spiral in the costs of civil litigation has not escaped the concerned eyes of the Judiciary. The Master of the Rolls appointed Lord Justice Jackson to lead a fundamental review of the costs of civil litigation. The Final Report of the Review of Civil Litigation Costs was published in 2009 and below some of Lord Justice Jackson's recommendations are considered.

13.2 GENERAL PRINCIPLES

In deciding which party should pay the costs of an interim application or the whole proceedings, there are two main principles as follows:

(a) the costs payable by one party to another are at the discretion of the Court (Senior Courts Act 1981, s 51 and CPR r 44.3(1)); and

(b) the general rule is that the unsuccessful party will be ordered to pay the costs of the successful party (CPR r 44.3(2)).

13.2.1 Exercise of discretion

The discretion granted by the Senior Courts Act 1981 is wide, and the Court shall oppose any limitation being imposed on it by rigid adherence to rules or practice.[1] The Court has the power to determine by whom and to what extent the costs of an application or proceedings are to be paid. In exercising its discretion the Court is required to have regard to all the circumstances and in particular (CPR, r 44.3(4) and (5)):

(a) the extent to which the parties followed any applicable pre-action protocol;

(b) the extent to which it was reasonable for the parties to raise, pursue or contest each of the allegations or issues;

(c) the manner in which the parties pursued or defended the action or particular allegations or issues;

(d) whether the successful party exaggerated the value of the claim;

(e) whether the party was only partly successful;

(f) any payment into Court or admissible offer to settle;

Such principles are therefore intended to ensure that whilst the Court has a wide discretion as to costs, that discretion should be exercised judicially and on reasons connected with the claim.[2] In many ways such principles reinforce the overriding objective of the CPR. Thus where, for example, a party fails to adhere to the applicable pre-action protocol ((a) above) and proceedings were commenced which otherwise might have been avoided, the defaulting party may be penalised in costs for failing to co-operate to avoid litigation. Factors (b) and (e) correspond with encouraging the parties to identify at an early stage the real issues in the case and only pursue those to trial. Factor (c) covers unreasonable conduct to ensure that the parties who fail to act co-operatively are at risk of an adverse order as to costs. Exaggeration of the value of the claim may not only make it difficult for a defendant to assess the true value of the claim but also protect its position by way of a Part 36 offer and therefore reduces the likelihood of early settlement. Further an inflated claim may also result in the action being allocated to a higher value track than it otherwise may have been and therefore falling within a more lucrative

---

[1] *Aiden Shipping Co. Ltd v Interbulk Ltd* [1986] AC 965.
[2] *Donald Campbell & Co Ltd v Pollock* [1927] AC 372.

costs regime.[3] Finally where a party is only partially successful on its claim, the Court may determine that it should only recover a percentage of its costs and thereby not recover for those issues on which it failed to succeed.[4]

13.2.2 The successful party

The party that succeeds on the application or on the claim shall usually recover their costs from the unsuccessful party (ie the costs follow the event). However 'success' is always relative and some cases shall require a detailed consideration and analysis to determine which party has succeeded and the extent of that success.

The outcome of the application or claim shall normally be the starting point. In *Scherer v Counting Instruments Ltd*[5] the Court of Appeal set out the following principles:

(a) The normal rule is that costs follow the event. The party which unjustifiably brings another party to Court or causes another party to have recourse to legal proceedings should recompense that other party in costs; but

(b) Pursuant to SCA 1981, s 51 the Court has an unlimited discretion to make what order as to costs he considers justice requires.

(c) A successful party shall have a reasonable expectation of obtaining an order as to costs from the opposing party but does not have a legal right to such an order.

(d) The discretion as to costs should not be exercised arbitrarily but must be exercised judicially in accordance with established principles and the facts of the case.

(e) The discretion must be exercised with proper and relevant grounds for otherwise it shall not be exercised well.

(f) The grounds must be connected with the case and can include any matters relating to the litigation, but no further. In relation to interim applications, the grounds must be connected with the application and should not extend to the whole of proceedings.

(g) If a party invokes the jurisdiction of the Court to grant him discretionary relief and although establishing the grounds for relief is denied the same by the exercise of discretion, the opposing party

---

[3] The costs recoverable on the Smalls Claim Track, the Fast Track and the Multi Track differ.
[4] *English v Emery Reimbold and Strick Ltd* [2002] 1 WLR 2409.
[5] [1986] 1 WLR 615.

may properly be ordered to pay the costs. However where the grounds for relief are not established, it is difficult to envisage a ground upon which the opposing party could properly be ordered to pay the costs.

Of course, there shall be some circumstances where even if a party is successful the Court will not award that party their costs. Whilst there is no limitation upon the circumstances where this may occur, there are broadly four situations where this may happen.

First a successful party may not recover its costs if the situation was of their own making or arose from their own default. For example, if a party successfully applies to set aside a default judgment or for reinstatement of struck out claim, the applying party should rightly bear the costs of the application and may be required to pay the opposing parties costs.

Secondly, where a party has claimed substantial damages but has only recovered nominal damages, the successful party will normally be ordered to pay the defendant's costs.[6] However where a Claimant recovers more than nominal damages, but only a small proportion of the sum claimed, the costs will usually follow the event.

Thirdly, a party may only achieve partial success and succeed on some but not all the issues in the claim. In such circumstances the Court is unlikely to award the whole of the costs of the claim to the successful party and may instead award the costs of proving the unsuccessful issues to the losing party. The usual approach in the event of partial success is to award the successful party a percentage of its costs rather than to attempt to make a convoluted issue based costs order which shall be difficult to disentangle upon assessment.[7]

Fourthly misconduct by the successful party may result in costs not following the event (CPR r 44.3(4)(a)). In assessing whether a party is guilty of misconduct, the Court can take into account conduct before and during proceedings (including the extent to which a party complied with the pre-action protocol) as well as the manner in which a party pursued or defended the claim or a particular issue or allegation. Much shall depend on the nature of the misconduct and its consequence upon the proceedings (particularly in increasing costs or negating the possibility of settlement). Whilst misconduct may justify depriving the successful of its costs it will not always justify an award of costs in favour of the unsuccessful party.[8]

---

[6]   *Texaco Ltd v Arco Technology Inc* (1989) TLR 13 October 1989.

[7]   *English v Emery Reimbold and Strick Ltd* [2002] 1 WLR 2409.

[8]   *Scherer v Counting Instruments Ltd* [1986] 1 WLR 615.

13.3   INTERIM COSTS ORDERS

For costs to be payable by one party to another, the Court must make an order as to costs. If the Court order is silent as to costs, none are payable in respect of the application or proceedings to which the order relates (CPR r 44.13(1)).

During the course of proceedings, the Court will usually make an order as to costs determining which party shall pay the costs of any interim application or hearing. There are a number of interim costs orders which the Court can make as set out in the table below. The choice of order shall usually be determined either by which party, in the Court's view, succeeded on the application or by the circumstances giving rise to the interim application.

Interim Costs Order	Effects
Costs in the case	The party in whose favour the Court makes an order for costs at the end of the proceedings is entitled to his costs of the interim application. Case management hearings or hearings where there is no obvious successful party result in an order for costs in the case as there is neither a winner nor a loser of the application/hearing.
Claimant's costs/Claimant's costs in any event	The Defendant shall pay the Claimant's costs of the application irrespective of the outcome of the proceedings.
Defendant's costs/Defendant's costs in any event	The Claimant shall pay the Defendant's costs of the application irrespective of the outcome of the proceedings.
Claimant's costs in the case	If the Claimant is awarded his costs at the end of proceedings, he shall be entitled to recover the costs of the interim application from the Defendant. However if the Claimant is not awarded his costs at the end of proceedings, he shall have to bear his own costs of the interim application.

Interim Costs Order	Effects
Defendant's costs in the case	If the Defendant is awarded his costs at the end of proceedings, he shall be entitled to recover the costs of the interim application from the Claimant. However if the Defendant is not awarded his costs at the end of proceedings, he shall have to bear his own costs of the interim application.
Costs reserved	The Court defers the decision as to the appropriate order as to costs until a later hearing. If the Judge at the second hearing makes no specific order as to costs arising from the first hearing, the costs of the first hearing shall be costs in the case.
Costs thrown away	Where for example, due to one party's default, a judgment or order is set aside, the party in whose favour the order is made is entitled to recover the costs which have been incurred as a consequence of the other party's default. Such costs usually include: (a) The costs of preparing for and attending any hearing at which the judgment or order subsequently set aside were made. (b) The costs of preparing for and attending any hearing at which the judgment or order are set aside. (c) The costs of preparing for and attending any adjourned relevant hearing. (d) The costs of any steps taken to enforce or comply with the original order or judgment.
Costs of and occasioned by	This is the usual order as to costs where a party seeks to amend a statement of case. It entitles the other party to recover their costs of preparing for and attending any hearing seeking permission to amend and any costs incurred amending their own statement of case.

Interim Costs Order	Effects
Costs here and below	The party in whose favour the costs order is made is entitled to their costs of the appeal and also their costs of the proceedings before the lower Court.
No order as to costs/each party bear their own costs.	Each party is liable for their own costs of any interim application and have no liability to pay the other party's costs.

13.4 FINAL COST ORDERS

Pursuant to CPR r 44.3(6) there are seven variations from the usual rule that the successful party shall recover the whole of its costs from the unsuccessful party. These variations are as follows:

(a)   that a party must pay only a proportion of another party's costs;

(b)   that a party must pay a specified amount in respect of the other side's costs;

(c)   that a party must pay costs from or until a specific date only;

(d)   that a party must pay costs incurred before proceedings have begun;

(e)   that a party must pay costs relating to only certain steps taken in the proceedings;

(f)   that a party must pay costs relating only to a certain distinct part of the proceedings; and

(g)   that a party must pay interest on costs from or until a certain date, including a date before judgment.

13.5 ORDERS FOR COSTS IN CLAIMS WITH MULTIPLE DEFENDANTS

Where a Claimant issues proceedings against two or more defendants, the Claimant may only succeed against one, or not all, of the defendants. In such circumstances, if costs were to follow the event, the unsuccessful defendant(s) would have to pay the Claimant's costs, but the Claimant would have to pay costs incurred by the successful Defendant(s). However, if the Court considers that it was reasonable to bring proceedings against more than one defendant, the Court may exercise its discretion and make the following orders:

***Bullock* Order**: This is where the Claimant is ordered to pay the costs of the successful Defendant(s) and, only once paid, the Claimant can recover such costs from the unsuccessful Defendant(s) in addition to the costs incurred in respect of the claim against the unsuccessful Defendant(s) (see *Bullock v London General Omnibus Company*).[9]

***Sanderson* Order**: This is where the unsuccessful Defendant(s) must pay the costs of not only the Claimant but also pay the costs of the successful defendant(s) directly (see *Sanderson v Blyth Theatre Company*.[10] Such an order is appropriate where the Claimant is legally aided or insolvent, as it shall ensure that the successful Defendant(s) shall recover his costs.

13.6   ORDER FOR COSTS IN CLAIMS INVOLVING ADDITIONAL PARTIES

In claims involving additional parties pursuant to CPR Part 20, the Court has the power to make such order as it thinks just. Although each case shall turn upon its facts the following guidance can usually be followed:

(a)   If the Claimant succeeds against the Defendant and the Defendant succeeds against the third party, the third party shall be liable for the Defendant's costs including the costs that the Defendant shall have to pay the Claimant.

(b)   If the Defendant has defended the Claimant's claim for his benefit, the Defendant may only be able to recover the costs of the additional claim against the third party.

(c)   The Claimant may have to pay all of the costs of the Defendant and the third party if unsuccessful on the claim and it was inevitable that the Defendant would issue an additional claim to meet the Claimant's claim.

(d)   If the Claimant is unsuccessful against the Defendant and consequently the Defendant is unsuccessful against the third party, the Claimant may not be liable for the third party's costs if the Defendant should not have issued the claim against the third party.

(e)   If the Claimant and the third party are both unsuccessful against the Defendant, it is likely that each shall have to bear the costs of the claim to which they were a party.

---

[9]   [1907] 1 KB 264, CA.
[10]   [1903] 2 KB 533, CA.

13.7 COSTS OF COUNTERCLAIMS AND SET-OFFS

It is appropriate for the Court to make separate orders for costs where the Claimant succeeds on the claim and the defendant succeeds on the counterclaim, or where both the Claimant and Defendant are unsuccessful on their respective claims (see *Medway Oil and Storage Co Ltd v Continental Contractors Ltd*[11] and *Universal Cycles plc v Grangebriar Ltd*[12]).

However, a single order for costs might be suitable where the counterclaim is a set-off or where the issues involved in the claim and counterclaim are so interwoven as to be substantially the same. In such circumstances it is likely that the Court shall make a single judgment for the balance between the claim and the counterclaim and then make a single order as to costs (see *Shell Engineering Ltd v Unit Tool and Engineering Co Ltd*).[13]

13.8 COST ORDERS AGAINST NON-PARTIES

Pursuant to s 51 of the Senior Courts Act 1981, the Court has the jurisdiction to make an order for costs against an individual who was not party to the substantive proceedings (see *Aiden Shipping v Interbulk*).[14] Such an order is referred to as a 'Non-Party Costs' order.

The Court of Appeal, in *Symphony Group v Hodgson*,[15] provided guidance as to the principles which the Court should apply in determining to exercise its discretion as to whether to make a non-party costs order. This guidance was as follows:

(a) An order for a non-party costs order will always be exceptional and should be treated with caution.

(b) Where the applicant had a cause of action against the non-party but elected not to join the non-party to the substantive proceedings, it shall be even more exceptional for a non-party costs order to be made.

(c) Even if the applicant can provide a good reason for not joining the non-party to the substantive proceedings, the applicant should forewarn the non-party at the earliest opportunity that such an order may be sought in order to enable the non-party to apply to be joined to the proceedings should he wish to.

---

[11] [1929] AC 88, HL.
[12] [2000] CPLR 42.
[13] [1950] 1 All ER 378, CA.
[14] [1986] AC 965.
[15] [1994] QB 179.

(d) An application for a non-party costs order should normally be determined by the trial judge and the fact that the trial judge may have expressed prior views on the conduct of the non-party shall not constitute bias.

(e) The normal rule of witness immunity from any form of civil action should be applied. Accordingly if the non-party against whom the order is later sought has given evidence at trial without first being joined to proceedings, the application for a non-party costs order is likely to fail.

There are now numerous examples of circumstances in which non-party costs orders have been made,[16] from which it appears that two broad themes can be identified in the exercise of the Court's discretion. First, whilst it is not necessary for the non-party to have funded the litigation, the non-party should either have effectively controlled the proceedings or sought to derive benefit from them. Secondly, where the non-party has funded the litigation, the motivation of the funder shall be highly relevant to the exercise of the Court's discretion. 'Pure Funders' (being those who fund litigation out of philanthropic or charitable motivation and whom derive no direct benefit from the litigation) shall generally be exempt from liability on the ground that such funding is often in the public interest, whereas 'Professional Funders' (being those who are contractually bound to fund the litigation) are more likely to be at risk of a non-party costs order up to the amount contributed to the unsuccessful party's litigation.[17]

Applications for non-party costs orders are made pursuant to CPR, r 48.2(1) which provides that: (a) an individual must be added as a party to the proceedings for the purposes of costs only; and (b) that an individual must be given a reasonable opportunity to attend a hearing at which the Court will consider the matter further. In practice, the application is usually made at the end of the trial or application and the Court shall adjourn for a further hearing before the same judge following the filing and service of written statements of case and responses.

---

[16] See for example *Re a Company (No 004055 of 1991)* [1991] 1 WLR 1003 where the directors of a company had improperly caused a party to incur costs in a winding-up petition, *CIBC Mellon Trust Co v Stolzenberg (No 3)* [2005] EWCA Civ 628, where a shareholder had been instrumental in commencing or defending proceedings for his own benefit.

[17] See *Hamilton v Al Fayed (No 2)* [2002] EWCA Civ 665 and *Arkin v Borchard Lins Ltd (Nos 2 & 3)* [2005] EWCA Civ 655.

13.9 COSTS ORDERS AGAINST LEGAL REPRESENTATIVES

The Court has the jurisdiction to make a 'wasted costs order' against legal representatives pursuant to s 51 of the Senior Courts Act 1981, as amended by s 4 of the Courts and Legal Services Act 1990.

'Wasted costs' are any costs incurred by a party as a result of 'improper, unreasonable or negligent act or omission' on the party of any legal representative or an employee of such representatives. 'Legal Representatives' are legal or other representatives exercising a right of audience or a right to conduct litigation on behalf of the party to proceedings.

In considering whether to make a wasted costs order, the Court must have regard to the three stage test set out in the Practice Direction to CPR r 48.7 that:

(a)   the legal representative has acted improperly, unreasonably or negligently;

(b)   his conduct has caused a party to incur unnecessary costs; and

(c)   it is just in all the circumstances to order him to compensate that party for the whole of part of those costs.

The first stage of the test requires 'improper, unreasonable or negligent' conduct. 'Improper' conduct covers, but is not confined to, conduct which would ordinarily be held to justify disbarment, striking off, suspension for practice or other serious professional penalty. It shall also cover a significant breach of a substantial duty imposed by a professional code of conduct. 'Unreasonable' conduct describes conduct which is vexatious and designed to harass the other side rather than advance resolution of the case. The test is whether the conduct permits reasonable explanation. 'Negligence' denotes the failure to act with the competence reasonably expected of an ordinary member of the profession.

The second stage of the test is concerned with causation. The applicant must show that the conduct complained of has caused the applicant to incur wasted costs. Where the conduct is proved but no waste of costs consequent upon the conduct is shown, the application shall fail.

The third and final stage of the test enables the Court to exercise its discretion having regard to the circumstances of the case in order that the Court's discretion shall not be fettered by previous decision.

An application for a costs order against a legal representative may be made orally or in accordance with the procedure set out in CPR, Part 23. Any application made in accordance with CPR, Part 23 must be supported by evidence in support setting out the alleged acts or omissions of the legal representatives which are the subject of the application. Although the Court can make a wasted costs order at any stage in the proceedings, applications are generally best left until the conclusion of the proceedings before the trial judge that determined the claim, as the judge shall be best placed to determine the application.

Generally, the Court shall determine whether to make a wasted costs order in two stages. First, the Court must be satisfied that it has evidence before it that, if unanswered, would be likely to lead to a wasted costs order being made and that the proceedings are justified. Secondly, the Court is likely to provide the legal representatives with the opportunity to make submissions as to whether a wasted costs order should be made. Accordingly, the legal representatives should not be called upon to show cause unless there is a strong prima facie case made against him. If the Court is satisfied that there is sufficient evidence, it shall usually make directions regarding the filing and serving of evidence by the legal representative to show cause.

13.10 QUANTIFICATION OF COSTS – SUMMARY ASSESSMENT AND DETAILED ASSESSMENT

Following the Court making the appropriate order as to costs, the amount of costs payable by a party to the other shall need to be quantified. This can be done either by agreement by the parties, the application of any fixed costs regime or by Court assessment. There are two processes of assessment, summary assessment and detailed assessment. A summary assessment occurs immediately at the conclusion of the application or final hearing and is conducted by the Judge who heard the application or trial. A detailed assessment usually involves leaving the quantification of costs to a formal assessment hearing before a costs officer after the proceedings have concluded, (although the Court has the power to order an assessment at an earlier stage).

13.10.1 Summary assessment or detailed assessment

Whilst the Civil Procedure Rules provided guidance as to when the Court should conduct a summary or detailed assessment, it is usually at the discretion of the Court. The general rule is that the Court should make a summary assessment of costs in the circumstances set out below (CPR Pt 44, PD 7A):

(a) At the conclusion of the trial of a case which has been dealt with on the fast track, in which case the order will deal with the costs of the whole claim.

(b) At the conclusion of any other hearing, which has lasted not more than one day, in which case the order will deal with the costs of the application or matter to which the hearing related. If the hearing disposes of the claim, the order may deal with the costs of the whole claim.

However even if the hearing lasts one day or less the Court should not order a summary assessment if:

(a) the costs are payable to an infant or protected party unless the solicitor acting for the infant or protected party has waived the right to claim any further costs directly from the infant or protected party (CPR Pt 48, PD 2); or

(b) the costs are payable to a Legal Service Commission funded client (CPR r 44.17);

(c) where the receiving party has entered into a funding arrangement (such as a conditional fee agreement) the Court may assess the base costs summarily but not the additional liability (such as any success fee) until the conclusion of the proceedings or part of the proceedings to which the funding arrangement relates;

(d) there is some other good reason not to do so. For example in *R v Cardiff County Council*,[18] costs were referred for a detailed assessment where there was a substantial dispute as to the appropriate hourly rate and whether the costs claimed infringed the indemnity principle).

A detailed assessment shall be ordered when the matter is unsuitable for summary assessment. Thus a detailed assessment is likely to be ordered at the conclusion of a multi-track trial and following an interim hearing that exceeds one day.

13.10.2 General considerations

Irrespective of whether the quantification of costs shall be by the summary or detailed assessment procedure, there are three general considerations which are relevant to the quantification of costs regardless of the method of assessment. These general considerations are the indemnity principle, the basis of assessment and proportionality.

13.10.3 The indemnity principle

The indemnity principle is the principle whereby the receiving party cannot recover more from the paying party than he is liable to pay his own

---

[18] 11 June 1999 (unreported).

lawyers. This is because costs between the parties are by law as an indemnity to the person entitled to them and are not imposed as a punishment on the party who pays the costs or given as a bonus to the party who receives them.[19] Thus, if the solicitors representing the receiving party have intimated to their client that he need 'not worry' about paying their fees, there is a prospect that the Court will find that the paying party does not have any liability for costs.[20]

The signature of the legal representative on the costs schedule shall usually be sufficient to satisfy the Court that the indemnity principle has not been breached (see *Bailey v IBC Vehicles Ltd*).[21] Accordingly the signature is not a mere formality but operates as a certificate by an officer of the Court that the receiving party's solicitors are not seeking to recover for each item more than they have agreed to charge their client. However the Court does have the power to order disclosure of documents and the provision of information to determine whether the indemnity principle has not been infringed but the jurisdiction to do so shall not be too readily applied.

If the issue of whether the indemnity principle has been breached is raised, the receiving party can ask the Court to rule whether there is a genuine issue regarding the alleged infringement. If the Court finds that there is no genuine issue that is the end of the matter. However if a genuine issue is raised (or the receiving party concedes that there is a genuine issue) the Judge shall have to rule as to whether the indemnity principle has been infringed. This is likely to require the receiving party to adduce documents (such as the client care letter, the retainer, any bills sent to the client) and the Court has the power to specifically direct the documents to be adduced. The documents will, in the first instance, be produced to the Court and thereafter the Court may ask the receiving party whether they wish to adduce such documents to the paying party or rely upon other evidence (e g a witness statement) in determining the issue. The production of documents necessarily raises issue of legal professional privilege which the receiving party shall be entitled to claim.

There are three exceptions to the indemnity principle. First, the Civil Legal Aid General Regulations allow a Legal Service Commission funded party to recover costs at the full going rate from the other party. Secondly, on the Fast Track, counsel's fees are fixed according to the value of the claim (see CPR Part 46) and the fixed amount is awarded irrespective of the indemnity principle. Thirdly, where the receiving party has entered into an enforceable conditional fee agreement, it is likely that the receiving party has very little financial outlay or risk to pay the solicitors costs in any event.

---

[19] See *Harold v Smith* (1860) 5 H&N 381.
[20] See *British Waterways Board v Norman* (1993) 26 HLR 232.
[21] [1998] 3 All ER 570.

13.10.4 The basis of assessment

The general approach adopted by the Court to summary and detailed assessment should be the same. On either method of assessment, the Court should not be seen to endorse disproportionate and unreasonable costs. Accordingly the Court must determine, when making the order as to costs, whether the costs should be assessed on the standard basis or on the indemnity basis (CPR r 44.4(1)).

The Standard Basis: This is the usual basis upon which costs are assessed and shall be less generous to the receiving party than the indemnity basis. If the Court orders costs to be paid on the standard basis it will not allow costs which have been unreasonably incurred or are unreasonable in amount and will only allow costs which are proportionate to the matters in issue. Further any doubt that the Court may have as to whether costs were reasonably incurred or reasonable in amount shall be resolved in favour of the paying party not the receiving party.

The Indemnity Basis: This basis of assessment is more generous to the receiving party than the standard basis. The Court may make an order that costs are payable on the indemnity basis to reflect the misconduct of the paying party or for the failure to achieve a greater award than a Part 36 Offer (although it should be noted that there are no set rules or guidance to determine when indemnity costs must be ordered). If the Court orders costs to be paid on the indemnity basis it will not allow costs which have been unreasonably incurred or are unreasonable in amount. However, unlike the standard basis, the Court will resolve any doubt it may have as to whether the costs were reasonably incurred or were reasonable amount in favour of the receiving party not the paying party.

It should be noted that if the Court orders the costs to be paid on the standard basis, the Court must have regard to the issue of proportionality. The question of proportionality does not expressly feature in considering the amount of costs payable on the indemnity basis (although proportionality is a pervasive feature of the overriding objective of the CPR).

13.10.5 Proportionality

Once the Court has determined the appropriate order as to costs and the basis of assessment, the Judge should then be in a position to assess the costs payable. However, if the costs are to be assessed on the standard basis, the Judge must step back and consider the proportionality of the costs claimed in accordance with the guidance in *Home Office v Lownds*.[22]

---

[22] [2002] 1 WLR 2450. Whilst *Home Office v Lownds* was a decision of the Court of Appeal in relation to detailed assessment proceedings, it has been held in *Harries v Summers* (unreported) 25 April 2007 that its guidance applies equally to the summary assessment of costs.

When considering the issue of proportionality, a two-stage approach is required:

> 'There has to be a global approach and an item by item approach. The global approach will indicate whether the total sum claimed is or appears to be disproportionate having particular regard to the considerations which Part 44.5(3) states are relevant. If the costs as a whole are not disproportionate according to that test, then all that is normally required is that each item should have been reasonably incurred and that cost for each item should be reasonable. If on the other hand the costs as a whole appear disproportionate then the Court will want to be satisfied that the work in relation to each item was necessary and, if necessary, that the cost of the item is reasonable.'

The rationale behind this approach is to ensure that the paying party is only liable to the receiving party for the reasonable costs if the litigation had been conducted proportionately. Consequently, where a bill is proportionate the test is only one of reasonableness, whereas if a bill is disproportionate the more stringent test of necessity and thereafter reasonableness is applied.

The factors to be considered in determining whether a bill is proportionate or disproportionate are set out at CPR r 44.5(3) and include the conduct of the parties, the amount or value of any money or property involved, the importance of the matter to the parties and the complexity of the issues. Further guidance can also be derived from CPR Pt 44, PD 5A at paras 11.1–11.4, which include:

(a)   The relationship between the total of the costs incurred and the financial value of the claim may not be a reliable guide. A fixed percentage cannot be applied in all cases of the value of the claim in order to ascertain whether or not the costs are proportionate.

(b)   In any proceedings there will be costs which will inevitably be incurred and which are necessary for the successful conduct of the case. Solicitors are not required to conduct litigation at rates which are uneconomic. Thus in a modest claim the proportion of costs is likely to be higher than in a large claim, and may even equal or possibly exceed the amount in dispute.

(c)   Where a trial takes place, the time taken by the Court in dealing with a particular issue may not be an accurate guide to the amount of time properly spent by the legal or other representatives in preparation for the trial of that issue.

Ultimately, it is a question of the Court's judgment as to whether a bill of costs is proportionate or disproportionate. In practice the Court shall often compare the statement of costs of the receiving and paying party to determine whether the receiving party's bill is proportionate or disproportionate. Practitioners are therefore well advised to file and serve statement of costs even when it is unlikely that an order for costs shall be made in their client's favour.

If the Court finds that the bill of costs is disproportionate, the paying party shall only recover for the items that were necessarily incurred and, if necessarily incurred, reasonably incurred. It is open to the Judge to determine the threshold of 'necessity'. The threshold of 'necessity' must clearly be higher than of 'reasonableness' but the Court must seek to avoid placing too high a threshold with the benefit of hindsight. Often, the conduct of the paying party shall be relevant to the determination of necessity, as if the paying party has acted unreasonably during the proceedings this may have necessitated greater work than otherwise would have been required by the receiving party. In the latter circumstances, the paying party cannot avoid the payment of costs which he has made necessary.

Finally, even if the Court finds at the first stage (the global approach) that the bill has a whole is proportionate, this does not prohibit the Court on the second stage (the item-by-item approach) from finding individuals items to be disproportionate and therefore applying the test of necessity to them alone (see *Giambrone v JMC Holidays*).[23]

13.11   SUMMARY ASSESSMENT – PRACTICE AND PROCEDURE

13.11.1   The statement of costs

It is likely that the Court shall make a summary assessment of costs at the conclusion of a fast track trial or any interim hearing that last less than one day. As its names suggest, a summary assessment adopts a rather broad brush and rough and ready approach to the sums payable to the receiving party.

For a summary assessment to occur, it is usual for the party who intends to claim costs to prepare a statement of costs in the form of a costs schedule (CPR Pt 44). The statement of costs should follow, as closely as possible, Form N260 and should show separately:

(a)   the number of hours claimed;

(b)   the hourly rate claimed;

(c)   the grade of fee earner;

---

[23]   [2003] 2 Costs LR 189.

(d) the amount and nature of any disbursement claimed other than counsel's fee for attending the hearing.

(e) solicitor costs claimed for attending or appearing at the hearing;

(f) counsel's fees claimed in respect of the hearing; and

(g) any VAT claimed on these amounts.

The statement of costs must be signed by the party or his legal representatives to satisfy the indemnity principle. The signature should certify that '*the costs estimated above do not exceed the costs which the (party) is liable to pay in respect of the work which this estimates covers*'. However, if the litigant is an assisted person or funded by the Legal Service Commission, the certificate at the end of the form need not be included.

The statement of costs must be filed at Court and served on the party against whom an order for costs is sought not less than 24 hours prior to the hearing. If the receiving party fails to comply with the above requirements, the Court can waive the requirement for a schedule, adjourn briefly for a schedule to be prepared, direct that a summary assessment take place on a later date (but must be before the same judge) or direct a detailed assessment.

Whilst the failure to comply with the requirement of service of the costs schedule 24 hours before the hearing does not justify the Court refusing to assess costs,[24] it should be noted by practitioners that the failure to comply with these requirements without reasonable excuse can be taken into account by the Court in deciding what order to make as to costs of the claim/application, the costs of any further hearing or the costs of any detailed assessment hearing that may be necessary as a result of the failure. Practitioners are therefore well advised to ensure that costs schedule meet the requirements and are filed and served in good time.

13.11.2 Procedure

The procedure for a summary assessment of costs is straightforward. Once the Court has determined the order as to costs and the basis of assessment, the Court shall hear representations from the paying and receiving parties' representatives as to the costs incurred and thereafter make a decision. Usually, the paying party shall make submissions first, followed by the receiving party and thereafter the paying party shall have the right to reply. Should the paying party submit that the cost schedule is disproportionate on a global basis, the Court shall often determine this as a preliminary issue before going on to consider item-by-item submissions.

---

[24] See *MacDonald v Taree Holdings* (2000) *The Times*, 28 December.

This is because whether the costs schedule on a global basis is proportionate or disproportionate will determine the approach the Court takes to the item-by-item assessment (see Proportionality above).

In conducting and determining a summary assessment the Court must focus on the detail breakdown of costs actually incurred by the receiving party. Whilst the Court is entitled to draw upon its general experience and knowledge of the costs incurred in comparable applications or cases to determinate whether the costs are reasonable and disproportionate, the Court is not entitled to apply a standard judicial tariff for different claims or applications based upon that experience.[25]

In determining the final amount of costs payable much shall turn upon the detail of the submissions made by legal representatives and any evidence filed in support or before the Court (eg invoices of disbursements, the brief, size of trial bundles etc). For points to be taken by the paying party to reduce the quantum of the costs payable to the receiving party, see the section below entitled 'Challenging the Bill of Costs'.

Costs assessed summarily are payable within 14 days unless the Court directs otherwise. A party seeking a longer period for payment must apply for it and, where appropriate, any such application must be supported by evidence (CPR rr 44.3 and 44.8). However, in practice, Judges are often content to allow 21 to 28 days for payment simply at the request of the paying party. This is particularly the case where the paying party is relying upon its insurers to pay the costs, as the Court is alive to the delay that can often occur in processing payments.

13.12 DETAILED ASSESSMENT – PRACTICE AND PROCEDURE

A detailed assessment is generally conducted at the conclusion of the proceedings (CPR, r 47.1). However the Court retains the discretion to order a detailed assessment at an earlier stage. A detailed assessment of costs is likely to be ordered in proceedings on the multi-track or interim applications which last more than one day. In addition, certain proceedings are inappropriate for summary assessment so the Court shall order a detailed assessment (see section entitled Summary Assessment or Detailed Assessment above).

13.12.1 The appropriate office

All applications and requests in detailed assessment proceedings must be made or filed at the 'appropriate office' (CPR r 47.3). In the High Court claims, this is usually the Senior Court Costs Office. The District Registry

---

25   See *1-800 Flowers Inc v Phonenames Ltd* [2001] EWCA Civ 721.

or the County Court shall usually be the appropriate office, if it was Court dealing with the case which made the judgment or order giving rise to the assessment. However, any Court can direct that the Senior Court Costs Office is the appropriate office (CPR r 47.3(2)) but should only doing so having regard to the size of the bill of costs, complexity, length of hearing and costs to the parties.

13.12.2 Starting detailed assessment proceedings

The procedure for commencing detailed assessment proceedings varies depending upon whether: (a) the right to recover costs was ordered by the Court; or (b) prior to the issue of proceedings the dispute was compromised with an agreement that one side shall pay the other party's costs.

Where the Court makes a judgment, order, award or other determination giving rise to the right to recover costs, the detailed assessment proceedings must be commenced within 3 months of the date of the order (CPR r 47.7). However the period can be extended or shortened by agreement between the paying party and the receiving party. Detailed assessment proceedings are commenced by the receiving party serving on the paying party a notice of commencement (Form N252) together with a copy of the bill of costs. The receiving party must also serve copies of counsel's fee notes, expert fee invoices and written evidence for all disbursements which exceed £250 and a statement giving the name and address for service of any person upon whom the receiving party intends to serve the notice of commencement (CPR Pt 47, PD 5, section 32.3).

The above procedure for commencing detailed assessment proceedings is only applicable where formal Court proceedings have already been issued and the Court has determined such proceedings. However disputes often settle prior to the issue of proceedings with the agreement that one side shall pay the other party's costs. Should the parties be unable to agree the quantification of costs, it will be necessary for the Court to adjudicate upon the amount of costs payable. In such circumstances the receiving party will need to commence 'Costs-Only' proceedings. In commencing 'Costs-Only' proceedings there are two options available to the receiving party.

The first option is that the receiving party could commence a CPR Part 7 claim for breach of the compromise agreement and seek damages in the amount of their reasonable costs. However, there are two potential difficulties with such an approach. First, the paying party could dispute their liability as to whether: (a) any compromise agreement was reached at all; or (b) the terms of that agreement as to costs. Secondly, even if liability is not in issue and judgment is entered for the receiving party, it is arguable that the Court shall need to determine the intention of the parties on the question of the 'reasonableness' by which the receiving party's costs should be judged. Such complications are best avoided.

The second option, and it is submitted the preferred option, is for the receiving party to commence CPR Part 8 proceedings seeking an order for costs. If such an order is made, there will then be a Court order for costs which can form the basis of the detailed assessment proceedings. The CPR Part 8 procedure is specifically provided for by CPR r 44.12A. A claim form issued under CPR r 44.12A must identify the dispute giving rise to the compromise, the date and terms of the compromise agreement, the amount of costs claimed and whether the costs are claimed on the standard or indemnity basis. Further any written evidence of the agreement or confirmation of the agreement must be attached to the claim form. It is unusual for the paying party (the defendant) to oppose the claim and it should be noted that a claim is not treated as opposed simply because the paying party disputes the amount of costs. Accordingly once the date of the paying party to file an acknowledgment of service of the claim has expired, the receiving party (the Claimant) should write to the Court seeking an order for a detailed assessment. Once the Court has made the order, the three-month time limit for commencing the detailed assessment (pursuant to CPR r 47.7) shall begin to run and the receiving party should serve the notice of commencement (Form N252) and related documents, as set out above.

There may be serious repercussions if the receiving party fails to serve a notice of commencement within the 3-month time limit the repercussions. First, the paying party can apply for an order that the receiving party must file the request for an assessment within a specified period and the Court can direct that, if there is a breach of the direction, the receiving party will lose all or part of the recoverable costs (CPR r 47.8(2)). Secondly, if the receiving party applies for an assessment hearing out of time (but without the paying party making an application for a request), the Court may impose a sanction on the receiving party by disallowing or all or part of the interest allowable on the recoverable costs (CPR r 47.8(3). Thirdly if the delay in commencing the proceedings is inordinate, inexcusable and has prejudiced the paying party, it may amount to misconduct such that all or part of the costs claimed should be disallowed (CPR r 44.14).[26]

13.12.3 The bill of costs

The receiving party's bill of costs must be served with the notice of commencement (CPR r 47.5(1)). The Schedule to the Costs Practice

---

[26] See *Botham v Khan, Lamb v Khan* [2004] EWHC 2602 (QB) and *Haji-Ioannou v Frangos & Ors* [2006] EWCA Civ 1663 which have addressed whether delay in commencing assessment proceedings can amount to 'misconduct' for the purposes of CPR r 44.14 such that costs should be disallowed or whether the more lenient penalty of disallowance of interest pursuant to CPR r 47.8 is appropriate.

Direction PD 43–48 includes four model forms of the bill of costs. Regard should be had to the guidance in the Senior Court Costs Office Guide as to the appropriate contents of the bill of costs. In particular practitioners are well advised to include a narrative of background information which sets out the issues in dispute between the parties and the key milestones in the running of the claim in order. This enables the Court to be fully appraised of the complexity of the claim, the length of the claim and the necessary steps taken to bring it to resolution. With such a detailed narrative before it, the Court can make a proper determination of the proportionality and reasonableness of the costs incurred.

It must be understood that both the Court and the parties shall use the bill of costs as a working document both before and during the detailed assessment hearing. The bill of costs should therefore be user friendly such that it is recommend that the format set out below is adhered to:

(a) Each item claimed in the bill must be consecutively numbered to ease identification.

(b) The bill should be divided into five columns – the first three columns should be headed, 'Item', 'Amount Claimed', 'VAT' and populated with the relevant information by the receiving party – and the last two columns should be headed 'Amount Allowed' and 'VAT' which are to be populated at the detailed assessment hearing.

(c) The bill should be divided into two or more parts to distinguish between times when the receiving party was acting in person, represented by different sets of solicitors or to signify any increase in hourly rates with the passage of time.

(d) It is useful to for each page to have a summary of the total costs claimed on each page and for there to be sub-totals of base costs, disbursements and VAT.

13.12.4 The points of dispute and default costs certificates

The paying party can dispute any item in the bill by serving the receiving party with points of dispute. Points of dispute should be short and to the point and must:

(a) identify each item in the bill of costs which is disputed;

(b) for each item disputed state the nature and grounds of dispute;

(c) where practicable suggest a figure to be allowed for each item in respect of which a reduction or deduction is sought;

(d) be signed by the party serving them or by paying party's solicitor.

It should be noted that the paying party at the assessment hearing may raise only items specified in the points of dispute unless the Court gives permission (CPR r 47.14(7)). Accordingly the paying party should ensure that the points of dispute are fully pleaded.

Points of dispute must be served on the receiving party (and any other party served with the notice of commencement) within 21 days of service of the notice of commencement (CPR r 47.9(2)). However the parties may extend or shorten the time for service by agreement.

If the paying party fails to serve points of dispute within the 21 day, or other agreed, time limit, there are two potential consequences. First the paying party may not be heard further in the detailed assessment proceedings unless the Court grants permission (CPR r 47.9(3). Secondly the receiving party can, on filing a request (Form N254), obtain a default cost certificate (CPR rr 47.9(4) and 47.11). A default costs certificate means that all of the costs claimed in the bill of costs shall be allowed.

However a default costs certificate cannot be obtained if prior to the issue of the certificate the points of dispute are served, even if the points of dispute are out of time (CPR r 47.9(5)). Further, if a default costs certificate is obtained, the paying party can apply for it to be set aside. The Court shall set aside the default costs certificate if there is good reason to do so and the application was made promptly (CPR r 47.12). In making an application to set aside, the paying party should ensure that draft points of dispute are before the Court.

13.12.5   The reply

The receiving party can elect, but is not obliged, to serve a reply to the points of dispute (CPR r 47.13). The purpose of the reply is effectively two fold. First, it provides the opportunity to undermine and counteract the points of dispute by allowing the receiving party to respond to any arguments raised by the paying party. Secondly, it allows the issues in dispute to be narrowed, as the receiving party can accept any of the reductions proposed by the paying party or make a counter offer on any issues in dispute.

The reply can take the form of annotations to the points of dispute or can be a separate document. The reply must be served on the paying party and any other parties to the detailed assessment within 21 days of service of the points of dispute (CPR r 47.13(2)).

13.12.6   Requesting the detailed assessment hearing

Following service of the points of dispute the receiving party must, within 3 months of the date of expiry of the period for commencing the detailed assessment proceedings, file a request for an assessment hearing (CPR r 47.14).

The repercussions for failing to comply with the time limit for requesting an assessment hearing can be severe for the receiving party. First, the paying party can apply for an order that the receiving party must file the request for an assessment within a specified period and the Court can direct that, if there is a breach of the direction, the receiving party will lose all or part of the recoverable costs (CPR r 47.14(4)). Secondly, if the receiving party applies for an assessment hearing out of time (but without the paying party making an application for a request), the Court may impose a sanction on the receiving party by disallowing or all or part of the interest allowable on the recoverable costs (CPR r 47.14(5)). However it is submitted that it is unlikely that such delay shall amount to misconduct pursuant to CPR r 44.14 such that costs should be disallowed in full or in part, as there is unlikely to be any prejudice to the paying party in conducting the assessment proceedings, as the points of dispute shall have already been drafted and the battle lines drawn.

13.12.7   The detailed assessment hearing

Whilst detailed assessment hearings are usually heard in public, district judges or costs judges in private rooms normally conduct them. The hearings are generally informal and rights of audience are necessarily extended to costs lawyers and costs draftsmen, who are treated as employees of the firm of solicitors instructing them.

The Court will usually consider any matters in the points of dispute on an item-by-item basis. Accordingly the Court shall hear oral representations from the paying party and the receiving party as to why the item should be allowed or disallowed, consider any evidence before it and give an oral decision on that item. The evidence before the Court shall include the receiving party's papers which are filed at Court prior to the assessment hearing.

The primary question for the Court to determine is whether the costs were reasonably incurred or were reasonable and proportionate in amount. In determining such issues, the Court shall have regard to all the circumstances and in particular the matters set out at CPR r 44.5(3). These are:

(a)   the conduct of the parties before, as well as, during the proceedings. This includes the efforts made to resolve the dispute;

(b)   the amount or value of money or property involved;

(c)   the importance of the matter to all the parties;

(d)   the complexity, difficulty or novelty of questions raised by the dispute;

(e)   the skill, effort, specialised knowledge and responsibility involved;

(f)   the time spent on the case; and

(g)   the place where and circumstances in which the work or any part of it was done.

Whilst perhaps an oversimplification, it would be fair to say that the Court needs to determine to what extent the work undertaken advanced the case and whether the time spent on that work was reasonable or proportionate. For points to be taken by the paying party to reduce the quantum of the costs payable to the receiving party, see **13.14.**

Once each item has been determined and adjudicated upon, the Court shall calculate the sum due and owing and a Final Costs Certificate shall be drawn in the relevant amount (CPR r 47.16).

13.12.8   Costs of the detailed assessment hearing

Pursuant to CPR r 47.18, the general rule is that the paying party must also pay the receiving party's costs of the detailed assessment proceedings. The costs of the detailed assessment are usually summarily assessed and then added to the final bill of costs payable. The receiving party does not have to provide a costs schedule of the costs of the detailed assessment in advance of the hearing unless the Court orders otherwise. In summarily assessing the costs, the Court may have regard to all the circumstances including the conduct of the parties, the amount (if any) by which the bill of costs is reduced and whether it was reasonable for particular items to appear in the bill or particular objections to be taken (CPR r 47.18).

Both the paying party and the receiving party can seek to protect their exposure to the costs of the detailed assessment proceedings by making an offer in writing to settle the costs in dispute pursuant to CPR r 47.19. The offer should be expressed to be 'without prejudice save as to the costs of the detailed assessment proceedings'. The offer should specify whether or not it is intended to be inclusive of the costs of preparation of the bill, interest and VAT in order that the terms of the offer are clear. If the offer is silent on whether it includes such items, the offer shall be taken to be inclusive of all these items (CPR Pt 47, PD 19A, Section 46.3).

Whilst there is no provision in the rules mandating the offeror to specify a date by which the offer should be made or accepted, the rules are intended to encourage early settlement. Accordingly an offer made by the paying party should usually be within 14 days of the date of service of the notice of commencement and an offer by the receiving party should usually be within 14 days of the date of service of the points of dispute (CPR Pt 47, PD 19A, Section 46). Offers made after these dates are likely to be given less weight by the Court in deciding what order as to costs to make unless there is good reason for the offer not being made until a later date (CPR Pt 47, PD 19A, Section 46.1).

The amount of the offer should not be communicated to the costs officer until the bill of costs has been assessed, following which the offer may be taken into account in deciding who should pay the costs of the assessment proceedings. It should be noted that the offer will only be 'taken into account' in deciding which party should pay the costs of the detailed assessment proceedings and shall not be determinative (CPR r 47.19(1)(b)). Consequently even if the receiving party recovers equal to, or less than, the paying party's offer, this does not necessarily mean that the receiving party shall be liable for the costs of the detailed assessment proceedings.[27] However, it is submitted that in such circumstances it would be unusual for the receiving party not to be liable for the paying party's costs of the assessment proceedings from the date of service of the offer.

In the event that an offer is accepted, an application should be made to the Court for a certificate in the agreed terms. Alternatively the bill may be withdrawn in accordance with the procedure when costs are agreed (CPR r 47, PD 19A, Section 46.3 and CPR r 47.10).

13.13   FINAL COSTS CERTIFICATE, INTEREST AND THE RIGHT TO APPEAL

Within 14 days of the conclusion of the detailed assessment hearing, the receiving party must file at Court a completed bill of costs to show the amount due following the detailed assessment. Upon receipt of the same the Court will issue a final costs certificate and serve it upon the parties to the detailed assessment hearing. The final costs certificate will include an order for the paying party to pay the costs to which it relates (see CPR r 47.16).

Interest on the costs of the claim normally runs for the date of the judgment or order disposing of the claim (see CPR rr 40.8 and 44.3(6)(g)). The final costs certificate shall not include this interest,

---

[27]   This therefore contrasts with the stricter provisions as to determining liability for costs of the substantive proceedings arising from offers made pursuant to CPR Part 36 within the substantive civil proceedings.

however the parties can apply for a certificate of the interest that has accrued and the daily rate of future interest. Interest on the costs of the detailed assessment proceedings runs from the date of the default or final costs certificate.

A party can appeal a decision made in detailed assessment hearings. Appeal from assessment decisions by district judges, masters, costs judges or circuit judges following the rules and procedure for appeals set out within CPR Part 52. However an appeal from an authorised officer are made to a costs judge or district judge of the High Court and there is no requirement to seek permission or for written reasons. The relevant procedure is set out within CPR r 47.22 and any appeal in such circumstances shall take the form of a rehearing of the assessment proceedings (CPR r 47.23).

13.14 CHALLENGING THE BILL OF COSTS

Whilst every summary or detailed assessment shall turn upon its particular facts and circumstances, below is a checklist of points which the paying party may consider taking in order to challenge the bill of costs at either a summary or detailed assessment. To resist such challenges the receiving party is well advised to ensure that both the bill of costs and reply to the points of dispute are comprehensively drafted and that all files of papers (letters and attendance notes) and invoices of disbursements are carefully maintained. In particular the receiving party should always seek to ensure that the narrative to the bill is detailed, sets out the substantive dispute between the parties in full and provides a chronology of the steps taken in the proceedings, so that that the Court is fully apprised of the context of the claim and its conduct.

The paying party may wish to consider taking the following points in challenging the bill of costs at any summary or detailed assessment of costs:

(a) **The retainer/indemnity principle**: The paying party should satisfy itself that there is a valid retainer between the receiving party and his or her solicitors. If not the indemnity principle shall have been breached and this may result in all, or part, of the costs being disallowed. See **13.10.3**.

(b) **Enforceability of Conditional Fee Agreement**: If the receiving party has conducted the claim under a conditional fee agreement, the paying party should satisfy itself that any such agreement has complied with the relevant legislative requirements and is not defective and therefore unenforceable.[28] If not, the indemnity principle shall have been breached and this may result in all, or part, of the costs being disallowed.

(c) **The success fee**: If the receiving party has conducted the claim under a conditional fee agreement, the paying party may wish to challenge the 'success fee' (this is the percentage uplift which the receiving party is entitled to on any profit costs). First, if the success fee is fixed by the Civil Procedure Rules, the party should ensure that the correct percentage uplift is claimed.[29] Secondly, if the success fee is not fixed by any rule, the Court must assess the reasonableness of the success fee at the time the CFA was agreed and not assess it with the benefit of hindsight.[30] Thus, if the paying party wishes to reduce the percentage uplift, it must focus on the likelihood (or lack of risk) of the receiving party succeeding on the claim at the date the agreement was entered into.

(d) **Proportionality**: If the Court finds that the bill of costs is disproportionate on a global basis, the Court will apply the more stringent test of whether, on an item-by-item basis, the costs incurred were necessary and, if necessary, whether the costs were reasonable.[31] A finding that the bill is disproportionate therefore places considerable pressure on the receiving party to justify the costs incurred. In making submissions (oral or written) as to the proportionality of the bill, the paying party should ensure its arguments are focused on the factors set out in CPR r 44.5(3). The paying party may also wish to place before the Court its bill of costs which, if considerably less than the receiving party's bill, may usefully illustrate to the Court that the receiving party's bill is disproportionate if the paying party were able to conduct the litigation more economically.

(e) **Solicitors' hourly rates**: The paying party is well advised to challenge the solicitors' hourly rates as if the challenge is successful it is likely to result in a significant reduction in the bill of costs. Although the solicitor and client may agree an hourly rate for the work undertaken, it does not follow that the Court shall consider this hourly rate to be reasonable and therefore recoverable. Alternatively,

---

[28] As stated in the Introduction, the enforceability of Conditional Fee Agreements is outside the scope of this work and regard should be had to specialist practitioner texts such as 'Cook on Costs'.

[29] CPR, Part 45 provides for fixed percentage uplifts in road traffic accidents occurring after 6 October 2003 and employers' liability claims for accidents after 1 October 2004.

[30] See *Atack v Lee* [2004] EWCA Civ 1712.

[31] See section entitled 'Proportionality' above and *Home Office v Lownds* [2002] 1 WLR 2450.

where no firm agreement has been reached between solicitor and client as to the charging rate, a reasonable amount should be allowed.[32]

In determining the reasonably hourly rate, the Court is likely to have regard to the guidelines of solicitor rates published by the Court Service. However, these are only guidelines and are not binding upon the Court and therefore the particular circumstances of the case may justify departure from the guideline rates. The guideline hourly rates are determined by two factors – the grade/experience of the fee earner[33] and the locality of the solicitor.[34]

Consequently, this allows for two avenues of attack by the paying party. First the paying party may seek to challenge the hourly rate on the ground that the issues in dispute did not justify the experience of a fee earner of a particular grade and that a lower grade fee earner could have reasonably conducted the litigation. Secondly that it was unreasonable for the receiving party to instruct a solicitor who was not local and who charged a higher rate than a local solicitor where there were local solicitors who were suitably qualified to undertake the work.[35]

(f) **Rates recoverable by Litigants in Person**: Litigants in Person can include a company or other corporation acting without a legal representative and barristers, solicitors or other authorised litigators acting for himself (see CPR r 48.6(6)). The rates recoverable by litigants in person depend upon whether he or she can prove a financial loss incurred in conducting the litigation.[36] If the litigant in person can prove a financial loss, he or she is entitled to the amount lost for time reasonably spent doing work, subject to a maximum of two-thirds of the amount which would have been allowed if the litigant in person had been represented by a legal representative (CPR r 48.6). If the litigant in person cannot prove a financial loss, he or she is entitled to recover for the amount of time reasonably spent on doing the work at the rate set out in the practice direction

---

[32] See *Joseph v Boyd & Hutchinson* (unreported) 16 January 2001, ChD.

[33] There are 4 grades of Fee Earners – A to D. Grade A is for solicitors with over 8 years post qualification experience, including 8 years litigation experience. Grade B is for solicitors and legal executives with over 4 years post-qualification experience, including 4 years litigation experience. Grade C is for other solicitors and legal executives not falling within grades A and B. Grade D is for trainee solicitors, paralegals and equivalent fee earners.

[34] Localities are divided into three bands for outside of London and a separate band for central and greater London. The logic being, that the overheads in parts of England and Wales shall be greater than in other localities and therefore justify a higher hourly rate in some areas than others.

[35] See *Truscott v Truscott, Wraith v Sheffield Forgemasters Ltd* [1998] 1 All ER 82.

[36] To prove a financial loss at a summary assessment, the Litigant in Person should file and serve any written evidence upon which he relies 24 hours prior to the hearing at which the question may be decided (CPR 48, PD 3A, Section 52.2). At a detailed assessment, the evidence should be served with the notice of commencement (CPR Pt 48, PD 3A, Section 52.3).

(CPR r 48.6(4)(b) – presently, this is £9.25 per hour). Where a litigant in person seeks to prove a financial loss, the party should rigorously test whether any loss has been suffered and, if so, the amount of that loss. It is not uncommon for litigants in person to have inflated ideals as to their loss which, if properly analysed, may amount to less than £9.25 per hour!

(g) **Duplication by fee earners**: Where the receiving party's case has been handled by a number of fee earners over the lifetime of the claim, it is likely that there shall be some inevitable duplication of work as fee earners familiarise themselves with the work undertaken by the colleagues. Such duplication of work is likely to be irrecoverable.

(h) **Correspondence and attendances**: The receiving party shall usually divide chargeable work between attendances upon the client, opponent, the Court, counsel etc and within each division the charges shall be separated for letters and telephone calls. Routine letters and telephone calls will generally be allowed on a unit basis of 6 minutes per letter or telephone call (ie charged at 1/10th of the hourly rate). The Court in its discretion may allow for the time recorded for preparing emails sent by the solicitors or allow for emails sent on a unit basis. The paying party should consider whether the number of letters and telephone calls is reasonable. There is no easy method of doing so, given that the paying party does not have access to the receiving party's files. However effective ways of assessing the reasonableness of the amount of work is either to establish the average number of attendances per month of the litigation or to compare with the paying party's own cost schedule. The latter is particularly effective when comparing attendances upon opponents.

Generally the Court will not allow for emails received, the cost for postage, couriers, faxes, outgoing telephone calls, the cost of copying documents or the cost of local travel by the solicitor (CPR Pt 43 PD 4 Section 4.6). Further, unless the case is unusual solicitors cannot charge for time spent 'looking up the law'.[37]

(i) **Work done on documents**: The receiving party's bill shall usually include a section for work done on documents. Whilst the bill should provide a total of the amount of time spent, there should be a schedule accompanying the bill which itemises the work done on documents. This schedule should be carefully scrutinised by the paying party for repetition of work over the lifetime of the claim, documents that were not actually drafted, documents which were drafted but not used in the proceedings or where the time spent considering documents appears excessive.

---

[37]   See *Perry v the Lord Chancellor* (1994) *The Times*, 26 May.

(j) **Solicitors attendance at court**: Not every case shall reasonably require a solicitor to attend at Court and the paying party should give consideration to this.

(k) **Counsel's fees**: Counsel's fees are based upon judgment.[38] Factors to be taken into account include the seniority of counsel, the number of documents perused, the specialist knowledge and skill of counsel, complexity of the work undertaken, the value of the claim and its importance, the responsibility involved and the place and circumstances where the work is performed. In determining whether a fee is reasonable, although the time spent on the case is a relevant factor, it is not appropriate to determine the fee by applying an hourly rate.[39] The normal rule is that work done after the delivery of the brief (eg meeting with experts, drafting closing submissions etc) should be included within the brief fee and should not be recoverable separately.[40] If Counsel has had to travel a significant distance to attend Court, the brief fee is likely to be higher than if local counsel were instructed. In such circumstances the Court shall need to consider whether the case required specialist counsel or could have been adequately dealt with by the local bar.

(l) **Other disbursements**: The receiving party must serve with the notice of commencement evidence of all disbursements which exceed £250. However, in practice, the receiving party would be advised to disclose all invoices of any disbursements as the failure to do so may lead to the paying party questioning whether the item was incurred.

(m) **Value Added Tax**: Although the solicitor/clients costs attract VAT, a receiving party who is registered for VAT can recover the VAT from H M Revenue & Customs as an input tax credit and therefore the paying party should not have to pay the VAT element in such circumstances. VAT should not be charged on disbursements (eg Court fees) unless the solicitor had to pay VAT on the disbursement (eg counsel's fees).

13.15 ENFORCEMENT OF AN AWARD OF COSTS

Where the paying party (the judgment debtor) refuses to comply with the order of the Court for payment of the receiving party's (the judgment creditor's) costs, there are a number of enforcement procedures available to the judgment creditor in the civil courts.

It should be noted that enforcement can be both costly and time consuming and before embarking upon any enforcement procedure, the

---

[38] See *Simpson Motor Sales (London) Ltd v Hendon BC* [1965] 1 WLR 112.

[39] See *XYZ v Schering Health Care: Oral Contraceptive Litigation* The Law Society Gazette, 30 September 2004.

[40] See *Loveday v Renton (No 2)* [1992] 3 All ER 184.

judgment creditor should be satisfied that the judgment debtor is refusing and/or unable to pay the recoverable costs. Accordingly once the period for payment has elapsed, the first step should be to write to the other party or their legal representatives and request payment. Often payment is not made within time due to inefficiency or incompetence rather than inability or refusal to pay.

13.15.1 Transfer of proceedings

If payment remains withheld, the second step is to consider whether it is necessary to transfer the proceedings before enforcement proceedings can be commenced. In considering whether the proceedings need to be transferred, it is important to note that the Senior Court Costs Office is a division of the High Court.

Proceedings will need to be transferred from the Senior Court Costs Office to the county court if:

(a)   execution against goods is sought of a judgment under £600;

(b)   a charging order is sought where the judgment debt is under £5,000

(c)   an attachment of earnings order is sought.

To transfer the proceedings the judgment creditor must make an application to the High Court in accordance for transfer of the proceedings in accordance with CPR, r 70.3. Where a charging order or attachment of earnings order is sought, the proceedings need to be transferred to the county court serving the district where the judgment debtor resides or carries on business.

Proceedings will need to be transferred from the county court to the county court serving the district where the judgment debtor resides or carries on business, if the judgment creditor wishes to apply for:

(a)   an oral examination;

(b)   a charging order;

(c)   an attachment of earnings order; or

(d)   a judgment summons

To transfer proceedings from one county court to another for enforcement, the judgment creditor must make a request in writing to the Court where the order for costs was made. A Court Officer will then transfer the proceedings unless a judge orders otherwise.

13.15.2 Enforcement proceedings

There are numerous means by which a judgment can be enforced. In deciding which method to pursue, the consideration for the judgment creditor are likely to be straightforward – which means of enforcement is most likely to secure payment of the costs in the shortest time frame? Below are details of some of the more common methods of enforcement:

(a) **Execution against goods**: This is the most common method of enforcement. In the High Court execution is effected through the writ of '*fi fa*' and in the County Courts by warrants of execution. In the High Court, the judgment creditor produces a draft writ, a praecipe and the judgment which is then issued by being sealed and served on the sheriff of the county where the debtor resides. In the County Court the judgment creditor sends a request for the issue of the warrant to the Court and the Court informs the bailiffs. The Sheriff's officers or bailiffs, following gaining lawful entry to the debtor's premises, seize sufficient goods to satisfy the judgment and the costs of enforcement. Thereafter, the threat of sale of the goods is usually sufficient to persuade the debtor to pay. However if the debtor refuses or is unable to pay, the goods will be sold at auction and the proceedings of sale distributed accordingly.

(b) **Administration orders**: The judgment creditor or debtor can apply for an administration order. Such an order has the effect of restricting creditors named in the order from joining in a bankruptcy petition against the debtor. The order will usually provide for the debtor to make specified payments by instalment. Administration orders remain in effect for three years.

(c) **Third party debt orders**: A third party debt order transforms a debt payable by a third party to the judgment debtor into an obligation to pay the debt to the judgment creditor. These are particularly effective where the debt to be attached is owed by a responsible individual, such as a bank or building society. The procedure for applying for a third party debt order is in set out in CPR Part 72. The first stage is a without notice application which is considered by the Judge on the papers and, if satisfied, the judge shall make an interim third party debt order directing the third party not to make any payment which reduces the amount he owes to the judgment debtor to less than the amount specified in the order. The second stage is for the Court to determine whether it should make a final third party debt order. At this stage the Judge shall consider any evidence filed by the third party or the judgment debtor which objects to the final order being made. At the hearing the Court make a final third party debt order, discharge the interim third party debt order, decide any issues or direct a trial on the issues.

(d) **Attachment of earnings**: Where a judgment debtor is employed, but has no other substantial assets, an attachment of earnings order is an effective means of enforcing the judgment. Such an order can only be made if the judgment debtor has failed to make one or more payments required by the relevant adjudication.[41] An attachment of earnings order will direct the debtor's employer to make periodical deductions from the debtor's earnings and to pay the amount deducted to the collecting officer of the Court. Earnings includes wages, salaries, fees, bonuses, commission and overtime payable under a contract of service, including occupational pensions and statutory sick pay. The application for such an order is made by filing a request in a standard form certifying the amount of money remaining due. The Court shall then send the debtor a questionnaire to complete as to his financial means and an administrative officer of the Court who may make the attachment of earnings order subsequently considers the questionnaire. If either party objects to the order, or the administrative officer decides not to make the order, the application is referred to a district judge to determine at a hearing. If the attachment of earnings order is made, it will be served on the debtor's employer to make the deductions ordered by the Court. Alternatively, the Court may suspend the attachment of earnings order, which will only be served on the debtor's employer, if the debtor fails to pay agreed instalments.

(e) **Charging orders**: A charging order secures a judgment debt, it does not of itself satisfy the judgment by producing any money. It enables a charge to be registered over the debtor's property and, if the debt remains unsatisfied, the an application can be made for sale of the property and, if allowed, the proceeds of sale will be applied to satisfy the debt. The procedure for applying for a charging order is in two stages, as set out in CPR Part 73. The first stage is to apply for an interim charging order by issuing an application notice in form N379 which is considered without a hearing by the Judge. If made and the interim order relates to land, the charge should be registered as a pending action at the Land Registry, before the order is served upon the debtor. The second stage is to apply for a final charging order at the final hearing. Any person objecting to a final order being made must file and serve written evidence setting out the grounds of the objection. At the hearing the Court may make the final charging order, discharge the interim charging order, decide any issues or direct a trial of any issues. Once the final charging order is made, if the property is owned solely by the debtor, the judgment creditor can commence CPR Part 8 proceedings for an order for sale of the property in accordance with CPR r 73.10. However, if the charged property is owned by more than one person, an application for an order for sale has to be made in accordance with s 14 of the Trusts of Land and Appointment of Trustees Act 1996.

---

[41]   See s 3(3) of the Attachment of Earnings Act 1971.

(f) **Insolvency**: Often the failure by the judgment debtor to satisfy the debt is evidence that the judgment debtor is insolvent. If the debt exceeds £750, it may be apt to bring bankruptcy or winding up proceedings rather than to apply for enforcement. Bankruptcy and Winding-Up proceedings can be brought in accordance with the procedure set out in the Insolvency Act 1986 and the Insolvency Rules 1986.

13.16   REVIEW OF CIVIL LITIGATION COSTS

Lord Justice Jackson's 'Review of Civil Litigation Costs' was published in December 2009. Running to 584 pages, Lord Justice Jackson's Report reviewed the rules and principles governing the costs of civil litigation and made recommendations in order to promote access to justice at proportionate costs. The Report's recommendations are wide ranging and include specific recommendations to manage and control the costs of litigation in particular practice areas, such as personal injury, intellectual property, and defamation amongst others. Whilst it remains to be determined whether Lord Justice Jackson's recommendations will be implemented, it is worthwhile briefly considering some of his recommendations.

(a) **Contingency Fee Agreements:** Lord Justice Jackson recommended that lawyers should be able to enter into contingency fee agreement with clients for contentious litigation. Presently lawyers are not permitted to act on a contingency fee basis in contentious litigation. A contingency fee agreement is an agreement whereby a lawyer is only paid if the client's claim is successful and the lawyer is paid out of the settlement sum or damages awarded. It is Lord Justice Jackson's view that such agreements should be permissible, in order to increase access to justice, provided that the terms of the agreement are regulated to safeguard the interests of the lay client.

(b) **Success Fees and After the Event Insurance:** In litigation conducted under conditional fee agreements, Lord Justice Jackson considered that disproportionate costs had resulted from such funding due to the success fees due to lawyers and after-the-event insurance premiums (being insurance which are taken out to cover the claimant against the risk of paying the defendant's costs). Presently both the success fee and the insurance premium (which may be staged) are recoverable from the paying party, should the Defendant be ordered to pay the Claimant's costs. Lord Justice Jackson has proposed that the success fee and after-the-event insurance premium should not be recoverable from the unsuccessful Defendant but rather that the liability for any success fee will rest with the successful Claimant. This is intended to ensure that Claimant's have an interest in the proportionality of their litigation costs, as any success fee may need to be funded out of any damages awarded.

(c) **Qualified One Way Costs Shifting**: Lord Justice Jackson has proposed an alternative to the usual rule that 'the costs will follow the event'. It is recommended that 'qualified one way costs shifting' should be introduced to certain categories of litigation where after-the-event insurance is currently prevalent (for example, potentially personal injury, clinical negligence, judicial review and defamation claims). Qualified one way costs shifting is whether the unsuccessful Defendant will be liable for the successful Claimant costs but an unsuccessful Claimant will not be liable for the successful Defendant's costs. The only exceptions to the latter would be if the Claimant had behaved unreasonably or unjustifiably or the financial resources available to both parties necessitated a different order as to costs. The intention of such a change in principle, is to increase access to justice for Claimants whilst removing the necessity to incur the considerable expense of after-the-event insurance to protect Claimants against the financial consequences of unsuccessful litigation.

(d) **Fixed Costs on Fast Track Litigation**: Civil claims allocated to the Fast Track are those with a value of up to £25,000. Lord Justice Jackson has recommended has recommended either that the costs recoverable are fixed for certain types of claims or that there is a financial limit on the costs recoverable. With the regard to the latter, he has proposed a figure of £12,000 as the limit for pre-trial costs, with this figure to be reviewed by a 'Costs Council.

(e) **Costs Management**: As an adjunct to case management (which is at the heart of the Civil Procedure Rules), Lord Justice Jackson has recommended 'costs management' whereby the Court, with input from the parties, actively attempts to control the costs of cases before it. To do so, it is suggested that parties should provide budgets of the costs incurred for the Court's approval and that these budgets should be updated from time to time. The Court will then be able to formulate directions and orders with a view to ensuring that costs remain proportionate. It is suggested that the Court could achieve this by limiting disclosure and/or the number of witnesses.

(f) **Summary and Detailed Assessment**: Lord Justice Jackson only recommended limited changes with respect to Summary and Detailed Assessment procedures. For Summary Assessment, it was suggested that Form N260, whilst suitable for interim applications, provides insufficient detail for the assessment of costs relating to the whole trial processes. Similar criticisms were also raised at the format of the bill of costs in Detailed Assessment proceedings. It is therefore recommended that a new format of bill of costs should be devised, which will be more informative and capable of yielding information at different levels of generality and it was suggested that computer software should be developed to assist in this process.

With regard to the procedure for Detailed Assessment, three particular recommendations merit attention. First that Points of Dispute and Points of Reply should have more focus without the need to plead to every individual item in the bill of costs. Secondly, the Paying Party should be required to make a compulsory offer in settlement of the costs of the claim, when it serves the Points of Dispute. Thirdly the provisions of CPR Part 36 (offers to settle) should apply to Detailed Assessment proceedings with the consequential liability for costs which flow from failing to do better than any offer made.

Whilst a number of the proposed changes set out above are significant, even if Lord Justice Jackson's recommendations are implemented it is unlikely to result in the death knell of costs litigation. No doubt lawyers, as ever, will find points (good and bad) to argue about.

APPENDIX

Employment Tribunals (Constitution and Rules of Procedure) Regulations 2004

SI 2004/1861

****

Schedule 1
The Employment Tribunals Rules of Procedure

Regulation 16

****

How To Bring A Claim

Costs Orders And Orders For Expenses

38 General power to make costs and expenses orders

(1) Subject to paragraph (2) and in the circumstances listed in rules 39, 40 and 47 a tribunal or Employment Judge may make an order ("a costs order") that –

(a) a party ("the paying party") make a payment in respect of the costs incurred by another party ("the receiving party");

(b) the paying party pay to the Secretary of State, in whole or in part, any allowances (other than allowances paid to members of tribunals) paid by the Secretary of State under section 5(2) or (3) of the Employment Tribunals Act to any person for the purposes of, or in connection with, that person's attendance at the tribunal.

(2) A costs order may be made under rules 39, 40 and 47 only where the receiving party has been legally represented at the Hearing or, in proceedings which are determined without a Hearing, if the receiving party is legally represented when the proceedings are determined. If the receiving party has not been so legally represented a tribunal or Employment Judge may make a preparation time order (subject to rules 42 to 45). (See rule 46 on the restriction on making a costs order and a preparation time order in the same proceedings.)

(3) For the purposes of these rules "costs" shall mean fees, charges, disbursements or expenses incurred by or on behalf of a party, in relation to the proceedings. In Scotland all references to costs (except when used in the expression "wasted costs") or costs orders shall be read as references to expenses or orders for expenses.

(4) A costs order may be made against or in favour of a respondent who has not had a response accepted in the proceedings in relation to the conduct of any part which he has taken in the proceedings.

(5) In these rules legally represented means having the assistance of a person (including where that person is the receiving party's employee) who –

    (a)   has a general qualification within the meaning of section 71 of the Courts and Legal Services Act 1990;

    (b)   is an advocate or solicitor in Scotland; or

    (c)   is a member of the Bar of Northern Ireland or a solicitor of the Court of Judicature of Northern Ireland.

(6) Any costs order made under rules 39, 40 or 47 shall be payable by the paying party and not his representative.

(7) A party may apply for a costs order to be made at any time during the proceedings. An application may be made at the end of a hearing, or in writing to the Employment Tribunal Office. An application for costs, which is received by the Employment Tribunal Office later than 28 days from the issuing of the judgment determining the claim, shall not be accepted or considered by a tribunal or Employment Judge unless it or he considers that it is in the interests of justice to do so.

(8) In paragraph (7), the date of issuing of the judgment determining the claim shall be either –

    (a)   The date of the Hearing if the judgment was issued orally; or

    (b)   If the judgment was reserved, the date on which the written judgment was sent to the parties.

(9) No costs order shall be made unless the Secretary has sent notice to the party against whom the order may be made giving him the opportunity to give reasons why the order should not be made. This paragraph shall not be taken to require the Secretary to send notice to that party if the party has been given an opportunity to give reasons orally to the Employment Judge or tribunal as to why the order should not be made.

(10) Where a tribunal or Employment Judge makes a costs order it or he shall provide written reasons for doing so if a request for written reasons is made within 14 days of the date of the costs order. The Secretary shall send a copy of the written reasons to all parties to the proceedings.

Amendments: SI 2005/1865; SI 2008/2683.

39 When a costs or expenses order must be made

(1) Subject to rule 38(2), a tribunal or Employment Judge must make a costs order against a respondent where in proceedings for unfair dismissal a Hearing has been postponed or adjourned and –

(a)   the claimant has expressed a wish to be reinstated or re-engaged which has been communicated to the respondent not less than 7 days before the Hearing; and

(b)   the postponement or adjournment of that Hearing has been caused by the respondent's failure, without a special reason, to adduce reasonable evidence as to the availability of the job from which the claimant was dismissed, or of comparable or suitable employment.

(2) A costs order made under paragraph (1) shall relate to any costs incurred as a result of the postponement or adjournment of the Hearing.

Amendments: SI 2005/1865; SI 2008/2683.

40 When a costs or expenses order may be made

(1) A tribunal or Employment Judge may make a costs order when on the application of a party it has postponed the day or time fixed for or adjourned a Hearing or pre-hearing review. The costs order may be against or, as the case may require, in favour of that party as respects any costs incurred or any allowances paid as a result of the postponement or adjournment.

(2) A tribunal or Employment Judge shall consider making a costs order against a paying party where, in the opinion of the tribunal or Employment Judge (as the case may be), any of the circumstances in paragraph (3) apply. Having so considered, the tribunal or Employment Judge may make a costs order against the paying party if it or he considers it appropriate to do so.

(3) The circumstances referred to in paragraph (2) are where the paying party has in bringing the proceedings, or he or his representative has in conducting the proceedings, acted vexatiously, abusively, disruptively or otherwise unreasonably, or the bringing or conducting of the proceedings by the paying party has been misconceived.

(4) A tribunal or Employment Judge may make a costs order against a party who has not complied with an order or practice direction.

Amendments: SI 2008/2683.

41 The amount of a costs or expenses order

(1) The amount of a costs order against the paying party shall be determined in any of the following ways –

(a)   The tribunal may specify the sum which the paying party must pay to the receiving party, provided that sum does not exceed £10,000;

(b)   The parties may agree on a sum to be paid by the paying party to the receiving party and if they do so the costs order shall be for the sum so agreed;

(c)   The tribunal may order the paying party to pay the receiving party the whole or a specified part of the costs of the receiving party with the amount to be paid being determined by way of detailed assessment in a County Court in accordance with the Civil Procedure Rules 1998 or, in Scotland, as taxed according to such part of the table of fees prescribed for proceedings in the sheriff court as shall be directed by the order.

(2) The tribunal or Employment Judge may have regard to the paying party's ability to pay when considering whether it or he shall make a costs order or how much that order should be.

(3) For the avoidance of doubt, the amount of a costs order made under paragraphs (1)(b) or (c) may exceed £10,000.

Amendments: SI 2008/2683.

Preparation Time Orders

42 General power to make preparation time orders

(1) Subject to paragraph (2) and in the circumstances described in rules 43, 44 and 47 a tribunal or Employment Judge may make an order ("a preparation time order") that a party ("the paying party") make a payment in respect of the preparation time of another party ("the receiving party").

(2) A preparation time order may be made under rules 43, 44 or 47 only where the receiving party has not been legally represented at a Hearing or, in proceedings which are determined without a Hearing, if the receiving party has not been legally represented when the proceedings are determined. (See: rules 38 to 41 on when a costs order may be made; rule 38(5) for the definition of legally represented; and rule 46 on the restriction on making a costs order and a preparation time order in the same proceedings).

(3) For the purposes of these rules preparation time shall mean time spent by –

(a)   The receiving party or his employees carrying out preparatory work directly relating to the proceedings; and

(b)   The receiving party's legal or other advisers relating to the conduct of the proceedings; up to but not including time spent at any Hearing.

(4) A preparation time order may be made against a respondent who has not had a response accepted in the proceedings in relation to the conduct of any part which he has taken in the proceedings.

(5) A party may apply to the tribunal for a preparation time order to be made at any time during the proceedings. An application may be made at the end of a hearing or in writing to the Secretary. An application for preparation time which is received by the Employment Tribunal Office

later than 28 days from the issuing of the judgment determining the claim shall not be accepted or considered by a tribunal or Employment Judge unless they consider that it is in the interests of justice to do so.

(6) In paragraph (5) the date of issuing of the judgment determining the claim shall be either –

    (a)   The date of the Hearing if the judgment was issued orally; or,

    (b)   If the judgment was reserved, the date on which the written judgment was sent to the parties.

(7) No preparation time order shall be made unless the Secretary has sent notice to the party against whom the order may be made giving him the opportunity to give reasons why the order should not be made. This paragraph shall not be taken to require the Secretary to send notice to that party if the party has been given an opportunity to give reasons orally to the Employment Judge or tribunal as to why the order should not be made.

(8) Where a tribunal or Employment Judge makes a preparation time order it or he shall provide written reasons for doing so if a request for written reasons is made within 14 days of the date of the preparation time order. The Secretary shall send a copy of the written reasons to all parties to the proceedings.

Amendments: SI 2008/2683.

43 When a preparation time order must be made

(1) Subject to rule 42(2), a tribunal or Employment Judge must make a preparation time order against a respondent where in proceedings for unfair dismissal a Hearing has been postponed or adjourned and –

    (a)   the claimant has expressed a wish to be reinstated or re-engaged which has been communicated to the respondent not less than 7 days before the Hearing; and

    (b)   the postponement or adjournment of that Hearing has been caused by the respondent's failure, without a special reason, to adduce reasonable evidence as to the availability of the job from which the claimant was dismissed, or of comparable or suitable employment.

(2) A preparation time order made under paragraph (1) shall relate to any preparation time spent as a result of the postponement or adjournment of the Hearing.

Amendments: SI 2005/1865; SI 2008/2683.

44 When a preparation time order may be made

(1) A tribunal or Employment Judge may make a preparation time order when on the application of a party it has postponed the day or time fixed for or adjourned a Hearing or a pre-hearing review. The preparation time

order may be against or, as the case may require, in favour of that party as respects any preparation time spent as a result of the postponement or adjournment.

(2) A tribunal or Employment Judge shall consider making a preparation time order against a party (the paying party) where, in the opinion of the tribunal or the Employment Judge (as the case may be), any of the circumstances in paragraph (3) apply. Having so considered the tribunal or Employment Judge may make a preparation time order against that party if it considers it appropriate to do so.

(3) The circumstances described in paragraph (2) are where the paying party has in bringing the proceedings, or he or his representative has in conducting the proceedings, acted vexatiously, abusively, disruptively or otherwise unreasonably, or the bringing or conducting of the proceedings by the paying party has been misconceived.

(4) A tribunal or Employment Judge may make a preparation time order against a party who has not complied with an order or practice direction.

Amendments: SI 2008/2683.

45 Calculation of a preparation time order

(1) In order to calculate the amount of preparation time the tribunal or Employment Judge shall make an assessment of the number of hours spent on preparation time on the basis of –

    (a)   information on time spent provided by the receiving party; and

    (b)   the tribunal or Employment Judge's own assessment of what it or he considers to be a reasonable and proportionate amount of time to spend on such preparatory work and with reference to, for example, matters such as the complexity of the proceedings, the number of witnesses and documentation required.

(2) Once the tribunal or Employment Judge has assessed the number of hours spent on preparation time in accordance with paragraph (1), it or he shall calculate the amount of the award to be paid to the receiving party by applying an hourly rate of £25.00 to that figure (or such other figure calculated in accordance with paragraph (4)). No preparation time order made under these rules may exceed the sum of £10,000.

(3) The tribunal or Employment Judge may have regard to the paying party's ability to pay when considering whether it or he shall make a preparation time order or how much that order should be.

(4) For the year commencing on 6th April 2006, the hourly rate of £25 shall be increased by the sum of £1.00 and for each subsequent year commencing on 6 April, the hourly rate for the previous year shall also be increased by the sum of £1.00.

Amendments: SI 2008/2683.

46 Restriction on making costs or expenses orders and preparation time orders

(1) A tribunal or Employment Judge may not make a preparation time order and a costs order in favour of the same party in the same proceedings. However where a preparation time order is made in favour of a party in proceedings, the tribunal or Employment Judge may make a costs order in favour of another party or in favour of the Secretary of State under rule 38(1)(b) in the same proceedings.

(2) If a tribunal or an Employment Judge wishes to make either a costs order or a preparation time order in proceedings, before the claim has been determined, it or he may make an order that either costs or preparation time be awarded to the receiving party. In such circumstances a tribunal or Employment Judge may decide whether the award should be for costs or preparation time after the proceedings have been determined.

Amendments: SI 2008/2683.

47 Costs, expenses or preparation time orders when a deposit has been taken

(1) When –

    (a)   a party has been ordered under rule 20 to pay a deposit as a condition of being permitted to continue to participate in proceedings relating to a matter;

    (b)   in respect of that matter, the tribunal or Employment Judge has found against that party in its or his judgment; and

    (c)   no award of costs or preparation time has been made against that party arising out of the proceedings on the matter;

the tribunal or Employment Judge shall consider whether to make a costs or preparation time order against that party on the ground that he conducted the proceedings relating to the matter unreasonably in persisting in having the matter determined; but the tribunal or Employment Judge shall not make a costs or preparation time order on that ground unless it has considered the document recording the order under rule 20 and is of the opinion that the grounds which caused the tribunal or Employment Judge to find against the party in its judgment were substantially the same as the grounds recorded in that document for considering that the contentions of the party had little reasonable prospect of success.

(2) When a costs or preparation time order is made against a party who has had an order under rule 20 made against him (whether the award arises out of the proceedings relating to the matter in respect of which the order was made or out of proceedings relating to any other matter considered with that matter), his deposit shall be paid in part or full settlement of the costs or preparation time order –

    (a)   When an order is made in favour of one party, to that party; and

(b)   When orders are made in favour of more than one party, to all of them or any one or more of them as the tribunal or Employment Judge thinks fit, and if to all or more than one, in such proportions as the tribunal or Employment Judge considers appropriate;

and if the amount of the deposit exceeds the amount of the costs or preparation time order, the balance shall be refunded to the party who paid it.

Amendments: SI 2008/2683.

Wasted Costs Orders Against Representatives

48 Personal liability of representatives for costs

(1) A tribunal or Employment Judge may make a wasted costs order against a party's representative.

(2) In a wasted costs order the tribunal or Employment Judge may –

(a)   Disallow, or order the representative of a party to meet the whole or part of any wasted costs of any party, including an order that the representative repay to his client any costs which have already been paid; and

(b)   Order the representative to pay to the Secretary of State, in whole or in part, any allowances (other than allowances paid to members of tribunals) paid by the Secretary of State under section 5(2) or (3) of the Employment Tribunals Act to any person for the purposes of, or in connection with, that person's attendance at the tribunal by reason of the representative's conduct of the proceedings.

(3) "Wasted costs" means any costs incurred by a party: –

(a)   As a result of any improper, unreasonable or negligent act or omission on the part of any representative; or

(b)   Which, in the light of any such act or omission occurring after they were incurred, the tribunal considers it unreasonable to expect that party to pay.

(4) In this rule "representative" means a party's legal or other representative or any employee of such representative, but it does not include a representative who is not acting in pursuit of profit with regard to those proceedings. A person is considered to be acting in pursuit of profit if he is acting on a conditional fee arrangement.

(5) A wasted costs order may be made in favour of a party whether or not that party is legally represented and such an order may also be made in favour of a representative's own client. A wasted costs order may not be made against a representative where that representative is an employee of a party.

(6) Before making a wasted costs order, the tribunal or Employment Judge shall give the representative a reasonable opportunity to make oral or written representations as to reasons why such an order should not be made. The tribunal or Employment Judge may also have regard to the representative's ability to pay when considering whether it shall make a wasted costs order or how much that order should be.

(7) When a tribunal or Employment Judge makes a wasted costs order, it must specify in the order the amount to be disallowed or paid.

(8) The Secretary shall inform the representative's client in writing: –

(a) Of any proceedings under this rule; or
(b) Of any order made under this rule against the party's representative.

(9) Where a tribunal or Employment Judge makes a wasted costs order it or he shall provide written reasons for doing so if a request is made for written reasons within 14 days of the date of the wasted costs order. This 14 day time limit may not be extended under rule 10. The Secretary shall send a copy of the written reasons to all parties to the proceedings.

Amendments: SI 2004/2351; SI 2008/2683.

****

INDEX

References are to paragraph numbers.